Christless
Christianity

Christless Christianity

The Alternative Gospel of the American Church

Michael Horton

BakerBooks

a division of Baker Publishing Group
Grand Rapids, Michigan

Published by Baker Books
a division of Baker Publishing Group
P.O. Box 6287, Grand Rapids, MI 49516-6287
www.bakerbooks.com

Printed in the United States of America

Library of Congress Cataloging-in-Publication Data
Horton, Michael Scott.
    Christless Christianity : the alternative gospel of the American church / Michael Horton.
        p.   cm.
    Includes bibliographical references (p.   ).
    ISBN 978-0-8010-1318-8 (cloth)
    1. Evangelicalism—United States. 2. United States—Religious life and customs. 3. Jesus Christ—History of doctrines—United States. I. Title.
BR1642.U5H674 2008
277.3'083—dc22   2008023631

To "our Lord Jesus Christ,
through whom we have
now received reconciliation"

Romans 5:11

Contents

Liberating a Captive Church

Here we are in the North American church—conservative or liberal, evangelical or mainline, Protestant or
Catholic, emergent or otherwise—cranking along just
fine, thank you. So we're busy downsizing, becoming culturally
relevant, reaching out, drawing in, making disciples, managing
the machinery, utilizing biblical principles, celebrating recovery,
user-friendly, techno savvy, finding the purposeful life, practicing peace with justice, utilizing spiritual disciplines, growing
in self-esteem, reinventing ourselves as effective ecclesiastical
entrepreneurs, and, in general, feeling ever so much better about
our achievements.

Notice anything missing in this pretty picture? *Jesus Christ!*

Jesus Christ indeed. In Flannery O'Connor's wild, wickedly
funny novella, *Wise Blood*, her antipreacher preacher, Hazel
Motes, preaches a 'Church without Christ" where nobody sheds
blood, and there's no redemption "'cause there ain't no sin to

redeem," and "what's dead stays that way."[1] I always thought O'Connor's book an outrageous, wildly improbable satire. Then Mike Horton comes along and names the "Church without Christ" as our pervasive ecclesial reality. Horton accuses us of achieving what has never transpired in the entire history of Christendom. Somehow we've managed to preach Christ crucified in such a way that few are offended, a once unmanageable God suddenly seems nice, and the gospel makes good sense—as we are accustomed to making sense. We just can't stand to submit to the machinations of a living God who is determined to have us on God's terms rather than ours, so we devise a god on our own terms. Flaccid, contemporary Christianity is the result.

This is a tough book, but well written, fast paced, and wonderfully grounded in classical Reformation Christianity. Our poor old, compromised, accommodating church is here subjected to withering theological critique. Here the roots of our current theological malaise are exposed and we see the wrong turns we took when we began taking ourselves more seriously than God. The boredom and conventionality of the contemporary church are assaulted. Michael Horton diagnoses our trouble in stunning, unavoidable candor. Therapeutic, utilitarian deism is named, nailed, and and defeated with the best weapon God has given us—the gospel of Jesus Christ. Presumptively evangelical Christianity is exposed as the latest recruit to the cause of insipid, culturally compromised liberalism. I am judged in the process. Robert Schuller's vapid ecclesiology is us all over. My sermons are only slightly less silly and compromised than Joel Osteen's. Mea culpa. Mea culpa. Mea culpa.

But this book is not all critique. Horton mounts a wonderfully hopeful argument. His sermon is not only tough but also invigorating and empowering. In the process of reading this Jesus-induced polemic, you will be recalled to the power of the gospel. God forgive us for selling out our great intellectual treasure—the gospel of *God with us*—for a mess of psychobabble and pragmatic, utilitarian, self-help triviality.

Horton joyfully reminds us that theological thinking is so much more interesting than all of the distractions that keep us busy but malnourished. The peculiar Good News of Jesus Christ is better than anything William James or Charles G. Finney and their innumerable heirs have to offer. The determination of God in Jesus Christ to love sinners and to enlist them in the invasion that is his kingdom is so much more relevant to our true condition than our inclination to meet the felt needs of narcissistic North American consumers.

Have a wonderful adventure reading this book. Enjoy being enticed into the strange new world of vibrant Christianity in Horton's spirited gospel recovery operation. In the process, you will be liberated from our cultural captivity so that again you will be free to worship, in word and deed, the risen Christ.

Let's put Christ back in Christianity.

William Willimon
Bishop of the United Methodist Church
Birmingham, Alabama

Acknowledgments

Although I have debts to many for this book, especially to those who have provided wonderful examples of faithfulness to the gospel over many years, I will limit acknowledgments here to the Baker team, including Bob Hosack and Mary Wenger, but especially to Jack Kuhatschek, whose encouragement and patient direction on this project proved invaluable. Finally, I am grateful to my Westminster Seminary California colleagues and students, to the White Horse Inn/ *Modern Reformation* staff, and Christ United Reformed Church, but especially to my wife, Lisa, and our children, James, Olivia, Matthew, and Adam, for always being a reminder to me of why these issues are so important.

Christless Christianity

The American Captivity of the Church

What would things look like if Satan really took control
of a city? Over a half century ago, Presbyterian minister Donald Grey Barnhouse offered his own scenario
in his weekly sermon that was also broadcast nationwide on CBS
radio. Barnhouse speculated that if Satan took over Philadelphia,
all of the bars would be closed, pornography banished, and
pristine streets would be filled with tidy pedestrians who smiled
at each other. There would be no swearing. The children would
say, "Yes, sir" and "No, ma'am," and the churches would be full
every Sunday . . . *where Christ is not preached.*

It is easy to become distracted from Christ as the only hope for
sinners. Where everything is measured by our happiness rather
than by God's holiness, the sense of our being sinners becomes
secondary, if not offensive. If we are good people who have lost
our way but with the proper instructions and motivation can

become a better person, we need only a life coach, not a redeemer. We can still give our assent to a high view of Christ and the centrality of his person and work, but in actual practice we are being distracted from "looking to Jesus, the founder and perfecter of our faith" (Heb. 12:2). A lot of the things that distract us from Christ these days are even good things. In order to push us off-point, all that Satan has to do is throw several spiritual fads, moral and political crusades, and other "relevance" operations into our field of vision. Focusing the conversation on us—our desires, needs, feelings, experience, activity, and aspirations—energizes us. At last, now we're talking about something practical and relevant.

As provocative as Barnhouse's illustration remains, it is simply an elaboration of a point made throughout the history of redemption. Wherever Christ is truly and clearly being proclaimed, Satan is most actively present in opposition. The wars between the nations and enmity within families and neighborhoods is but the wake of the serpent's tail as he seeks to devour the church. Yet even in this pursuit, he is more subtle than we imagine. He lulls us to sleep as we trim our message to the banality of popular culture and invoke Christ's name for anything and everything but salvation from the coming judgment. While undoubtedly stirring his earthly disciples to persecute and kill followers of Christ (with more martyrdoms worldwide in an average year now than in any previous era), Satan knows from experience that sowing heresy and schism is far more effective. *While the blood of the martyrs is the seed of the church, the assimilation of the church to the world silences the witness.*

I think that the church in America today is so obsessed with being practical, relevant, helpful, successful, and perhaps even well-liked that it nearly mirrors the world itself. Aside from the packaging, there is nothing that cannot be found in most churches today that could not be satisfied by any number of secular programs and self-help groups.

Christless Christianity. Sounds a bit harsh, doesn't it? A little shallow, sometimes distracted, even a little human-centered rather than Christ-centered from time to time, but *Christless*? Let me be a little more precise about what I am assuming to be the regular diet in many churches across America today: "do more, try harder." I think that this is the pervasive message across the spectrum today. It can be exhibited in an older, more conservative form, with a recurring emphasis on moral absolutes and warnings about falling into the pit of worldliness that can often make one wonder whether we are saved through fear rather than faith. Heaven and hell still figure prominently in this version. Especially on the "high holy days" of the American church calendar (that is, Memorial Day, Independence Day, Father's Day, and Mother's Day), often complete with giant American flags, a color guard, and patriotic songs, this sterner version of "do more, try harder" helped get the culture wars off the ground. At the same time, more liberal bodies could be just as shrill with their "do more, try harder" list on the left and their weekly calls to action rather than clear proclamation of Christ.

Reacting against this extreme version of fundamentalist and liberal judgmentalism, another generation arose that wanted to soft-pedal the rigor, but the "do more, try harder" message has still dominated—this time in the softer pastels of Al Franken's "Stuart Smalley" than in the censorious tone of Dana Carvey's "Church Lady," both of *Saturday Night Live* fame. In this version, God isn't upset if you fail to pull it off. The stakes aren't as high: success or failure in this life, not heaven or hell. No longer commands, the content of these sermons, songs, and best-selling books are helpful suggestions. If you can't get people to be better with sticks, use carrots.

Increasingly, a younger generation is taking leadership that was raised on hype and hypocrisy and is weary of the narcissistic (i.e., "me-centered") orientation of their parents' generation. They are attracted to visions of salvation larger than the legalistic individualism of salvation-as-fire-insurance. Yet they are also fed up with the consumeristic individualism of salvation-as-personal-improvement. Instead, they are desperately craving authenticity and genuine transformation that produces true community, exhibiting loving acts that address the wider social and global crises of our day rather than the narrow jeremiads of yesteryear.

Despite significant differences across these generations and types of church ministry, crucial similarities remain. The focus still seems to be on us and our activity rather than on God and his work in Jesus Christ. In all of these approaches, there is the tendency to make God a supporting character in our own life movie rather than to be rewritten as new characters in God's drama of redemption. Assimilating the disruptive, surprising, and disorienting power of the gospel to the felt needs, moral crises, and socio-political headlines of our passing age, we end up saying very little that the world could not hear from Dr. Phil, Dr. Laura, or Oprah.

Besides the preaching, our practices reveal that we are focused on ourselves and our activity more than on God and his saving work among us. Across the board, from conservative to liberal, Roman Catholic to Anabaptist, New Age to Southern Baptist, the "search for the sacred" in America is largely oriented to what happens inside of us, in our own personal experience, rather than in what God has done for us in history. Even baptism and the Supper are described as "means of commitment" rather than "means of grace" in a host of contemporary systematic theologies by conservative as well as progressive evangelicals. Rather than letting "the word of Christ dwell in you richly, teaching and admonishing one another in all wisdom, singing psalms and hymns and spiritual songs, with thankfulness in your hearts to God" (Col. 3:16), the purpose of singing (the "worship time") seems today more focused on our opportunity to express our own individual piety, experience, and commitment. We come to church, it seems, less to be transformed by the Good News than to celebrate our own transformation and to receive fresh marching orders for transforming ourselves and our world. Rather than being swept into God's new world, we come to church to find out how we can make God relevant to the "real world" that the New Testament identifies as the one that is actually fading away.

Most Americans believe in God, affirm that Jesus Christ is in some sense divine, and believe that the Bible is the Word of God. Evangelical pollster George Barna found that 86 percent of American adults describe their religious orientation as Christian, while only 6 percent describe themselves as atheist or agnostic.[1] Judging by its commercial, political, and media success, the evangelical movement seems to be booming. But is it still *Christian*?

I am not asking that question glibly or simply to provoke a reaction. My concern is that we are getting dangerously close to the place in everyday American church life where the Bible is mined for "relevant" quotes but is largely irrelevant on its own terms; God is used as a personal resource rather than known, worshiped, and trusted; Jesus Christ is a coach with a good game plan for our victory rather than a Savior who has already achieved it for us; salvation is more a matter of having our best life now than being saved from God's judgment by God himself; and the Holy Spirit is an electrical outlet we can plug into for the power we need to be all that we can be.

As this new gospel becomes more obviously American than Christian, we all have to take a step back and ask ourselves whether evangelicalism is increasingly a cultural and political

19

movement with a sentimental attachment to the image of Jesus more than a witness to "Jesus Christ and him crucified" (1 Cor. 2:2). We have not shown in recent decades that we have much stomach for this message that the apostle Paul called "a stone of stumbling, and a rock of offense," "folly to Gentiles" (Rom. 9:33; 1 Cor. 1:23). Far from clashing with the culture of consumerism, American religion appears to be not only at peace with our narcissism but gives it a spiritual legitimacy.

Before I launch this protest, I should carefully state up front what I am *not* saying. First, I acknowledge that there are many churches, pastors, missionaries, evangelists, and distinguished Christian laypeople around the world proclaiming Christ and fulfilling their vocations with integrity. I apologize in advance for not telling this other side of the story, with its truly remarkable exceptions. However, I doubt that they will mind, since many of them register similar worries about the state of Christianity in America.

Second, I am not arguing in this book that we have *arrived* at Christless Christianity but that we are well on our way. There need not be explicit abandonment of any key Christian teaching, just a series of subtle distortions and not-so-subtle distractions. Even good things can cause us to look away from Christ and to take the gospel for granted as something we needed for conversion but which now can be safely assumed and put in the background. Center stage, however, is someone or something else.

I will refer to recent studies demonstrating that it does not really matter any longer whether one has been raised in an evangelical family and church—understanding the basic plot of the biblical drama and its lead character is as unlikely for churched as for unchurched young people. God and Jesus are still important, but more as part of the supporting cast in our own show. More interested in our own thin plots, we are losing our confidence in what English playwright Dorothy Sayers called "the greatest story ever told." So much of what I am calling "Christless Christianity" is not profound enough to constitute heresy. Like the easy-listening Muzak that plays ubiquitously in the background in other shopping venues, the message of American Christianity has simply become trivial, sentimental, affirming, and irrelevant.

Third, I am not questioning American Christianity at the level of *zeal*. The call of Christian leaders to "deeds, not creeds" is doubtless motivated by a serious concern to be witnesses to Christ in a broken world. I do not question the sincerity of those who say that we have the correct doctrine but are not living it out. Rather, I simply do not agree with their assessment. I think our doctrine has been forgotten, assumed, ignored, and even misshaped and distorted by the habits and rituals of daily life in a narcissistic culture. We are assimilating the disrupting and disorienting news from heaven to the banality of our own immediate *felt needs*, which interpret God as a personal shopper for the props of our life movie: happiness as entertainment, salvation as therapeutic well-being, and mission as pragmatic success measured solely in terms of numbers.

So, in my view, we *are* living out our creed, but that creed is closer to the American Dream than it is to the Christian faith. The claim I am laying out in this book is that the most dominant form of Christianity today reflects "a zeal for God" that is nevertheless without knowledge—particularly, as Paul himself specifies, the knowledge of God's justification of the wicked by grace alone, through faith alone, in Christ alone, apart from works (Rom. 10:2, see vv. 1–15).

Fourth, there are a lot of issues I would like to address about our American captivity that will not be taken up here. Most of these issues I have treated elsewhere, especially in *Made in America*, *Power Religion*, and *Beyond Culture Wars*.[2] The idols that identify the Christian cause with left-wing or right-wing political ideology are merely symptoms that Christ is not being regarded as sufficient for the church's faith and practice today. As the media follows the growing shift among many younger evangelicals from more conservative to more progressive politics, the real headline should be that the movement is going back to church to grow in the grace and knowledge of Jesus Christ rather than becoming a demographic block in the culture wars. So my focus in this book is on whether Christ is even being widely proclaimed in the nation where half the population claims to be evangelical.

Where the gospel is not taken for granted, it is often a means to an end, like personal or social transformation, love and service to our neighbors, and other things that in themselves are marvelous effects of the gospel. However, the Good News concerning Christ is not a stepping-stone to something greater and more relevant. Whether we realize it or not, there is nothing in the universe more relevant to us as guilty image-bearers of God than the news that he has found a way to be "just and the justifier of the one who has faith in Jesus" (Rom. 3:26). It is "the power of God for salvation" (Rom. 1:16), not only for the beginning, but for the middle and end as well—the only thing that creates the kind of new world to which our new obedience corresponds as a reasonable response.

In the following chapters I offer statistics supporting the remarkable conclusion that those who are raised in "Bible-believing" churches know as little of the Bible's actual content as their unchurched neighbors. Christ is ubiquitous in this subculture, but more as an adjective (*Christian*) than as a proper name. While we swim in a sea of "Christian" things, Christ is increasingly reduced to a mascot or symbol of a subculture and the industries that feed it. Just as you don't really need Jesus Christ in order to have T-shirts and coffee mugs, it is unclear to me why he is necessary for most of the things I hear a lot of pastors and Christians talking about in church these days.

I do not think we realize the extent of our schizophrenia: annually decrying the commercialization of Christmas by the culture while we assume a consumer-product-sales approach in our own churches every week. We lament the growing secularization of American society while we ensure that the generations currently under our care will know even less than their parents and be less shaped by the covenantal nurture that sustains life in Christ over generations. While calling our capitulation to a narcissistic culture *mission* and *relevance*, we charge secularists with emptying public discourse of beliefs and values that transcend our instant gratification.

While we take Christ's name in vain for our own causes and positions, trivializing his Word in all sorts of ways, we express outrage when a movie trivializes Christ or depicts Christians in a negative light. Although professing Christians are in the majority, we often like to pretend we are a persecuted flock being prepared for an imminent slaughter through the combined energies of Hollywood and the Democratic Party. But if we ever were really persecuted, would it be because of our offensive posturing and self-righteousness or because we would not weaken the offense of the cross? In my experience, substantiated by countless stories of others, believers who challenge the human-centered process of trivializing the faith are more likely to be persecuted—or at least viewed as troublesome—by their church. My concern is not that God is treated so lightly in American culture but that he is not taken seriously in our own faith and practice.

Killing Us Softly

My argument in this book is not that evangelicalism is becoming theologically liberal but that it is becoming theologically vacuous. Far from engendering a smug complacency, core evangelical convictions—centering on "Christ and him crucified"—drove three centuries of evangelical missions. The ministry of John Stott, a key leader of this postwar consensus, has embodied this integration of Christ-centered proclamation with missional passion. Yet when asked in a recent issue of *Christianity Today* how he evaluates this worldwide movement, Stott could only reply, "The answer is 'growth without depth.'"[3]

There certainly are signs that the movement's theological boundaries are widening—and I will touch on a few examples in this book. Furthermore, vacuity and liberalism have typically gone hand-in-hand when it comes to the church's faith and practice. Liberalism started off by downplaying doctrine in favor of moralism and inner experience, losing Christ by degrees. Nevertheless, it is not heresy as much as silliness that is killing us softly. God is not denied but trivialized—used for our life programs rather than received, worshiped, and enjoyed.

Christ is a source of empowerment, but is he widely regarded among us today as the source of redemption for the powerless? He helps the morally sensitive to become better, but does he save the ungodly—including Christians? He heals broken lives, but does he raise those who are "dead in trespasses and sins" (Eph. 2:1 NKJV)? Does Christ come merely to *improve* our existence in Adam or to *end* it, sweeping us into his new creation? Is Christianity all about spiritual and moral makeovers or about death and resurrection—radical judgment and radical grace? Is the Word of God a resource for what we have already decided we want and need, or is it God's living and active criticism of our religion, morality, and pious experience? In other words, is the Bible God's story, centering on Christ's redeeming work, that rewrites our stories, or is it something we use to make our stories a little more exciting and interesting?

Conservatives and liberals moralize, minimize, and trivialize Christ in different ways, of course, with different political and social agendas, showing their allegiance either to elite culture or popular culture, but it is still moralism. According to Methodist bishop William Willimon,

> Lacking confidence in the power of our story to effect that of which it speaks, to evoke a new people out of nothing, our communication loses its nerve. Nothing is said that could not be heard elsewhere. . . . In conservative contexts, gospel speech is traded for dogmatic assertion and moralism, for self-help psychologies and narcotic mantras. In more liberal speech, talk tiptoes around the outrage of Christian discourse and ends up as an innocuous, though urbane, affirmation of the ruling order. Unable to preach Christ and him crucified, we preach humanity and it improved [4]

Liberals may have pioneered the theory that there is salvation in other names than Jesus Christ, but no group in modern history has wanted the general public to pray nonsectarian prayers—that is, with or without Jesus Christ—as much as the conservative evangelicals. When it comes to *getting God back into our schools*, we can even leave Jesus behind.

Jesus has been dressed up as a corporate CEO, life coach, culture-warrior, political revolutionary, philosopher, copilot, cosufferer, moral example, and partner in fulfilling our personal and social dreams. But in all of these ways, are we reducing the central character in the drama of redemption to a prop for our own play?

Like the liberals of yesteryear, a growing number of evangelical leaders are fond of setting Jesus's teaching on the kingdom—especially the Sermon on the Mount—over against the more doctrinal emphasis found especially in Paul's epistles. Many celebrate this emphasis on Christ-as-example rather than Christ-as-Redeemer as the harbinger of *a new kind of Christian*, but is it really an old kind of moralist? Regardless of whether Christ's death is regarded as a vicarious sacrifice, discipleship—*our* cross-bearing—becomes the more interesting topic. Never mind that disciples are people who learn something before they set out to make a splash by their zealous activity. Again, I'm not saying that these brothers and sisters are liberals but that there is no discernable difference for our witness whether we ignore or deny the message of Christ and his cross. When the focus becomes "What would Jesus do?" instead of "What has Jesus done?" the labels no longer matter. Conservatives have been just as prone to focus on the former rather than the latter in recent decades.

Religion, spirituality, and moral earnestness—what Paul called "the appearance of godliness but denying its power" (2 Tim. 3:5)—can continue to thrive in our environment precisely because they avoid the scandal of Christ. Nobody will raise a fuss if you find Jesus helpful for your personal well-being and relationships, or even if you think he was the greatest person in history—a model worthy of devotion and emulation. But start talking about the real crisis—where our best efforts are filthy rags and Jesus came to bear the condemnation of helpless sinners who place their confidence in him rather than in themselves—and people begin shifting in their seats, even in churches.

Discipleship, spiritual disciplines, life transformation, culture-transformation, relationships, marriage and family, stress, the spiritual gifts, financial gifts, radical experiences of conversion, end-times curiosities that seem to have less to do with Christ's bodily return than with matching verses to newspaper headlines, and accounts of overcoming significant obstacles through the power of faith. This is the steady diet we're getting today, and it is bound to burn us out because it's all about us and our work rather than about Christ and his work. Even important biblical exhortations and commands become dislocated from their indicative, gospel habitat. Instead of the gospel giving us new thoughts, experiences, and a motivation for grateful obedience, we lodge the power of God in our own piety and programs.

I do not expect to get everything right. Some of my judgments may turn out to be too sweeping or ill-informed. I hope not, because these issues are too important to be treated casually. Readers will certainly find a lot of good news interspersed between the bad news in this book, but I admit from the outset that on balance it is not a cheerful missive. I'm counting on the indulgence of readers to wait for this book's more constructive sequel. If this book will have only raised questions that provoke us to deeper analysis of our witness in the world today, it will be sufficient.

My aim is not to target any particular wing, movement, person, or group. We are all victims as well as accomplices in our captivity. In fact, my sense of urgency is motivated by my impression that "Christless Christianity" is pervasive, crossing the conservative-liberal spectrum and all denominational lines. In fact, when I wrote up some of the thoughts in this book for an article in a magazine recently, a Catholic editor exclaimed, "He's writing about us!"

Actually, I *am* writing about "us"—all of us who profess the name of Christ both as ministers and witnesses. It would be easier if we could identify one particular writer, circle of writers, or movement as an isolated nemesis. However, no tradition is free of this captivity, including my own, and no person, including myself. There is therefore no position of antiseptic purity that I can pretend to occupy, from which I can mop up the rest of the floor. The most that any of us can do is to say with Isaiah, as he beheld a vision of God in his holiness, "Woe is me! For I am lost; for I am a man of unclean lips, and I dwell in the midst of a people of unclean lips; for my eyes have seen the King, the LORD of hosts!" (Isa. 6:5).

Naming Our Captivity

Moralistic, Therapeutic Deism

several years ago a mainline theologian told me of his experience at an evangelical megachurch. He was visiting
his children and grandchildren during spring break. In the
church they attended Easter Sunday, nothing visibly suggested
that it was a Christian service, but this distinguished theologian tried to rein in his judgments. There was no greeting from
God or sense that this was God's gathering. The songs were
almost exclusively about us, our feelings, and our intentions to
worship, obey, and love, but it was not clear whom they were
talking about or why. He concluded, "Well, evangelicals don't
really have a liturgy. They put all of the content into the sermon,
so I'll wait."

However, his patience was not rewarded. Although it was
Easter, the message (with no clear text) was on how Jesus
gives us the strength to overcome our obstacles. Lacking even

a benediction, this theologian left discouraged. He had come to an evangelical church at Easter, and instead of meeting God and the announcement of a real victory over sin and death by Jesus Christ, he encountered other Christians who were being given fellowship and instructions for making their own Easter come true in their life.

Pressed with leading questions by his son-in-law as to his reaction to the service (such as, "Did it touch your heart?"), the theologian broke his silence: "I assume you're trying to 'evangelize' me right now," he said. "But there was no 'gospel' anywhere in that service that might convert me if I were unconverted. . . . Not even in the most liberal churches I've been in was the service so devoid of Christ and the gospel. It's like 'God *who*?'"

Since then, a mainline Methodist theologian told me of an almost identical experience—curiously, also at Easter—in a conservative Presbyterian church that was known around the university for its "Bible-believing" and "Christ-centered" ministry. He too left disappointed (the sermon was something about how Jesus overcame his setbacks and so can we), further substantiating his appraisal that evangelicals are as likely as mainliners today to talk pop psychology, politics, or moralism instead of the gospel.

But are these isolated anecdotes that could be culled from any period of church history?

Substantiating the Charge

Based on numerous studies conducted by his research group, George Barna concludes, "To increasing millions of Americans, God—if we even believe in a supernatural deity—exists for the pleasure of humankind. He resides in the heavenly realm solely for our utility and benefit. Although we are too clever to voice it, we live by the notion that true power is accessed not by looking upward but by turning inward."[1]

Unless something changes, Barna thinks,

> It will be every man for himself, with no second thoughts or regrets about the personal or societal implications of this incredibly selfish, nihilistic, narcissistic way of life. . . .
>
> Most Americans have at least an intellectual assent when it comes to God, Jesus Christ, and angels. They believe that the Bible is a good book filled with important stories and lessons. And they believe that religion is very important in their lives. But this same group of people, including many professing Christians, also believe that people are inherently good; that our primary purpose is to enjoy life as much as possible.[2]

Eighty-two percent of Americans (and a majority of evangelicals) believe that Benjamin Franklin's aphorism, "God helps those who help themselves," is a biblical quotation. A majority believe that "all people pray to the same god or spirit, no matter what name they use for that spiritual being" and that "if a person is generally good or does enough good things for others during their life, they will earn a place in heaven."[3] It should not surprise us, then, when President Bush says, "I believe that all the world, whether they be Muslim, Christian, or any other religion, prays to the same God. That's what I believe."[4]

After citing a series of reports, Barna concludes,

> In short, the spirituality of America is Christian in name only. . . . We desire experience more than knowledge. We prefer choices to absolutes. We embrace preferences rather than truths. We seek comfort rather than growth. Faith must come on our terms or we reject it. We have enthroned ourselves as the final arbiters of righteousness, the ultimate rulers of our own experience and destiny. We are the Pharisees of the new millennium.[5]

31

Among the false assumptions "killing the ministry" today are that "Americans have a firm understanding of the basic tenets of Christianity," that "people who believe in God believe in the God of Israel" known in Scripture, or that non-Christians are interested in salvation, since most Americans "are relying instead on their own good deeds, their good character, or the generosity of God" apart from Christ.[6]

Barna's studies suggest that most Americans value time and efficiency over everything else, minimizing long-term commitments, maintaining "independence and individuality at all costs," even to the point of being skeptical of institutions, people, and authorities. After all, people are being told every day, "You are unique" and you shouldn't submit to the expectations of others. Above all, *"Trust your feelings to guide you.* Relying upon absolute principles places unrealistic limitations on you. Only you know what's right or best for you at any given moment, in those circumstances." Finally, *"Set goals and achieve them. . . . Have fun. . . . Stay in good health. . . . Discover and revel in the purpose of your life."*[7] These are the principal values according to Barna's surveys of American adults today. In spite of his diagnosis, however, Barna's own prescriptions (which I take up in a later chapter) are more likely to aggravate the illness rather than cure it.

Over a decade ago, I had the opportunity to interview Robert Schuller on our radio program. During our two-hour conversation, the best-selling author and televangelist reiterated his arguments in *Self-Esteem: The New Reformation.* A church, he says, can afford to think in a God-centered fashion, but a mission must put humans at the center. "It was appropriate for Calvin and Luther to think theocentrically," writes Schuller, but now "the scales must tip the other way" toward a "human needs approach." In fact, "classical theology has erred in its insistence that theology be 'God-centered,' not 'man-centered.'" *Sin* is defined as "any act or thought that robs myself or another human being of his or her self-esteem. . . . And what is 'hell'? It is the loss of pride that naturally follows separation from God—the ultimate and unfailing source of our soul's sense of self-respect. . . . A person is in hell when he has lost his self-esteem." "The Cross sanctifies the ego trip."[8]

I asked Dr. Schuller how he would interpret the following admonition from Paul to Timothy:

> But understand this, that in the last days there will come times of difficulty. For people will be lovers of self, lovers of money, proud, arrogant, abusive, disobedient to their parents, ungrateful, unholy, heartless, unappeasable, slanderous, without self-control, brutal, not loving good, treacherous, reckless, swollen with conceit, lovers of pleasure rather than lovers of God, having the appearance of godliness, but denying its power.
>
> 2 Timothy 3:1–5

Before I was even able to compose my own question, my distinguished guest immediately responded to these apostolic words by saying, "I hope you don't preach that. It will hurt a lot of beautiful people."

The challenge before us as Christian witnesses is whether we will offer Jesus Christ as the key to fulfilling our narcissistic preoccupation or as the Redeemer who liberates us from its guilt and power. Does Christ come to boost our ego or to crucify our ego and raise us up as new creatures with our identity in him? According to the apostle Paul, there is glory awaiting us, to be sure, but it is the glory that comes to us by virtue of our being in Christ: "For you have died, and your life is hidden with Christ in God. When Christ who is your life appears, then you also will appear with him in glory" (Col. 3:3–4). Our righteousness before a holy God is not inherent; it is a gift to those who are in themselves unrighteous.

By the way, I do not think this means that we simply write off the desire for fulfillment and happiness. The gospel neither meets our narcissistic goals nor denies the truth of which they are a perversion. People were created for meaning, purpose, joy, and fulfillment. As C. S. Lewis reminds us, it's not that our desires are too strong but that they are too weak.[9] While God wants to give us everlasting life, we settle for trivial satisfaction of superficial *needs* that are to a large extent created within us by the culture of marketing.

Only when God's law—his holiness, majesty, and moral will—creates in us a sense of our moral offensiveness to God does the gospel communicate deeper answers that our felt needs and cheap cravings only mask. Hardly unique, my children would be delighted if I told them that instead of their usual three meals today we would provide a variety pack of candies. When my wife and I decline their urges, it is because we know that they will make themselves sick if they just follow their immediate desires. Similarly, God wants to fill our lives with joy, but before we allow him to tell us the story, we have already decided within the narrow confines of our limited experience what joy is from.

Reacting against a legalistic and self-righteous tendency in their childhood, many Americans have abandoned church altogether. Those who return often do so on their own terms. The message must be light and affirming; the form in which it is presented must be entertaining and inspirational. They are ready for something useful and helpful but not something jarring and disturbing. As David Brooks has observed concerning the postwar generation generally, Boomers are part *Leave It to Beaver*, bourgeois moralists with a vague sense of values and nostalgia for community and part Bohemian revolutionaries of the sixties and seventies, who resist the traditions, commitments, convictions, and structures that genuine community requires.[10]

34

In this context, as *Newsweek* reported, churches "have developed a 'pick and choose' Christianity in which individuals take what they want . . . and pass over what does not fit their spiritual goals. What many have left behind is a pervasive view of sin."[11] A decade later, *Newsweek* added in yet another cover story on the search for the sacred,

> Disguised in the secular language of psychotherapy, the search for the sacred has turned sharply inward—a private quest. The goal, over the last forty years, has been variously described as "peace of mind," "higher consciousness," "personal transformation" or—in its most banal incarnation—"self-esteem." . . . In this environment, many searching Americans flit from one tradition to the next, tasting now the nectar of this traditional wisdom, now of that. But, like butterflies, they remain mostly up in the air.[12]

It was secular psychologist Karl Menninger who pointed out (in a book titled *Whatever Became of Sin?*) that the growing suppression of the reality of guilt in churches was actually contributing to neuroses rather than avoiding them.[13] Not long ago, I read a *Wall Street Journal* article with a similar report, bearing the headline, "To Hell with Sin: When 'Being a Good Person' Excuses Everything."[14] Isn't it slightly odd when the world has to complain that the churches are no longer talking about sin?

More recently, Robert Jay Lifton, a pioneer in neuropsychology, has argued that today's self is restlessly bent on reinvention mainly in order to get rid of a nagging sense of guilt that creates tremendous anxiety despite its unknown origins. The implication of his essay is that when people know why they feel guilty and are able to find an answer to it, they actually become more stable in their identity.[15] As C. FitzSimons Allison has alleged, exchanging the biblical categories of sin and grace for such therapeutic categories as dysfunction and recovery represents "pastoral cruelty."[16] If we *feel* guilty, maybe it is because we really *are* guilty. To change the subject or downplay the seriousness of this condition actually keeps people from the liberating news the gospel brings. If our real problem is bad feelings, then the solution is good feelings. The cure can only be as radical as the disease. Like any recreational drug, *Christianity Lite* can make people feel better for the moment, but it does not reconcile sinners to God.

Ironically, secular psychologists like Menninger are writing books about sin, while many Christian leaders are converting sin—a condition from which we cannot liberate ourselves—into dysfunction and salvation into recovery. In his best-seller, *The Triumph of the Therapeutic*, Philip Rieff describes how pop psychology has transformed our entire worldview, including religion. "Christian man was born to be saved," he writes. "Psychological man is born to be pleased."[17]

Neil McCormick, a columnist for London's *Daily Telegraph*, recounts the religious education classes he and his childhood friend, U2's Bono, received at a nondenominational but mainly Protestant school in Dublin. The classes were "characterized by a kind of wooly Christian liberalism, presided over by a well-meaning, but—as far as I was concerned—drippily ineffective young teacher named Sophie Shirley." McCormick recalls,

> There would be Bible readings and class discussions in which Jesus took on the character of a beatific hippie while God seemed to be personified as an avuncular old geezer who only wanted the best for His extended family—if that was the case, I wondered, why was I being kept awake at night wondering if the torments of Hell awaited me when I died? I would fire this and related questions at my long-suffering teacher but I never received satisfactory answers, just platitudes about Jesus loving me.[18]

Just yesterday I saw a scene from NBC's *ER* that powerfully underscores McCormick's experience. Lying in his hospital bed while he is dying from cancer, a retired police officer confesses to a chaplain his long-held guilt over allowing an innocent man to be framed and executed. He asks, "How can I even hope for forgiveness?" and the chaplain replies, "I think sometimes it's easier to feel guilty than forgiven." "Which means *what*?" "That maybe your guilt over his death has become your reason for living. Maybe you need a new reason to go on." "I don't want to 'go on,'" says the dying man. "Can't you see that I'm dying? The only thing that is holding me back is that I'm afraid—I'm afraid of what comes next." "What do you think that is?" the chaplain gently inquires. Growing impatient, the man answers, "*You tell me*. Is atonement possible? What does God *want* from me?" After the chaplain replies, "I think it's up to each one of us to interpret for ourselves what God wants," the man stares at her in bewilderment. "So people can do anything? They can rape, they can murder, they can steal—all in the name of God and it's OK?" Growing intense, the dialogue draws to its climax. "No, that's not what I'm saying," the chaplain responds. "Then what *are* you saying? Because all I'm hearing is some New Age, God-is-Love, have-it-your-way crap! . . . No, I don't have time for this now." "You don't understand," the chaplain counters. "No, *you* don't understand! . . . I want a *real* chaplain who believes in a *real* God and a *real* hell!" Missing the point of this man's struggle, the chaplain collects herself and says in the familiar tone of condescension disguised as understanding, "I hear that you're frustrated, but you need to ask yourself—" "No," the man interrupts, "I don't need to ask myself anything. I need *answers* and all of your questions and all your uncertainty are only making things worse." With no more to evaluate than his tone, she encourages calm. "I know you're upset," she begins, provoking his final outburst of frustration: "God, I need someone who will look me in the eye and tell me how to find *forgiveness*, because *I am running out of time*!"

Recently interviewed for a *USA Today* article for the Easter weekend, I was asked how Christ's resurrection could still hold any meaning when it doesn't seem to answer the kind of problem that we used to think was beyond us. The published story, "Is Sin Dead?" began by reporting a growing concern: "How can Christians celebrate Jesus' atonement for their sins and the promise of eternal life in his resurrection if they don't recognize themselves as sinners?"[19]

The writer quotes various social researchers who agree that "sin" is being defined by our own standards and goals rather than by any objective measurement in relation to God. While agreeing that there is such a thing as sin, they say that most people define it in "'a very personal and self-congratulatory manner'—I have to do what's best for me; I am not as sinful as most." Ironically, while Robert Schuller, ordained in the Reformed Church in America, encourages people to exchange the categories of sin and justification for those of shame and self-esteem, this article quotes Pope Benedict XVI's concern that the world today "is losing the notion of sin." The pope counsels, "People who trust in themselves and in their own merits are, as it were, blinded by their own 'I,' and their hearts harden in sin. On the other hand, those who recognize themselves as weak and sinful entrust themselves to God, and from him obtain grace and forgiveness."

One person is quoted who, though raised in the conservative Lutheran Church Missouri Synod, describes himself now as an atheist. "But I think the Bible has a lot of good stories. And I do connect with the story of Easter, of redemption and rebirth. It tells me you are going to make mistakes, and you will get another chance to do right in the future." (Yet something close to this interpretation was offered by evangelical leader Rick Warren last Christmas, when he told a national TV audience that Christ came into the world to give us a "do-over," as in golf.)

The article includes a quote from Barry Kosmin, a public policy professor who studies secularism. "Secular people still believe there's sin, judgment and punishment," he says, but secularism defies any universal standard established by God, much less moral culpability before this God. Of course, people make mistakes and hurt each other. "But if people are held guilty, the punishment, of course, has to be in this world, not the next. Secular people don't burn in hell, they burn in the court of public opinion."

Whether expressed in the sterner tones of fundamentalism or the softer tones of sentimentalism, the type of religion that these examples exhibit is what Paul called "the righteousness that is based on the law" as opposed to "the righteousness based on faith" (Rom. 10 5–6). "I bear them witness that they have a zeal for God, but not according to knowledge. For, being ignorant of the righteousness that comes from God, and seeking to establish their own, they did not submit to God's righteousness. For Christ is the end of the law for righteousness to everyone who believes" (vv. 2–4).

I realize that a lot of people who might gravitate toward a more therapeutic approach to life, including their faith, would nevertheless balk at the accusation of *works-righteousness*. The key to my criticism however, is that once you make your peace of mind rather than peace with God the main problem to be solved, the whole gospel becomes radically redefined. More than that, a therapeutic worldview gravely distorts the terms of the gospel even as the same words are still employed. Feeling good is more important than being good; in fact, normative judgments external to the self are out of place. One may *feel* guilty, but no one actually *is* guilty before God. The very thing that God's law comes to do—namely, to strip us of our pretensions of having it all together—can only be considered a violent aggression against the core value of self-esteem.

"How can I, a sinner, be right before a holy God?" is simply off the radar in a therapeutic mind-set. Once the self is enthroned as the source, judge, and goal of all of life, the gospel need not be denied because it's beside the point. But people need to see—for their own good—that self-realization, self-fulfillment, and self-help are all contemporary twists on an old heresy, which Paul identified as works-righteousness.

Diagnosing the Illness: Moralistic, Therapeutic Deism

Americans have always been can-do people. Pulling ourselves up by our own bootstraps, we assume that we are good people who could do better if we just had the right methods and instructions. Add to this the triumph of the therapeutic in popular culture and we end up with what sociologist Christian Smith has called "Moralistic, Therapeutic Deism."[20]

Besides psychologists, sociologists are documenting the fact that Christianity in America—including evangelicalism—is less interested in truth than in therapy and less focused on consumers than on making disciples. James Davison Hunter, Robert Bellah, Wade Clark Roof, and numerous others have made these points in their extensive studies of religion in America. However, there are two relatively recent sociologists who have contributed significantly to the spiritual condition that I am highlighting in this chapter: Christian Smith and Marsha Witten.

From 2001 to 2005, University of North Carolina (now Notre Dame) sociologist Christian Smith led a team in a remarkable study of teen spirituality in America today. From his extensive interviews, Smith concluded that the dominant form of religion or spirituality of American young people today is "moralistic, therapeutic deism." It is difficult to define this somewhat amorphous spirituality, especially and ironically since "22 percent of teen 'deists' in our survey reported feeling very or extremely close to God (yet the God they believe is not involved in the world today)."[21] Apparently God's involvement is restricted to the inner sphere of one's private world.

Smith observed that most teens—including those reared in evangelical churches who said their faith is "very important" and makes a big difference in their lives—are "stunningly inarticulate" concerning the actual content of that faith.[22] "Interviewing teens," he relates, "one finds little evidence that the agents of religious socialization in this country"—parents, pastors, and teachers—"are being highly effective and successful with the majority of their young people."[23] In contrast to previous generations that at least had some residual knowledge of the Bible and basic Christian teachings, it seems there is very little serious ability to state, reflect upon, or examine their beliefs, much less to relate them to daily life. Many young people seem to be living on the hype and the familiar circle of friends in the youth group, both of which eventually lose their influence, especially in college.

Smith defines *moralistic, therapeutic deism* as expressing this sort of working theology:

1. God created the world.
2. God wants people to be good, nice, and fair to each other, as taught in the Bible and most world religions.
3. The central goal of life is to be happy and to feel good about oneself.
4. God does not need to be particularly involved in one's life except when needed to resolve a problem.
5. Good people go to heaven when they die.[24]

The sense one gets from reading Smith's study corresponds with my own anecdotal experience of popular religion in America

41

today. Basically, the message is that God is nice and we are nice, so we should all be nice.

Do young people raised in evangelical homes and churches really believe this? According to Barna's reports, not to mention the studies of sociologists such as Smith, James Hunter, Wade Clark Roof, and others, the tragic answer is *yes*.[25] This approach, Smith says, reflects similar studies of their parents' generation. Smith points out that in the working theology of those he studied, "being religious is about being good and it's not about forgiveness. . . . It's unbelievable the proportion of conservative Protestant teens who do not seem to grasp elementary concepts of the gospel concerning grace and justification. . . . It's across all traditions."[26] Even Lutheran young people who were active in the church could not define *grace* or *justification*, he says, highlighting the disparity between what churches say they believe and what they are actually communicating week in and week out.

Whatever churches *say* they believe, the incoherent answers offered by those entrusted to their ministry substantiate my argument that a moralistic religion of self-salvation is our default setting as fallen creatures. If we are not explicitly and regularly taught out of it, we will always turn the message of God's rescue operation into a message of self-help.

Recently I came across a story in the newspaper on the remarkable success of a website called dailyconfession.com. "Chat rooms and confessional sites are exploding in popularity—dailyconfession.com receives as many as 1.3 million hits a day—as young people become more comfortable sharing intimate secrets and seeking advice online." One nineteen-year-old user of the site related, "The idea of confessing isn't necessarily about right and wrong. It's about unloading a burden. It's almost cathartic."[27]

We recognize here the confluence of Gnostic spirituality (individualistic, disembodied, private) and moralistic, therapeutic deism. According to a biblical worldview, confession of sin *is* about right and wrong. Real sins are really forgiven by a God who is intimately involved in our everyday lives. In a therapeutic worldview, there is no sin and guilt to be forgiven by God but only burdens and feelings of guilt for failing to live up to the expectations of oneself or other human beings. In other words, for Christianity there is objective guilt and justification; in moralistic therapy there is only subjective guilt and a cathartic release simply by telling someone else about it.

"Kate, a 23-year-old from Texas who describes herself as spiritual but not religious has visited daily confession almost every day for five years. 'I like reading people's confessions because it's nice to know that I'm not any more selfish, petty, conceited, weird or macabre than everyone else in America,' she wrote in an e-mail to a reporter."[28] But this means that confession is not a matter of being brokenhearted by offenses toward God and receiving his forgiveness; rather, it is a matter of justifying oneself as no worse than the average.

As much as we might talk about a *personal relationship* with God through Jesus Christ, there doesn't actually seem to be much of a relationship at all, except with the self. Confession is *good for the soul*—that is to say, a form of therapy. Perhaps the result of all of this emphasis on *my personal relationship with Jesus* means, finally, that Jesus really becomes my alter ego.

Far different is David's confession in Psalm 51: "Against You, You only, I have sinned and done what is evil in Your sight. . . . I was brought forth in iniquity, and in sin my mother conceived me. . . . Do not cast me away" (vv. 4–5, 11 NASB). Although the confession follows his adultery against Bathsheba and murder of her husband, Uriah, the fact that makes sin so utterly sinful is that it is ultimately against God. It is that vertical relationship with God (law and gospel) that will not allow us to reduce confession to the horizontal plane of our neighbors (moralism) or our inner self (therapy).

43

A Theological Diagnosis

The theological term for this malady is *Pelagianism*. A fourth-century British monk named Pelagius was appalled by the immorality he saw when he arrived in Rome, the center of Christendom. Assuming that the emphasis of the African bishop Augustine on human helplessness and divine grace was at the root, Pelagius and his followers denied original sin. Sin is not a universal human condition but simply a choice that each of us makes. With our free will we can choose to follow Adam's bad example or Jesus's good example. Although it was officially condemned by the church (even in its softer "semi-Pelagian" form), Pelagianism has always been a perennial threat. After all, it is our most natural theology.

While affirming that it is in our own power to be good or bad—and so merit eternal life or death—semi-Pelagianism nevertheless believed that some assistance of divine grace was necessary. Arminianism, named after a late sixteenth-century Dutch theologian who rejected Calvinism, was nevertheless one more step removed from Pelagian convictions, affirming the necessity of grace. Nevertheless, Arminianism still holds that salvation is a cooperative effort of God and human beings.

As I will make clearer at various points throughout this book, ever since the Second Great Awakening, especially evident in the message and methods of evangelist Charles G. Finney, American Protestantism has been more Pelagian than Arminian. In fact, Arminian theologian Roger Olson has recently made a similar point.[29]

Denying original sin, Finney asserts that we are only guilty and corrupt when we choose to sin.[30] Christ's work on the cross could not have paid our debt but could only serve as a moral example and influence to persuade us to repent. "If he had obeyed the law as our substitute, then why should our own return to personal obedience be insisted upon as a sine qua non of our salvation?" The atonement is simply "an incentive to virtue." Rejecting the view that "the atonement was a literal payment of a debt," Finney can only concede, "It is true, that the atonement, of itself, does not secure the salvation of any one."[31]

Justification by the imputation of Christ's righteousness is not only "absurd," says Finney, but undermines all motivation for personal holiness. The new birth is not a divine gift but the result of a rational choice to turn from sin to obedience. Christians can perfectly obey God in this life if they choose, and only in this way are they justified. In fact, he says that "full present obedience is a condition of justification." No one can be justified "while sin, any degree of sin, remains in him." Finney declares concerning the Reformation formula, "simultaneously justified and sinful." "This error has slain more souls, I fear, than all the universalism that ever cursed the world." For "whenever a Christian sins, he comes under condemnation and must repent and do his first works, or be lost."[32]

> As has already been said, there can be no justification in a legal or forensic sense, but upon the ground of universal, perfect, and uninterrupted obedience to law. . . . The doctrine of an imputed righteousness, or that Christ's obedience to the law was accounted as our obedience, is founded on a most false and nonsensical assumption, for Christ's righteousness could do no more than justify himself. It can never be imputed to us. . . . It was naturally impossible, then, for him to obey in our behalf. Representing the atonement as the ground of the sinner's justification has been a sad occasion of stumbling to many.[33]

Referring to "the framers of the Westminster Confession of faith" and their view of an imputed righteousness, Finney wonders, "If this is not antinomianism, I know not what is."[34]

It should be noted that these positions are far more radically antithetical to Reformation theology (with which evangelicalism supposedly identifies itself) than the condemnations of the Reformers' views by Rome at the Council of Trent. Finney's message was certainly *moralistic*. Through various methods, the evangelist could induce repentance, through constant crisis experiences that generated self-transformation. It was indeed a *therapeutic* orientation. And, as his critics observed, it was a system of religion that did not even seem to require God. Salvation and moral improvement were entirely in the hands of the evangelist and the convert. The *deistic* implications are also apparent. Even if the gospel is formally affirmed, it becomes a tool for engineering personal and public life (salvation by works) rather than an announcement that God's just wrath toward us has been satisfied and his unmerited favor has been freely bestowed in Jesus Christ. God's direct, personal, miraculous intervention for our salvation seems unnecessary, as suggested in the title of one of Finney's most famous sermons, "Sinners Bound to Change Their Own Hearts."

This concern I have expressed is hardly limited to a few grumpy Calvinists and Lutherans. "Self-salvation is the goal of much of our preaching," according to United Methodist bishop William Willimon.[35] Willimon perceives that a great deal of contemporary preaching, whether mainline or evangelical, assumes that conversion is something we generate through our own words and sacraments. "In this respect we are heirs of Charles G. Finney," who thought that conversion was not a miracle but a "'purely philosophical [i.e., scientific] result of the right use of the constituted means.'"

We have forgotten that there was once a time when evangelists were forced to defend their "new measures" for revivals, that there was once a time when preachers had to defend their preoccupation with listener response to their Calvinist detractors who thought that the gospel was more important than its listeners. I am here arguing that revivals are miraculous, that the gospel is so odd, so against the grain of our natural inclinations and the infatuations of our culture, that nothing less than a miracle is required in order for there to be true hearing. My position is therefore closer to that of the Calvinist Jonathan Edwards than to the position of Finney.[36]

Nevertheless, "The homiletical future, alas, lay with Finney rather than Edwards," leading to the kind of marketing pragmatism expressed by George Barna:

Jesus Christ was a communications specialist. He communicated His message in diverse ways, and with results that would be a credit to modern advertising and marketing agencies. . . . He promoted His product in the most efficient way possible: by communicating with the "hot prospects." . . . He understood His product thoroughly, developed an unparalleled distribution system, advanced a method of promotion that has penetrated every continent, and offered His product at a price that is within the grasp of every consumer (without making the product so accessible that it lost its value).[37]

The question that naturally arises in the face of such remarks is whether it is possible to say that Jesus made anything new.

"Alas," adds Willimon, "most 'evangelistic' preaching I know about is an effort to drag people even deeper into their subjectivity rather than an attempt to rescue them from it." Our real need, whether we feel it or not, is that we systematically distort and ignore the truth. This is why we need "an external word. . . . So in a sense, we don't discover the gospel, it discovers us. 'You did not choose me but I chose you' (John 15:16)." Willimon concludes, "The story is *euangelion, good news,* because it is about grace. Yet it is also news because it is not common knowledge, not what nine out of ten average Americans already know. Gospel doesn't come naturally. It comes as Jesus."[38]

Again, though, I am not pointing fingers at any one tradition. This pervasive tendency toward Pelagianism in American Christianity is evident even in churches that trace their history directly to the Reformation. Sociologists of religion such as Christian Smith and James D. Hunter remind us that Lutheran and Reformed laypeople today share many of these same assumptions. It is worth observing that Norman Vincent Peale was ordained in the Reformed Church in America, as is Robert Schuller. Furthermore, I have heard sermons in more conservative Presbyterian and Reformed churches that could easily fit Smith's profile of moralistic, therapeutic deism. Brian Gerrish, a mainline theologian at the University of Chicago, states the crisis: "The Reformed witness to grace may be even more needed today than it was in the sixteenth century, since now Pelagianism seems comfortably at home in the Reformed churches."[39]

How Preaching Reveals This Secularizing Trend

The Pelagian tendency of popular Christianity in our day—which Smith called "moralistic, therapeutic deism"—can be further substantiated by the studies of sociologist Marsha Witten. In *All Is Forgiven: The Secular Message in American Protestantism*, Witten reveals her results from studying the texts of forty-seven sermons on the parable of the prodigal son (Luke 15:11–32) delivered from 1986 to 1988 by various pastors in two denominations: the Presbyterian Church (USA) and the Southern Baptist Convention. She begins the book by recounting an afternoon on Good Friday 1990. While she was listening to Bach's *St. Matthew Passion*, "with antiphonal choirs calling

48

out sorrowfully to Jesus in his grave," the daily mail arrived and Witten opened the thickest envelope first. It was promotional material for a new Baptist church launching in her area:

Hi Neighbor!

At last! A new church for those who have given up on church services! Let's face it. Many people aren't active in church these days.

WHY?
Too often
—the sermons are boring and don't relate to daily living
—many churches seem more interested in your wallet than in you
—members are unfriendly to visitors
—you wonder about the quality of the nursery care for your little ones

Do you think attending church should be enjoyable?
WELL, WE'VE GOT GOOD NEWS FOR YOU!

Valley Church is a new church designed to meet your needs in the 1990s. At Valley Church you
—meet new friends and get to know your neighbors
—enjoy exciting music with a contemporary flavor
—hear positive, practical messages which uplift you each week
  • How to feel good about yourself
  • How to overcome depression
  • How to have a full and successful life
  • Learning to handle your money without it handling you
  • The secrets of successful family living
  • How to overcome stress
—trust your children to the care of dedicated nursery workers

WHY NOT GET A LIFT
INSTEAD OF A LETDOWN THIS SUNDAY?[40]

Witten, who describes herself as a non-Christian, uses this anecdote—*St. Matthew Passion* contrasted with the new church's promotional materials—to frame the conclusions she arrives at after extensive studies. While the former is fed by a rich sense of God's majesty, holiness, and mercy as well as the genuine struggle of faith, the latter is "optimistic, untroubled, purely mundane," like any other advertisement for a product. American Christianity today lives in this contradiction between "the spiritual and the psychological, the transcendent and the pragmatic."[41]

According to the well-known "secularization theory" of Max Weber, religion—under the conditions of modernity—goes through various stages. First, religion is *privatized*, its domain shrunk to the island of private subjectivity. Statements such as "Jesus is alive" and "Jesus is Lord" are no longer regarded as objective, public claims based on historical events but become references to one's personal experience. As for "Jesus is alive," in the words of a famous gospel song, "You ask me how I know he lives? He lives within my heart." And typically, "Jesus is Lord" refers to my personal decision to make Jesus my Lord and Savior. While the apostles testified to historical events of which they were eyewitnesses, "giving your testimony" in evangelical Christianity today typically means talking about one's inner experience and moral transformation. Once privatized, religion becomes *relativized*. No longer *truth*, it is *your* truth. Since religious beliefs are no longer claims about public events, they can only be justified now in terms of what each individual finds meaningful, useful, and transformative.[42]

The creedal, objective, and historical faith of traditional Christianity could not be translated into purely subjective terms. However, precisely because American religion has long cherished its opposition to more traditional forms of Christianity in favor of the sovereign inner experience of the individual, it not only *survives* but *thrives* in the atmosphere of this secularizing process.

A type of religion that most premodern Christians would have considered nearly heretical can become, in the American experience, the epitome of orthodoxy. So these same processes of modern secularization that led to the rejection of traditional Christian (i.e., creedal) faith and practice in Europe become the engine of perpetual religious revival in America.

As a result, religious speech becomes assimilated to the pragmatic rationality of rules, steps, techniques, and programs for personal transformation and well-being. As philosopher William James made explicit, the test for truth is "its cash-value in experiential terms."[43] Yet long before James, the history of revivalism was already assimilating Christian claims to pragmatic efficiency, measurable not only in numbers of converts but in dollars. "What I'm paid for my work makes it only about $2 a soul," evangelist Billy Sunday calculated, "and I get less proportionately for the number I convert than any other living evangelist."[44] In his Pulitzer Prize–winning *Anti-Intellectualism in American Life*, Richard Hofstadter contrasted the highly literate culture of New England Puritans and that of later revivalism. "Anything that seriously diminished the role of rationality and learning in early American religion would later diminish its role in secular culture," he notes. "The feeling that ideas should above all be made to work, the disdain for doctrine and for refinements in ideas, the subordination of men of ideas to men of emotional power or manipulative skill are hardly innovations of the twentieth century; they are inheritances from American Protestantism."[45]

If Christianity is about public truth delivered through an external Word, then ministry and evangelism require educated leaders who can expound and apply that truth for the benefit of those under their care. By contrast, if Christianity is reduced to personal experience, then its leadership will consist of the most successful entrepreneurs and managers of extraordinary staged events. In his recent book, *Head and Heart*, Catholic historian Garry Wills observes,

> The camp meeting set the pattern for credentialing Evangelical ministers. They were validated by the crowd's response. Organizational credentialing, doctrine purity, personal education were useless here—in fact, some educated ministers had to make a pretense of ignorance. The minister was ordained from below, by the converts he made. . . . The do-it-yourself religion called for a make-it-yourself ministry.[46]

Wills repeats Hofstadter's conclusion that "the star system was not born in Hollywood but on the sawdust trail of the revivalists."[47] Where American Transcendentalism and Romanticism (the nineteenth century's equivalent of the New Age movement) attracted Boston's intellectuals, Charles Finney and his revivalistic legacy represents "an alternative Romanticism," a popular version of self-reliance and inner experience, "taking up where Transcendentalism left off." Emerson wrote, "The height, the deity of man is to be self-sustained, to need no gift, no foreign force"—no external God, with an external Word and sacraments or formal ministry.[48] And revivalism in its own way was popularizing this distinctly American religion on the frontier. William James was proclaiming the sovereign value of pragmatic usefulness at Harvard, while Finney and his heirs had already been baptizing American Protestantism into pragmatism on the ground. Efficiency was the rule for success in religion as in business, and ever since evangelicals have judged new movements by whether they "work" in terms of subjective experience and moral transformation.

Witten's study supports this interpretation.[49] First, the transcendent God of majesty and holiness succumbed to a casual familiarity. Although only one in ten Americans say that they have ever doubted God's existence, most say that they view God exclusively as a friend rather than as a King and "only a small minority" report having ever experienced fear of God. Second, as religion is privatized into a kind of therapeutic usefulness, sin and redemption are translated in subjective rather than objective categories. Christ, then, is an answer to bad feelings, not to any actual state of enmity or guilt before God. Everything that used to be considered a sovereign work of God, through his appointed means of preaching and sacrament, is now attributed to the self (or the evangelist) working through the most efficient steps and techniques. We recognize this pragmatic orientation in the "how-to" literature that lines the shelves of Christian bookstores and pastors' studies. Even Billy Graham wrote a best-seller titled, *How to Be Born Again*.

Witten points out that "Christian self-help books . . . arose in the 1940s and 1950s with the publication of Norman Vincent Peale's *The Power of Positive Thinking* and Joshua Loth Liebman's *Peace of Mind*." To the pragmatism of revivalism was joined the therapeutic revolution that was sweeping the halls of liberal divinity schools.

> The focus on inner states also invites speech oriented largely to the present—to "natural" life, life on earth. Concern with the pragmatic business of life stands to diminish attention to affairs of the "hereafter." Coupled with cultural forces that de-emphasize notions of divine punishment for wrongdoing, the "now" orientation reduces the strength of talk about sin and its consequences. . . . An extreme formulation is the case of "Sheila-ism," a private religion invented by one of the interview subjects cited in *Habits of the Heart*: The tenets of Sheila's faith consist of the messages of "her own little voice."

No longer "martyrs"—that is witnesses—to God's unique intervention in history in Christ's incarnation, life, death, and resurrection, we become satisfied customers who offer testimonials to how much a personal relationship with Jesus has improved our life. In this pragmatic and therapeutic context, it makes little sense to talk about Jesus as "the way, the truth, and the life" (John 14:6) apart from whom there is no salvation. We would rather commend Christ as someone whom we have found personally helpful and meaningful as we encounter life's challenges.

Growing churches and growing businesses follow the same standard procedures of pragmatic efficiency. Not only evangelism, but the Christian life can also be accommodated to modern secularization and routinization. There are standard procedures that work, whether in producing conversions and moral improvement or in producing the greatest number of widgets for the least expenditure. Of course no one has to explicitly deny any article of the Christian creed in order to shift the focus from the public truth content of Christianity to the subject, pragmatic, and therapeutic categories of "how-to" religion. Christ may still be called *Savior*, but we really save ourselves by knowing and following the steps of the new birth and "victorious living."

Witten substantiates these observations, adding, "Taken to the extreme, this talk constitutes a 'do-it-yourself' guide for personal satisfaction, with a few mentions of God or faith or prayer tossed in to mark itself as 'religious.'" As a result of these processes, says Witten, "A religion's teachings no longer give meaning to their adherents' life in the world; their life in the world determines both the meanings and meaningfulness of their creed."[50]

As we can see then, the process of secularization is far more pervasive than theological differences between conservatives and liberals. It is not secular humanists but we ourselves who are secularizing the faith by transforming its odd message into something less jarring to the American psyche. This may mean, however, that precisely the most numerically successful versions of religion will be the least tethered to the biblical drama of redemption centering on Christ.

Witten's studies reveal that there was little difference between mainline Presbyterian and Southern Baptist sermons that she sampled. "The Calvinist roots of religious practice in Colonial America," she writes, were gradually eaten away by "popular ideologies of voluntarism, democratism, and pragmatism," making the view that human beings cannot "contribute to their own salvation seem less plausible."

While confessional Reformed and Presbyterian pastors and theologians in the mid-1800s challenged the emphasis on the self rather than God and human will over God's gracious initiative, revivalism finally won the field. As a result, "The major categories of evangelical talk about God tend to emphasize one's personal experience of an immanent deity." Witten adds, "When God is seen in transcendent terms at all, his fearsome qualities are either deemphasized or banished from the discourse and replaced by portraits of a clear-thinking, well-organized 'super-administrator,' one of whose primary functions is to plan efficiently the affairs of the universe."

This thinking, no doubt, contributes to the phenomenon that Smith characterizes as *moralistic, therapeutic deism.* God is basically the ideal Secretary of Homeland Security—*Homeland* defined as my own personal happiness, or national health, whether defined by the political left or right. Of course, when the affairs of the universe center on me and my happiness, this generic deism becomes therapeutic, especially focusing on "'God as daddy' and 'God as sufferer.'"

In a therapeutic paradigm, not only the parishioner but even God is put on the couch as we empathetically interpret his feelings. God is never angry or judgmental toward people; in fact, he is more anguished than we are, since he knows how much our actions can harm us. He is simply waiting for us to come to our senses, like the father in the parable of the prodigal son. We might even be inclined to feel sorry for this deity.

These sermon samples treated God exclusively as the *extravagant lover*. In fact, love overwhelms law; God sets aside any question of merit, duty, or achievement and simply embraces the prodigal. God never really surprises us, because his behavior is always predictable: he would never do anything to offend us. Consequently, there is no suggestion that we need a mediator at all, according to these sermons. God's love need not be correlated with his holiness, righteousness, and justice. Everything is okay—without any mention of Christ's self-sacrifice as the only way of reconciliation. Since, as a rule, God's love apparently overwhelms his justice and holiness, the "good news" offered here eliminates any need for the actual story recorded in the Gospels. If God's love so easily ignores his justice, holiness, and righteousness, then Christ's death on the cross seems like a cruel waste.

Witten writes, "The relatively weak notion of God's fearsome capabilities regarding judgment is underscored by an almost complete lack of discursive construction of anxiety around one's future state." It is "negative feelings," not an objectively negative danger, that these sermons stress as solved by the gospel. "The transcendent, majestic, awesome God of Luther and Calvin—whose image informed early Protestant visions of the relationship between human beings and the divine—has undergone a softening of demeanor throughout the American experience of Protestantism, with only minor interruptions."

When we adopt a human-centered approach that assimilates God to our own experience and happiness, the world is no longer God's creation; it too, like God, exists for our own personal well-being. Everything that exists is there for us to consume for our happiness. So, for example, drugs and sexual promiscuity are not wrong because they offend God, according to most of these sermons, but because they cannot compare with the joy and happiness of living God's way. They're not wrong as much as unfulfilling; they wear off. All the emphasis is on *celebration* and *happiness*, as in one sermon's assertion, "It feels good to be a Christian." When you are trying to sell a product like therapeutic transformation, there can be no ambiguity, no sense of anxiety, tension, or struggle.

In these sermons, another recurring emphasis is that human beings are victims and being *lost* no longer means damned but lacking direction in life. In the Southern Baptist sermons, the world is the pigpen in which the prodigal wasted his inheritance, with many sermons going into greater detail than Jesus on "cocktail parties, watching the vileness of Sodom in their living rooms, trying to escape reality with cocaine." Meanwhile, the church is the family.

The Southern Baptist sermons were far more likely to focus on the sins of the prodigal, centering on his rebellion against the home and its values, often going into great detail in order to make the wayward son as relevant to contemporary adolescents as possible. The most common summary of his fault in these sermons was that he rejected his own dignity and self-respect. "For Presbyterian speakers, on the other hand, it is the dutiful, religiously obedient, yet joyless older brother who is more likely to serve as the emblem of sin."

When the pastors sampled in these sermons do talk about sin, Witten relates, they depersonalize it, generalize it, and typically deflect it to outsiders. Without condoning their sin, says one Southern Baptist pastor, "We should go out to the poor, the blacks, the Hispanics, the beer drinkers, and the divorced." The deflection of sin to "outsiders" could hardly be more obvious. The main Presbyterian strategy, however, was to resist offering evaluations and empathize with both brothers. None of the sermons talk about sin in theological terms, "exemplified in the omission of the foundational doctrine of original sin."

Finally, Witten takes up what seems to be the main emphasis in these sermons: "the transformed self." While earlier preaching in America had an important place for transformation, she notes, it was "only through God's grace": the death of the old self and life of the new self in Christ. "This Augustinian vocabulary prevailed in Calvinist speech throughout the early years of American Protestantism," but it quickly succumbed to "modification that continues to the present day." Where the earlier notions identified self-love as the root of original sin, revivalists appealed to it as the motivation for conversion. With rising confidence in human ability more generally and "an emphasis on Arminian doctrines of free will," sin became transformed "into notions of sin as mistakes in behavior, amenable to correction by appropriate moral education." Like all behaviors, sin could be managed according to predictable principles.

Where the older views regarded the attempt to autonomously construct our own identities as part of the futility of being, in Augustine's words, "curved in on ourselves," Witten found that many of the sermons she evaluates assume the "self-crafted self" of secular culture. God *helps* in this endeavor, but the sense of the self as created for God's purposes, fallen in sin, and redeemed and refashioned by God, is at least muted by the original (autonomous and therapeutic) assumption. Increasingly, Americans came to see the church—with its appointed *means of grace* as secondary to "Bible classes, prayer meetings, and benevolent groups—in other words, parachurch organizations." Therefore, faith became increasingly privatized, with opportunities to express one's feelings, the language of faith "frequently laced with sentimentality."

Liberals and revivalists both de-emphasize God's transcendence and tend to see God's Word as something that wells up within a person rather than as something that comes to a person from outside. "The key to salvation thus lies *within* the self; the charge to the individual person is to listen and be receptive to this *inner voice*. Also, since sin was regarded largely as error or ignorance (consonant with liberal beliefs in the essential goodness of humankind), the view prevailed that behavioral change can come about through education about ethical and moral concerns" (emphasis added).

This opened the door to a psychologized understanding of faith in God "as a kind of therapy that would help men and women deal with the demands of the real world." Conservatives and liberals may argue over specific questions related to integrating theology and psychology, but both assume significantly psychologized interpretations of their creed. Conversion is basically self-fulfillment.

The central narrative of the Baptist sermons was "transformation through conversion," but both spoke in therapeutic terms. Conversion is up to us, but it's relatively easy to attain. It only requires "emotional self-awareness, openness, and receptivity," of which, of course, all people are entirely capable. Conversion will bring about "bonding with God," meaningful relationships, and triumph over one's daily problems.

The emphasis on transformation rests on important theological shifts: The first is an emphasis on free will. A recurring theme is that nothing is more essential to the self than free will. As one Southern Baptist preacher said, "In great love, God has set us free to become and to be, to take charge and be responsible for our own destinies." A second emphasis of this shift is "innate human goodness." One Presbyterian put it this way: "When Jesus says that [the prodigal son] came to himself, He pays us the highest of compliments, for He suggests that there is something within the human being which innately wants goodness and love, which wants to be at home and in harmony with the will of God." A Southern Baptist sermon includes the following quote:

When you get what you want in your struggle for wealth
  And the world makes you king for a day,
Then go to the mirror and look at yourself
  And see what that guy [or gal] has to say.
For it isn't your father or mother or wife
  Who judgment upon you must pass,
The fellow whose verdict counts most in your life
  Is the guy staring back from the glass.

Notice how "the fellow whose verdict counts most" is oneself rather than God.

A further element in this emphasis on transformation is the "psychology of openness, trust and self-disclosure, authenticity." The focus is almost exclusively human-centered rather than God-centered, and the view of human beings is basically Pelagian or at least semi-Pelagian. "Thus far, the speech of these sermons has identified a fundamental human nature at the core of every person: innately good, open to self-understanding, and in need of release from the artifice hiding its true identity." Although this is identified as the Christian doctrine of conversion, Witten's verdict is difficult to challenge: there is nothing here that couldn't be found in secular alternatives. The consistent message running throughout these sermons is, reach out to God; become vulnerable. But there is nothing here that would give a reason as to why "receiving God into the heart" is "the *only* possible recourse to realizing true selfhood."

For this transforming process of conversion, there are always effective procedures that become routinized and standardized. Witten points out that especially in the Southern Baptist sermons, the speech itself "collapses into a technical appendix, into which preachers insert talk about the procedures of getting saved." One pastor formalizes them from the parable: recognition, realization, responsibility, and restoration. Restoration is basically a human achievement of will and action. In fact, by the time they have stated the "effective procedures," which necessitate "human effort on a variety of fronts," conversion finally seems "not as easy as advertised." Among the typical concluding remarks are the following: "Open yourself to the salvation that God wants to work in your life."

So instead of introducing people to a majestic God who nevertheless condescended in mercy to save those who cannot save themselves, these sermons—even with the parable of the prodigal son as their text—proclaim a message that can be summarized as moralistic, therapeutic deism. As a product, the *God experience* can be sold and purchased with confidence that the customer is still king. Therefore, statements that would have appalled previous generations of mainline Protestants are assumed as a matter of course even among evangelicals today, such as George Barna's defense of "a fundamental principle of Christian communication: the audience, not the message is sovereign."[51]

Our Natural Heresy

I have identified Pelagianism as the default setting of the human heart: the religion of self-salvation. Much of Christianity in America, as elsewhere, stops short of being fully Pelagian. If asked directly whether we can save ourselves by moral effort apart from grace, I suspect most evangelicals would answer in the negative. However, grace is primarily seen by evangelicals as much as by the medieval church as divine *assistance* for the process of moral transformation rather than as a one-sided divine *rescue*.

If we are merely wayward, we only need direction; merely sick, we need medicine; merely weak, we need strength. Radical grace, on the other hand, answers to radical sinfulness—not simply to moral mistakes, lack of zeal, or spiritual lethargy, but to the condition that the Bible defines as nothing less than condemned, "children of wrath," "dead in trespasses and sins" (Eph. 2:1, 3).

In most cases, I suggest, it is semi-Pelagianism that dominates American Christianity, just as it did the medieval church. While Augustinianism affirms that God does all of the saving and Pelagianism crowns our moral achievement with the "grace" of acceptance, semi-Pelagianism says that salvation is a process that depends on the coworking of God and humans. The technical term for this position is *synergism* (working together). Donald Bloesch laments, "It must be acknowledged . . . that in much popular Protestantism synergism (salvation through both grace and free will) is even more evident than in Catholicism, and human reason and experience figure more prominently than Scripture in determining the norms for faith."[52]

Where we land on these issues is perhaps the most significant factor in how we approach our own faith and practice and communicate it to the world. If not only the unregenerate but the regenerate are always dependent at every moment on the free grace of God disclosed in the gospel, then nothing can raise those who are spiritually dead or continually give life to Christ's flock but the Spirit working through the gospel. When this happens (not just once, but every time we encounter the gospel afresh), the Spirit progressively transforms us into Christ's image. Start with Christ (that is, the gospel) and you get sanctification in the bargain; begin with Christ and move on to something else, and you lose both.

This means that no matter what methods, gimmicks, or excitements one might employ, no matter how much energy is invested in making the message relevant, our witness will fall on deaf ears unless God graciously intervenes. By contrast, if we adopt Pelagian or semi-Pelagian assumptions, we will carry the burden of trying to produce conversions, relying on our own cleverness and communicative power rather than on God's Word and Spirit.

But if reformation and repentance from our captivity to American religion is to really occur, there must be a rediscovery of sin. Original sin, as G. K. Chesterton observes, is 'the only part of Christian theology which can really be proved.' Later he says, "All the real argument about religion turns on the question of whether a man who was born upside down can tell when he comes right way up. The primary paradox of Christianity is that the ordinary condition of man is not his sane or sensible condition; that the normal itself is an abnormality."[53] Yet we suppress this truth with great sophistication, putting a comfortable spin on our lives in spite of our nagging sense of guilt. Making the gospel relevant can easily take the form of conforming it to the abnormal condition that we have come to regard as normal.

Jesus lamented that the religious leaders of his day were like children playing the funeral game and the marriage game, but they could neither mourn over their sins when John the Baptist came, nor dance in celebration at the arrival of the Son of Man (Matt. 11:16–19). Similarly today, the preaching of the law in all of its gripping judgment and the preaching of the gospel in all of its surprising sweetness merge into a confused message of gentle exhortation to a more fulfilling life. Consequently, we know neither how to mourn nor how to throw a real party. The bad news no longer stands in sharp contrast with the good news; we become content with so-so news that eventually fails to bring genuine conviction or genuine comfort but keeps us on the treadmill of anxiety, craving the next revival, technique, or movement to lift our spirits and catapult us to heavenly glory.

Without a serious recognition of original sin, Chesterton adds, we can easily become passive pawns in the game of dictators and democrats alike. It is the doctrine of human perfectibility that has brought tyrants to the world stage with the worshipful applause of the masses, but biblical teaching awakens us from our moralistic slumbers, identifying God as the only reliable object of our faith.[54]

Obviously it is a generalization, but Chesterton is basically correct when he says that Christianity's "outer ring" is despair—awareness of the tragic sense of life because of original sin, while its "inner ring" is "life dancing like children, and drinking wine like men; for Christianity is the only frame for pagan freedom. . . . But in the modern philosophy the case is the opposite; it is its outer ring that is obviously artistic and emancipated; its despair is within." Because its chief article is that life has no *transcendent* meaning or purpose, "it cannot hope to find any romance; its romances will have no plots. . . . One can find no meanings in a jungle of skepticism; but the man will find more and more meanings who walks through a forest of doctrine and design. Here everything has a story tied to its tail, like the tools or pictures in my father's house; for it is my father's house. I end where I began—at the right end. I have entered at least the gate of all good philosophy. I have come into my second childhood."[55] The funeral game is but the warm-up for the wedding game.

Smooth Talking
and Christless Christianity

We Americans are not well-known in the world as people who know how to blush. On the contrary, we are a very self-confident people. The last thing we want is to be told that we cannot do anything to save ourselves from the most serious problem that we have ever or will ever encounter—that we are entirely at God's mercy. Apart from a miracle, religious success in this atmosphere will always go to those who can effectively appeal to this can-do spirit and push as far to the background as possible anything that might throw our swaggering self off-balance. When looking for ultimate answers, we turn within ourselves, trusting our own experience rather than looking outside ourselves to God's external Word.

In the days of Judah's unfaithfulness, God upbraided the false prophets for craving affection and popularity. "They have healed the wound of my people lightly, saying, 'Peace, peace,' when there is no peace. . . . No, they were not at all ashamed; they did not know how to blush" (Jer. 6:14–15). Similarly, Paul had to defend his ministry against those whom he called the "super-apostles," who drew away disciples for themselves through their superior communication skills and a message more palatable to Greeks.

> For if someone comes and proclaims another Jesus than the one we proclaimed . . . or a different gospel . . . , you put up with it readily enough. I consider that I am not in the least inferior to these super-apostles. Even if I am unskilled in speaking, I am not so in knowledge; indeed, in every way we have made this plain to you in all things.
>
> 2 Corinthians 11:4–6

In the closing of his letter to the Romans, Paul appeals to the saints "to watch out for those who cause divisions and create obstacles contrary to the doctrine that you have been taught; avoid them. For such persons do not serve our Lord Christ, but their own appetites, and by smooth talk and flattery they deceive the hearts of the naive" (Rom. 16:17–18). Out of self-love, Paul warned Timothy, people will gather teachers who will tell them exactly what they want to hear (2 Tim. 3:2–4; 4:3–5). Much of what we call relevance Paul refers to in that passage as godlessness.

"Smooth talk and flattery" is part of the staple diet of successful American religion today. And it is almost always advertised simply as more effective mission and relevance.

"Playing fast and loose with the Bible needed a liberal audience in the days of Norman Vincent Peale," notes Yale theologian George Lindbeck, "but now, as the case of Robert Schuller indicates, professed conservatives eat it up."[1] Catapulted into prominence through his best-selling book, *The Power of Positive Thinking*, Peale was scolded by conservative Protestants for leaving out the most important aspects of Christian proclamation in favor of an upbeat message of self-help.

Robert Schuller, founding pastor of the Crystal Cathedral and Peale's most prominent disciple, helped to make this quintessentially American gospel more successful in evangelical circles. Spurred by his television ministry, Schuller's best-sellers include *Self-Esteem: The New Reformation, Self-Love, Believe in the God Who Believes in You*, and the *Be-Happy Attitudes*. Not only have evangelicals caught up with their liberal rivals in accommodating religion to secular culture, they are now clearly in the lead. No secular self-help guru comes close to the sales of evangelical rivals.

Taking a step beyond generic "positive thinking," a version of Pentecostalism known as the Word of Faith movement is spreading the *prosperity gospel* to the ends of the earth. Largely through their broadcasting and print empires, this message is spreading rapidly in the two-thirds world, especially in Africa. In an essay on mission and globalization, Wanyeki Mahiaini observes, "If you ask our televangelists why they agree with T. D. Jakes, for example, or Benny Hinn, and why they disagree with John Stott or other credible Bible teachers, you will find that the conclusions they have reached are not actually their own. They are merely repeating the biases and the prejudices that are common in the West."[2] Celebration of the much-advertised expansion of Christianity in the two-thirds world (most notably in recent years in Philip Jenkins's *The Next Christendom*) should at least be tempered by the fact that the prosperity gospel is the most explosive version of this phenomenon.

A number of theologians have pointed out the striking similarities between this prosperity message and ancient Gnosticism.[3] Like the ancient heresy, the Word of Faith message assumes a sharp dualism between spirit and matter, promising mastery over one's external circumstances by learning the secret principles of the invisible realm. Although creation itself is corrupt (referred to frequently as "the natural"), these teachers claim that the inner self is divine. "You don't have a God living in you," instructs Kenneth Copeland. "You are one. You are part and parcel of God."[4]

Perhaps no greater example of the church's American captivity can be discerned than in the remarkable success of Joel Osteen. To the extent that it reflects any theology at all, his message represents a convergence of Pelagian self-help and Gnostic self-deification. If a bland moralism from Protestant liberalism became part of the evangelical diet through Schuller, Osteen has achieved the dubious success of making the "name-it-claim-it" philosophy of Kenneth Copeland and Benny Hinn mainstream.

Osteen represents a variety of the moralistic, therapeutic deism that in less extreme versions seems to characterize much of popular religion in America today. Basically, God is there for you and your happiness. He has some rules and principles for getting what you want out of life, and if you follow them, you can have what you want. Just *declare it* and prosperity will come to you.[5] God as *personal shopper*.

Although explicit proponents of the prosperity gospel may be fewer than their influence suggests, its big names and best-selling authors (T. D. Jakes, Benny Hinn, Joel Osteen, and Joyce Meyer) are purveyors of a pagan worldview with a peculiarly American flavor. It's basically what Luther called the "theology of glory": How can I climb the ladder and attain the glory here and now that God has actually promised for us after a life of suffering? The contrast is the *theology of the cross*: the story of God's merciful descent to us at great personal cost—a message that the apostle Paul acknowledged was offensive and foolish to Greeks.

The attraction of Americans to this version of the "glory story" is evident in the astonishing success of Joel Osteen's runaway best-seller, *Your Best Life Now: Seven Steps to Living at Your Full Potential*, and the sequel, *Become a Better You*. Beyond his charming personality and folksy style, Osteen's phenomenal attraction is no doubt related to his simple and soothing sampler of the American gospel: a blend of Christian and cultural elements that he picked up not through any formal training, but as the son and television producer of a Baptist-turned-prosperity evangelist who was a favorite on the Trinity Broadcasting Network (TBN).

The pastor of Lakewood Church in Houston, which now owns the Compaq Center, does not come across as a flashy evangelist with jets and yachts but as a charming next-door neighbor who always has something nice to say. There are no televised healing lines, blessed prayer cloths, or other eccentricities of yesterday's televangelism. Nevertheless, the key tenets of Word of Faith dominate his teaching, although it is communicated in the terms and ambiance that might be difficult to distinguish from most megachurches and other seeker-driven ministries.

Law-Lite: Salvation from Unhappiness by Doing Your Best

There is no *condemnation* in Osteen's message for failing to fulfill God's righteous law. On the other hand, there is no *justification*. Instead of either message, there is an upbeat moralism that is somewhere in the middle: Do your best, follow the instructions I give you, and God will make your life successful. "Don't sit back passively," he warns, but with a gentle pleading he suggests that the only reason we need to follow his advice is because it's useful for getting what we want. God is a buddy or partner who exists primarily to make sure we are happy. "You do your part, and

God will do his part." "Sure we have our faults," he says, but "the good news is, God loves us anyway." Instead of accepting God's just verdict on our own righteousness and fleeing to Christ for justification, Osteen counsels readers simply to reject guilt and condemnation. Yet it is hard to do that successfully when God's favor and blessing on my life depend entirely on how well I can put his commands to work. "If you will simply obey his commands, He will change things in your favor."[6] That's all: *simply* obey his commands.

Everything depends on us, but it's easy. Osteen seems to think that we are basically good people and God has a very easy way for us to save ourselves—not from his judgment, but from our lack of success in life—with his help. "God is keeping a record of every good deed you've ever done," he says—as if this is *good* news. "In your time of need, *because of your generosity*, God will move heaven and earth to make sure you are taken care of."[7]

It may be *Law Lite*, but make no mistake about it: behind a smiling Boomer evangelicalism that eschews any talk of God's wrath, there is a determination to assimilate the gospel to law, an announcement of victory to a call to be victorious, indicatives to imperatives, Good News to good advice. The bad news may not be as bad as it used to be, but the Good News is just a softer version of the bad news: Do more. But this time, it's easy! And if you fail, don't worry. God just wants you to do your best. He'll take care of the rest.

So who needs Christ? At least, who needs Christ as "the Lamb of God who takes away the sin of the world" (John 1:29)? The sting of the law may be taken out of the message, but that only means that the gospel has become a less demanding, more encouraging law whose exhortations are only meant to make us happy, not to measure us against God's holiness.

As Marx said of a market-driven culture, "All that is solid melts into the air."[8] God, too, becomes a commodity—a product or therapy that we can buy and use for our personal well-being. Exemplifying the moralistic and therapeutic approach to religion, Osteen's message is also a good example of the inability of Boomers to mourn in the face of God's judgment or dance under the liberating news of God's saving mercy. In other words, all *gravity* is lost—both the gravity of our problem and of God's amazing grace. According to this message, we are not helpless sinners—the ungodly—who need a one-sided divine rescue. (Americans, but especially we Boomers, don't take bad news well.) Rather, we are good people who just need a little instruction and motivation.

So while many supporters offer testimonials to his kinder, gentler version of Christianity than the legalistic scolding of their youth, the only real difference is that God's rules or principles are easier these days and it's all about happiness here and now, not rescue from God's wrath by God's grace. In its therapeutic milieu, sin is failing to live up to our potential, not falling short of God's glory. It is "sin" not to believe in ourselves, and the wages of such sins is missing out on our best life now. But it's still a constant stream of exhortation, demands, and burdens: follow my steps and I guarantee your life will be blessed.

A *Time* magazine story in 2006 observed that Osteen's success has reached even more traditional Protestant circles, citing the example of a Lutheran church that followed *Your Best Life Now* during Lent, of all times, when, as the writer notes, "Jesus was having his worst life then."[9] Even churches formally steeped in a theology of the cross succumb to theologies of glory in the environment of popular American spirituality. We are swimming in a sea of narcissistic moralism: an easy-listening version of salvation by self-help.

This is what we might call the false gospel of "God Loves You Anyway." There's no need for Christ as our mediator since God is never quite as holy and we are never quite as morally perverse

71

as to require nothing short of Christ's death in our place. God is our buddy. He just wants us to be happy, and the Bible gives us the road map.

I have no reason to doubt the sincere motivation to reach non-Christians with a relevant message. My concern, however, is that the way this message comes out actually trivializes the faith at its best and contradicts it at its worst. We hear nothing that might offend a non-Christian, much less a believer in Christ; nothing about God's holiness, our condemnation, or Christ bearing our condemnation in our place. There is nothing in his message about the Trinity or the resurrection of the dead and the age to come. In fact, there is very little mention of Christ at all—a point that even reporters have pressed in interviews with Osteen. The televangelist shrugs off such concerns by saying that different people have different "giftings" and his mission is to help people live better. Osteen frequently points to the fact that adherents of other religions embrace his message (apparently without sensing any need for conversion) as a sign of his success.

There is little in Osteen's message that we have not heard before, repeatedly, from the culture of American optimism, expressed well by Disney's Jiminy Cricket: "If you wish upon a star, all your dreams will come true." While Osteen is hardly unique, his message is one of the clearest examples of moralistic, therapeutic deism. Is it possible to have evangelism without the evangel? Christian outreach without a Christian message?

If God matters, according to this outlook, it is for the most trivial concerns—or at least those quite secondary to the real crisis that the gospel addresses. One could easily come away from this type of message concluding that we are not saved by Christ's objective work for us but by our subjective *personal relationship with Jesus* through a series of works that we perform to secure his favor and blessing. God has set up all of these laws, and now it's up to us to follow them so we can be blessed.

As we lose a sense of God's gravity, sin loses its reference point. No longer falling short of God's glory (Rom. 3:23), sin is now falling short of the glory of the self. Everything is under control quite well without Christ. God is still keeping score—but only of the *good* things that we do, and the stakes are not quite as high: No longer an issue of our place in the life to come, it's just a question of getting the best out of life here and now.

Osteen reflects the broader assumption among evangelicals that we are saved by making a decision to have a personal relationship with God. The gospel seems to be that you can have a personal relationship with Jesus. Yet given the lack of any serious account of the human predicament before a holy God, it is unclear what this personal relationship might accomplish. Christ nowhere appears in Osteen's books (thus far at least) as a mediator between God and human beings. One searches in vain to find a substitute for sinners who fulfilled the law in their place and bore their guilt so that his righteousness could be imputed to them. It is not obvious how or why an average American today would even care to have a personal relationship with a Jewish rabbi who lived in the Middle East two thousand years ago. Living in the Bible Belt, I suppose, where "Jesus" is a rallying point for football games and the grand opening of shopping malls, the significance of Jesus can be taken for granted. The result, however, is a vague, sentimental attachment to someone who is more like an invisible friend than the incarnate, dead, raised, ascended, and reigning Savior of the ungodly.

In this context, Jesus becomes whatever you want him to be in your life. If one's greatest problem is loneliness, the good news is that Jesus is a reliable friend. If the big problem is anxiety, Jesus will calm us down. Jesus is the glue that holds our marriages and families together, gives us a purpose to strive toward, and provides wisdom for daily life. There are half-truths in all of these pleas, but they never really bring hearers face-to-face with their real problem: that they stand naked and ashamed before a holy God and can only be acceptably clothed in his presence by being clothed, head to toe, in Christ's righteousness.

This gospel of *submission, commitment, decision,* and *victorious living* is not good news about what God has achieved but a demand to save ourselves with God's help. Besides the fact that Scripture never refers to the gospel as having a *personal relationship with Jesus* nor defines faith as a decision to *ask Jesus to come into our heart,* this concept of salvation fails to realize that *everyone* has a personal relationship with God already: either as a condemned criminal standing before a righteous judge or as a justified coheir with Christ and adopted child of the Father.

"How can I be right with God?" is no longer a question when my happiness rather than God's holiness is the main issue. Joel Osteen is simply the latest in a long line of self-help evangelists who appeal to the innate American obsession with pulling ourselves up by our own bootstraps. Salvation is not a matter of divine rescue from the judgment that is coming on the world but rather a matter of self-improvement in order to have your best life now.

Osteen on *Larry King Live*

In his interview with Larry King (CNN, June 20, 2005), Osteen said he is not sure what happens to people who reject Christ. King followed up with the question about Jews, Moslems, and other non-Christians. "They're wrong, aren't they?" Osteen replied, "Well, I don't know if I believe they're wrong. I believe here's what the Bible teaches and from the Christian faith this is what I believe. But I just think that only God will judge a person's heart. I spent a lot of time in India with my father. I don't know all about their religion but I know they love God. And I don't know. I've seen their sincerity. So I don't know. I know for me, and what the Bible teaches, I want to have a relationship with Jesus."

King (and a caller) gave him a few more chances to answer the question, but it kept coming back to the heart: "God's got to look at your heart." Evidently the last judgment will be based not on God's standard of holiness and justice but on the purity of our hearts.

Certainly there is truth in this position. God will expose all the secrets of our hearts on the last day. But where Osteen seems to think that God's judgment of our heart (like his record keeping) is good news, Scripture treats it as the worst possible report since "the heart is deceitful above all things and desperately wicked. Who can know it?" (Jer. 17:9 NKJV). Jesus adds, "For out of the heart proceed evil thoughts, murders, adulteries, fornications, thefts, false witness, blasphemies" (Matt. 15:19 NKJV). My heart has conceived and committed sins that my hands have never carried out. Far from being a relatively unspoiled beach of sanctity, the heart is the citadel from which our mutiny against God and neighbor is launched. Even when I have done the right thing as far as other people are concerned, if my *sincerity* were weighed, it would actually count against my righteousness. So it is a dangerous mistake to think that our trial before God's all-knowing justice can somehow turn in our favor by examination of our heart or the record of our life. I keep thinking of St. Anselm's great response to those who thought that Christ's death was not a vicarious substitution: "You have not yet considered how great your sin is." Osteen's outlook may resonate with Americans steeped in a sentimentalized version of the Pelagian heresy of self-salvation. But it is not Christianity.

When asked by Larry King if he uses the word *sinners*, Osteen replied, "I don't use it. I never thought about it, but I probably don't. But most people already know what they're doing wrong. When I get them to church I want to tell them that you can change." What's remarkable is that he has not even thought about it.

The first move in Osteen's trivialization of sin is to shift its focus from an offense against God with eternal consequences to an offense against oneself that keeps us from health, wealth, and happiness right now. While his predecessors preached hell-fire-and-brimstone to get people to stop smoking, drinking, and participating in sexual immorality, Osteen's goal is to get people to follow his practical principles so they can have their best life now. It's not heaven in the hereafter but happiness here and now—and it is still up to you to make it happen. By doing certain things, you determine whether God's favor and blessing will come your way.

The second move in this trivialization of sin is to reduce it to actions (negative behaviors) that can be easily overcome by instruction rather than a condition from which we are helpless to free ourselves. If I can stop committing sin x, then it is at least logically possible that I can stop committing sin y, and so on, until I am at least avoiding all known sins. If, however, sin is first of all a condition and only secondarily actions, then no matter how many *sins* I "conquer," I'm still *sinful*! No matter what advances I think I've made, according to God, "There is no one righteous, not even one; there is no one who understands; no one who seeks God" (Rom. 3:10–11 NIV; quoting Pss. 14:1–3; 53:1–3). "Our *righteousness*"—never mind our sins!—"is like filthy rags" (Isa. 64:6 NKJV; emphasis added). So now we can no longer rest confidently in our own behaviors, standards, Judeo-Christian ethics, virtues, discipleship, deeds of love and kindness, and pious spirituality. We can no longer divide the world neatly into *decent* and *disgusting*; we must take our place with the prostitutes and publicans rather than with the Pharisees in order to enter the kingdom of God.

Wouldn't Osteen's message have a lot in common with what I've just said? In tone, perhaps. Instead of considering us Christians just as disqualified from heaven on our own merits as publicans and prostitutes, however, his message assumes that deep down we are all—including publicans and prostitutes—pretty good people who could just be a little better. Ironically, he shares with his hellfire-and-brimstone forebears an assumption that sin is not an all-encompassing condition from which we cannot free ourselves but instead particular actions that we can overcome through good instructions. And he too has his own lists. He may include some of the older taboos, but the main *sins* are failing to put God's principles for success into practice.

There are important differences, of course. First of all, *sins* seem to lack any clear vertical dimension. That is, it is not obvious that sin, in Osteen's view, is an offense against God. That's why he does not speak of sins but of mistakes or failure to be all we can be. According to the Bible, it is their offensiveness to God that makes such attitudes and actions sins in the first place. Without that *vertical* (God-oriented) dimension, even sinful actions lose their moral context. Instead, they become translated into the therapeutic language of *dysfunction*—unhealthy behaviors that fail to merit God's favor on us in our daily search for good parking spaces. But sinful actions, in this view, even lack the usual *horizontal* dimension: an offense against our neighbors. Even the social gospel, which made sin more of an offense against our fellow humans rather than first and foremost against God, at least recognized it as a failure to give to someone else the love and service that I owe. In the increasingly pervasive message of preachers like Osteen, however, sins become offenses I commit against myself that keep me from realizing my own expectations. It is therapeutic narcissism: I have failed to live up to my potential, to secure God's best for my life, or to follow the instructions that lead to the good life. Can we even comprehend in our human-centered universe of discourse today the God-centered orientation of David's confession to God: "Against you, you alone, have I sinned, and done what is evil in your sight" (Ps. 51:4 NRSV)?

Second, Osteen does not even use the words *sin* or *sinners*, as he himself observed above. In their place apparently is something like *mistake*. No longer "falling short of the glory of God" (see Rom. 3:23), sin is falling short of my best life now. "Is it hard to lead a Christian life?" asked Larry King. "I don't think it's that hard," Osteen replied. "To me it's fun. We have joy and happiness. . . . I'm not trying to follow a set of rules and stuff. I'm just living my life."

Again we meet the swinging pendulum: recoiling from the decidedly *un-fun* legalism of his youth, Osteen rebounds into the arms of antinomianism (no law). No wonder he does not speak of sins (much less the sinful condition that renders us all—even believers—sinners), since there is apparently no divinely given *set of rules* that might identify such an offense. The standard is not righteousness, but fun; not holiness before God, but happiness before oneself.

It is not obvious that Christ—at least his incarnation, obedient life, atoning death, and justifying and life-giving resurrection—is necessary at all in Osteen's scheme. "But you have rules, don't you?" King pressed, to which Osteen replied, "We do have rules. But the main rule is to honor God with your life. To live a life of integrity. Not be selfish. You know, help others. But that's really the essence of the Christian faith." Notice how Osteen's happy, fun-filled Christian life without rules suddenly becomes the most demanding religion possible. He is certainly correct when he says that God commands a life of integrity and helping others, not being selfish. In fact, Jesus excoriated the Pharisees for substituting their own petty laws for God's commands, which actually served some good purpose for our neighbors. But this is precisely what God's law prescribes. Jesus summarizes "the whole law": "love the Lord your God with all your heart, and with all your soul, and with all your mind and with all your strength, . . . [and] love your neighbor as yourself" (Mark 12:30–31). Osteen apparently thinks this is *easier* than following "a set of rules." In truth, as the rich young ruler learned, it is not. I may keep from literally killing my neighbor, but if I have not sacrificed everything for my neighbor's good, I have not really loved him or her. Osteen thinks that loving our neighbor is easier than "a lot of rules," but Jesus showed us that it's the other way around. One may appear sexually pure to one's friends, but God knows whether adultery has been committed in one's heart.

Osteen said that perhaps talk of God's judgment "was for a time," a generation ago. "But I don't have it in my heart to condemn people. I'm there to encourage them. I see myself more as a coach, as a motivator to help them experience the life God has for us."

At first glance, this sounds humble—and perhaps it is when compared to some of the moralistic and self-righteous jeremiads of yesteryear who threatened God's judgment for drinking a glass of wine or going to a movie. But the answer to bad law-preaching is good law-preaching, not its elimination. To say, "I don't have it in my heart to condemn people" is to point to one's own niceness rather than to the judgment that holds us all accountable as transgressors before God.

The proper preaching of the law—God's holiness, righteousness, glory, and justice—will not create an *us* versus *them* self-righteousness but will expose the best works, done from the best motives of the best among us, as filthy rags before God's searching judgment. *Bad law-preaching levels* some *of us; Osteen's omission of the law levels* none *of us; biblical preaching of the law levels* all *of us.*

It is actually arrogant for ambassadors to create their own policies, especially when they directly counter the word of the one who sent them. Osteen seems to admit that Jesus Christ is in some way unique and important, but he presumes ignorance of a point that Christ made perfectly clear: namely, that he is the only way of salvation from the coming judgment.

Was Jesus's message—however radically different from the rambling jeremiads of fundamentalism—only "for a time" as well? Did Jesus think that people are basically good when you look at their heart? Did he think that sincerity and moral effort would suffice as our clothing when we appear before the Judge of all the earth?

If Jesus and the apostles clearly proclaimed the total depravity of the human heart and redemption by Christ alone through faith alone, then Osteen is not being humble when he declines to represent that central announcement. It was Jesus who said that anyone who does not trust in him "stands condemned already" (John 3:18 NIV). That was because for Jesus, the judgment he came to save us from by enduring it for us had God and his glory, not me and my temporal happiness, as its reference point. The ditch we had dug for ourselves was so deep that only God incarnate could pull us out of it by falling in and climbing back out of it himself as our Substitute and Victor. For Osteen, the good news is that on judgment day God will look at our heart. According to Scripture, that is actually the bad news. The good news is that for all who are in Christ, God looks on the heart, life, death, and resurrection of his Son and declares us righteous in him. It is not a cheap gift, but it is a free gift.

Become a Better You

More recently, Osteen has written *Become a Better You: 7 Keys to Improving Your Life Every Day*. Under the Library of Congress identification, this book is classified as "1. Self-actualization (Psychology)—Religious Aspects—Christianity." Even the Library of Congress seems to know what sort of message this represents.

"You can be better," Osteen invites. "The question is: 'How? What must I do to become a better me?' In my first book, *Your Best Life Now*, I presented seven steps to living at your full potential." But with *Become a Better You*, he wants to go a little deeper. "I'm hoping to help you *look inside yourself* and discover *the priceless seeds of greatness that God has placed within you*. In this book, I will reveal to you *seven keys* that *you can use to unlock* those seeds of greatness, allowing them to burst forth in an abundantly blessed life. . . . Remember, God has put in you everything you need to live a victorious life. Now, it's up to you to draw it out. . . . What does it mean to become a better you? First, you understand that God wants you to become all that He created you to be. Second, it is imperative that you realize that God will do His part, but you must do your part as well" (emphasis added).[10] So the worst news you are likely to hear from Osteen is nothing that you didn't already know, and the best news is that by following his advice you can have more.

The *seven keys* are not gospel indicatives. In other words, announcements of God's saving work in Christ—such as prophetic anticipation of the Messiah; the incarnation; Christ's active obedience in the place of sinners; his sin-bearing death and victorious resurrection as the head of a body; Christ's ascension to represent us before the Father and send his Spirit into our hearts as a down-payment on the resurrection of our bodies at the end of the age when he returns in glory to judge the living and the dead. Rather, they are imperatives (commands) that could be generated from a host of sources without any appeal to the Bible: "To become a better you, you must: (1) Keep pressing forward. (2) Be positive toward yourself. (3) Develop better relationships.

(4) Form better habits. (5) Embrace the place where you are. (6) Develop your inner life. (7) Stay passionate about life." These are all things for you to do, without any mention of the Good News of what has been done for us by God.

The theme is "coming up higher," again in line with the theology of glory: our self-confident ascent rather than God's humble and sacrificial descent to us. From beginning to end, Osteen addresses his vast readership as though each person is "a child of the Most High God," with no mention of Christ as the Mediator of this relationship. Rather, it is simply by virtue of being created in God's image that everyone has these "seeds of greatness" planted within them—this divine DNA: "It's all in you. You are full of potential. But you have to do your part and start tapping into it. . . . You have the seed of Almighty God on the inside of you. . . . We have to believe that we have what it takes." The aberrant teaching of prosperity evangelists like Kenneth Copeland and other TBN notables, namely that we are "little gods" who have the essence of divinity within us, is promoted in less detailed yet explicit terms.

It is indeed true that there are appeals to the Bible scattered throughout Osteen's book. In nearly every case, however, a verse either is torn from its context and turned into a fortune cookie kind of promise that one can *name and claim* for oneself or is actually misquoted to serve Osteen's point. Whereas in Genesis 3:11 God asks Adam, "Who told you that you were naked?" in order to convict him of his sin, Osteen makes it sound as though it was Satan who told Adam that he had failed the test and didn't have what it takes to succeed.

As in his earlier book, Osteen here never speaks of sin as falling short of God's glory but of falling short of our own potential. In fact, Osteen's attachment to the prosperity gospel is even more explicit in *Become a Better You*. As if the fall never happened, Osteen writes, "He has programmed you with everything you need for victory," although *achieving* that victory is up to you. It requires daily self-talk: "I have what it takes. I am more than a conqueror. I am intelligent; I am talented. I am successful; I am attractive; I am an overcomer."

Whereas in Galatians 3:29 Paul argues that the inheritance of eternal life comes through the promise (Christ) rather than by the law, Osteen again lifts a single verse out of its context as a promise of temporal prosperity. This is a clear example of how Osteen turns even the most obvious references to *Christ* (as the fulfillment of Old Testament prophecy) into timeless examples of what can happen to us if we name and claim our blessings. He does not *interpret* Scripture; he *uses* it as a book of quotations to serve his own prosperity message.

The book is shot through with the lingo of the prosperity gospel: we are to *declare* God's blessing, *speak* prosperity, and *prophesy* health, wealth, and happiness into our lives. All of this creates the impression that God has set up everything for our victory, but it is up to us to actually plug into the power source and create our blessings by following the proper principles and procedures.

So in spite of the supernatural rhetoric, at the end of the day it all sounds deistic: God has set up everything, with the laws of prosperity in place, and now the ball is in our court. Following a well-worn path of *victorious life* teachers, Osteen speaks of *tapping into* the eternal realm. In this way even religion becomes a species of technology: by knowing the right principles, formulas, and steps, prosperity, blessing, and favor can be yours here and now. Once again, the Gnostic brand of spirituality is readily apparent:

He wants us to have a little heaven on earth, right where we are. . . . You can accomplish your dreams before you go to heaven! How can you do that? By tapping into God's power inside of you. . . . Please understand that those are all things from which you have already been set free. *But here's the catch*: If you don't appreciate and take advantage of your freedom, if you don't get your thoughts, your words, your attitudes going in the right direction, it won't do you any good. You may be sitting back waiting on God to do something supernatural in your life, but the truth is, God is waiting on you. You must rise up in your authority, have a little backbone and determination, and say, "I am not going to live my life in mediocrity, bound by addictions, negative and defeated" [emphasis added].

God may be the source of this blessing in an ultimate sense, since he set things up, but whether we actually receive God's favor and blessings depends entirely on our attitude, action, and obedience.

Osteen devotes a chapter to "Making Your Words Work for You," offering examples of people whose "positive declarations" brought them health, wealth, and happiness. In a chapter titled "Have Confidence in Yourself," Osteen repeats his mantra, again misquoting the Bible: "The Scripture says, 'Our faith is made effectual when we acknowledge everything good in us.' Think about this: Our faith is not effective when we acknowledge all our hurts and pains. It's not effective when we stay focused on our shortcomings or our weaknesses. Our faith is most effective when we acknowledge the good things that are in us."

The closest thing I have been able to find to the wording cited by Osteen is Paul's statement in 2 Corinthians 12:9: "But he [Jesus] said to me, 'My grace is sufficient for you, for my power is made perfect in weakness.' Therefore I will boast all the more gladly of my weaknesses, so that the power of Christ may rest upon me." Of course if this is the verse Osteen has in mind, it says exactly the opposite of his paraphrase. In fact, it is part of a larger explanation of why Paul, in contrast to the "super-apostles" who were leading the Corinthians astray with their "smooth talk and flattery," would "not boast about myself, except of my weaknesses." In fact, Paul says that God gave him a "thorn in the flesh . . . to keep me from exalting myself" (2 Cor. 12:5, 7 NASB: see vv. 5–10). In times of weakness, distress, and difficulty, Paul says, where we lose our self-confidence to handle our situation before God, we are actually in the best position for God to show his power.

In the only clear reference to trusting in Christ that I came across in this book, Osteen still feels compelled to include us as the object of faith: "When we believe in God's Son, Jesus Christ, *and believe in ourselves*, that's when our faith comes alive. When we believe *we* have what it takes, we focus on *our* possibilities" (emphasis added).

Even when the concepts of sin and redemption are employed, they are redefined. Sin is not a condition of rebellion that we inherit from Adam; it is diseases, poverty, and bad attitudes that we inherit from our family line. In the Bible, a *curse* has its proper place in the context of the covenant. For example, in ancient Near Eastern treaties, which form the pattern of covenantal thinking employed in the Bible, an emperor could bring judgment on a rebellious tribe or nation under his rule. This sanction would be called a *curse*: the emperor's invocation of the penalties that were threatened for violators of the treaty.

In the prosperity gospel, however, *curse* is more nearly related to the world of magic—the way we usually speak of curses in our culture today. So where the curses that God invokes upon humanity as a result of Adam's sin in the garden are a judicial sentence, Osteen speaks of "generational curses" that have no obvious reference to divine judgment. Sin is transformed into the language of dueling DNA. You may have inherited your grandmother's genes, which include the curse of diabetes, but "you need to put your foot down and say, 'Grandmother may have had it [diabetes]. Mother may have had it. But as for me and my house, we're redeemed from diabetes. I'm going to live under the blessing and not the curse. . . . This type of blessing is for believers, not doubters." It would not be surprising, then, if such teaching led a sincere follower to conclude that a failure to be healed or to become financially prosperous was the result of his or her own disobedience.

If I am diagnosed with Grandma's diabetes, am I a doubter rather than a believer? "The Bible calls it an *iniquity*," Osteen writes. Accordingly, sin is not a condition of inherent corruption and guilt that generates sinful thoughts, desires, and actions; rather, it is diseases and destructive patterns of behavior passed down through one's bloodline—"until somebody rises up and puts a stop to it." Obviously, that "somebody" is *you*, not *Christ*.

The ethical character of sin as both a condition and specific actions of transgressing or failing to conform to God's law is exchanged for a magical conception. At the same time, our victory over generational curses is entirely manageable through the spiritual technology that God has designed. "God has given you free will. You can choose to change. . . . Thank God, you and I can do something about it." This is the *good* news?

Osteen redefines redemption as freedom from pain, illness, and poverty as well as the bad attitudes and negative habits that our parents or grandparents passed on to us. "Think of it like this: Each of us has a spiritual bank account. By the way we live, we are either storing up equity or storing up iniquity. Equity would be anything good: our integrity, our determination, our godliness. That's storing up blessings. On the other hand, iniquity includes our bad habits, addictions, selfishness, lack of discipline."

In Philippians 3 the apostle Paul uses the spiritual bank account analogy to confess that although he was a Pharisee of Pharisees, scrupulously observing the law, he now places his own righteousness in the debit column (calling it "dung," v. 8 KJV) and clings exclusively to Christ's righteousness imputed to him through faith alone. For Osteen, however, it is exactly the opposite: "Your faithfulness is noticed in heaven. You are storing up equity for both yourself and generations to come." In fact, this theme of storing up equity by self-improvement runs throughout *Become a Better You*: "Get up every day and give it your best effort. If you will do that, not only will you rise higher and accomplish more, but God has promised that your seed, your family line for up to a thousand generations, is going to have the blessings and the favor of God—all because of the life that you've lived." Elsewhere he says, "God is keeping the records. He sees every act of kindness you show. He sees every time you are good to somebody. He hears every encouraging word you speak. God has seen all the times you went out of your way to help somebody who never said thank you. Your good deeds do not go unnoticed by Almighty God."

Make no mistake about it, behind all of the smiles there is a thorough-going religion of works-righteousness: "God's plan for each of our lives is that we continually rise to new levels. But how high we go in life, and how much of God's favor and blessings we experience, will be directly related to how well we follow His directions." God "is waiting for your obedience so He can release more of His favor and blessings in your life. . . . My question to you is: How high do you want to rise? Do you want to continue to increase? Do you want to see more of God's blessings and favor? If so, the higher we go, the more disciplined we must be; the quicker we must obey."

In fact, it is not simply that God makes the first move and then leaves the next move to us. Grace is a reward for our works. "You don't get the grace unless you step out. You have to make the first move. . . . Remember: How high you go in life will be directly related to how obedient you are."

And if anyone has any questions about whether this plan is workable, Osteen offers himself as an example: "I know I'm not perfect, but I also know this: My conscience is clear before God. I know that I'm doing my best to please Him. That's why I can sleep well at night. That's why I can lie down in peace. That's why I have a smile on my face. Friend, keep your conscience tender, and you will discover that life keeps getting better and better."

By contrast, Jesus and his apostles taught that the searching judgment of God through his law brings conviction, pricking my conscience that I have fallen short of God's glory. My conscience does not render a positive verdict in God's courtroom when I look inside myself. The only reason I can sleep well at night is that even though my heart is still filled with corruption and even though I am not doing my best to please him, I have in heaven at the Father's right hand the beloved Son, who has not only done his best for himself but has fulfilled all righteousness for me in my place.

So we see once again that Osteen has not abandoned the legalism of previous generations. If anything, he intensifies it. But his followers do not recognize the tightening noose or the mounting burden because he makes it sound so easy. It is not easy, however, to be told that our health, wealth, and happiness—as well as our victory over sin and death—depend on the extent of our determination and effort. A weak view of sin fails to bring us to the end of our rope; instead, it encourages us to try just a little bit harder to save ourselves. It's easy. *Really.*

Where Jeremiah says that the heart is more deceitful than anything else (Jer. 17:9), Osteen says that his confidence before God is in the righteousness of his own heart: "I may not have a perfect performance, but I know my heart is right. . . . Similarly, as long as you're doing your best and desire to do what's right according to God's Word, you can be assured God is pleased with you. Certainly, He wants you to improve, but He knows that we all have weaknesses." Sin is reduced to "human foibles and imperfections" that "poke through *our idealism*" rather than failing to conform to *God's law*. "*As long as we're doing our best*, we don't have to live condemned even when we make mistakes or fail" (emphasis added). But that's the *problem*: I don't do my best—not just on bad days, but on good ones. If according to Scripture our best is "filthy rags" (Isa. 64:6 NIV), Osteen's condition is actually condemnation.

The Good News of the Scriptures is that God does not judge us according to our record but according to Christ's. But Osteen repeatedly argues that God judges us—or rather, unfailingly approves us—on the basis of our inherent goodness and best efforts. Osteen believes that God "is smiling down on me right now" not because of Christ but because even though he is not perfect, "I know my heart is right. To the best of my ability, I'm doing what pleases Him. . . . Frankly, it's not because of what you have or haven't done; God loves you because of who you are and because of who he is. God is *love*."

Osteen's God is uncomplicated. Characterized by only one attribute (love), God's forgiveness is cheap. His love does not require consistency with his justice, holiness, and righteousness. Therefore, it is not *merciful* love—that is, compassion toward those who deserve judgment.

By contrast, the God of the Bible is far more interesting and majestic. Finding a way to love sinners that does not violate his holy character, God gave his Son to fulfill the law and bear our judgment in our place. The biblical plot of the redemptive drama is rich, while Osteen's story is thin—with me rather than God at the center

Once again, Osteen's message—though perhaps a bit more explicitly oriented toward the prosperity gospel than most—is not all that different from the general drift of a lot of popular religion and spirituality that pervades even our own evangelical circles today. The focus is on us rather than on God, on our happiness apart from God's holiness, on our *ascending higher* by moral effort rather than on our being receivers of God's saving work in Jesus Christ. Osteen reassures his readers, "I know, too, even when my plans don't work out, even when things don't go my way, because I am honoring God and striving to keep the right attitude, God will make it up to me."

Having exchanged the gospel of Christ's doing, dying, and rising for a pep talk for our doing, declaring, and rising, Osteen can say, "The world does not need to hear another sermon nearly as much as it needs to see one." Now *we* are the Good News.

But once we are placed back under the law for righteousness, on what basis can Osteen claim that God only counts the good works? Is there a single passage in the Bible that separates God's record-keeping in this way, so that our good works can bring God's favor and blessing but our sins do not count at all? If we are going to inherit God's promises by the "righteousness that is by the law" (Rom. 10:5 NIV), then Osteen's pleasant outlook hardly seems justified.

Just as Joel Osteen has decided for himself the message he will preach, he has also tailored his own vocation. In interviews, he has said that he is not called to explain the Scriptures or expound doctrine. In this book he adds, "I'm not called to explain every minute facet of Scripture or to expound on deep theological doctrines or disputes that don't touch where real people live. My gifting is to encourage, to challenge, and to inspire."

Ambassadors do not get to choose what they say. As ministers of the gospel, our *gifting* is to preach "the whole counsel of God" (Acts 20:27). As Paul says in Romans 10, we do not ascend to God; he descends to us in grace. He sends ambassadors who will preach the Good News that they have been *appointed* to preach. They do not send themselves but are sent on someone else's errand. "For faith comes by hearing, and hearing by the word of God" (v. 16 NKJV).

Glory and the Cross

Grab all the glory now. No cross, no wrath, no judgment. Just be all you can be. We are constantly bombarded in our culture by appeals to our native narcissism. The religious version of this message—purveyed for some time by liberals and many evangelicals today—makes God a means to an end rather than the end for whom we exist. In all of its varieties, this is the theology of glory. But it is not the glory that the gospel promises up ahead for those who in this life share in Christ's suffering and humiliation. It is the glory that we demand here and now by our own efforts, denying the reality of sin and death.

It is clear that Osteen is reacting against the scolding legalism of a previous generation, which beat people down over rules. Yet Osteen's alternative is to tell people to "lighten up and give yourself a break," asking God to "help me to do better next time." The biblical message is far deeper and richer, however, both in its bad news and its good news. The bad news is far worse than making mistakes or failing to live up to the legalistic standards of fundamentalism. It is that the best efforts of the best Christians, on the best days, in the best frame of heart and mind, with the best motives fall short of that true righteousness and holiness that God requires. Our best efforts cannot satisfy God's justice. Yet the good news is that God has satisfied his own justice and reconciled us to himself through the life, death, and resurrection of his Son. God's holy law can no longer condemn us because we are in Christ.

Instead of pointing us to Christ, where God's record-keeping was justly satisfied and the court transcription was nailed to the cross (Col. 2:14), Osteen gets rid of the idea of any negative record. God is only keeping records of "what you're doing right," your "conscious decision to be better, to live right, and to trust Him. He is pleased that you are kind and courteous to people." So nothing can count against us (not because of Christ but because God simply does not record shortcomings), but God's favor does depend on his record of our *good* deeds. Doesn't this mean that if I do *not* obey I will not receive God's blessing? And doesn't that imply that God is in fact keeping a record of sins?

Far from Paul's struggle in Romans 7, Osteen makes it sound as if we can manage the sin problem by our own positive outlook. "If you want to sin, you can sin. I sin all I want to," he says. "The good news is that I don't want to. . . . Stop dwelling on everything that's wrong with you and taking an inventory of what you're not. The Scripture says in Hebrews, 'To look away from everything that distracts.'" Once again, Osteen misquotes the Bible to make his point. Hebrews 12:1–2 actually reads, "Therefore, since we have so great a cloud of witnesses surrounding us, let us also lay aside every encumbrance and the sin which so easily entangles us, and let us run with endurance the race that is set before us, *fixing our eyes on Jesus*, the author and perfecter of faith, who for the joy set before Him endured the cross, despising the shame, and sat down at the right hand of the throne of God."

In other words, the counsel in Hebrews is to look away from ourselves—both our sins and our good works—and not let anything distract us *from Christ*. Yet Osteen's entire message represents a distraction from Christ. Who needs Christ if this is the gospel: "You're not perfect, but you are trying to live better, and God looks at your heart. He sees the inside, and He is changing you little by little"?

The bad news is far worse than that we are not experiencing health, wealth, and happiness now. It is that we are actually dying and nothing can reverse this fact. It gets worse. Death is just a symptom. We will all have a different cause of death listed on the medical certificate. Death, however, itself is the result of a condition we all share: "The wages of sin is death" (Rom. 6:23); "The sting of death is sin, and the power of sin is the law" (1 Cor. 15:56). Notice that it is not sins (particular actions) but *sin* (a condition) that requires our death. Even now we are falling apart on our way toward death—even if we are having our best life now.

At the same time, the Good News is far greater than finding a way to mask our symptoms. In both passages just cited, it is the counterpoint to the bad news: "For the wages of sin is death, *but the free gift of God is eternal life in Christ Jesus*" (Rom. 6:23; emphasis added). "The sting of death is sin, and the power of sin is the law. *But thanks be to God, who gives us the victory through our Lord Jesus Christ*" (1 Cor. 15:56–57; emphasis added). The victory promised here is far greater than relief from stress, sadness, loneliness, disappointment, and even illness leading to death. It is the victory over everlasting death through the resurrection on the last day, as we share in Christ's victory over the grave: "When the perishable puts on the imperishable, and the mortal puts on immortality, then shall come to pass the saying that is written: 'Death is swallowed up in victory.' 'O death, where is your victory? O death, where is your sting?'" (1 Cor. 15:54–55). Christ did not deal with symptoms; he went right to the source: the curse that his law justly imposes as the penalty for our participation in Adam's sin. As the first Adam brought death, the last Adam brought eternal life (1 Cor. 15:20–24).

Far greater than living longer and enjoying ourselves and our circumstances is the unfathomable richness of our life together with God, reconciled even while we were enemies, made alive even while we were spiritually dead, brought near even while we were strangers, and adopted as coheirs of the entire estate even while we were hostile to the things of God. Even now we begin to enjoy a foretaste of this feast, as those for whom "there is therefore now no condemnation" (Rom. 8:1).

You do not need Christ for the things that Osteen and many other preachers today promise. You do not need the Bible, just Tony Robbins. You do not need the kind of redemption that is promised in the Gospels. It is not even clear why you would need God simply to have a more positive outlook on life. Joel Osteen's message is representative of a much broader phenomenon of assimilating the gospel to culture. Whatever doctrines to which one might give assent, the story in which American religion lives and moves and has its being makes the message sound basically the same whether it comes from conservatives or liberals, Baptists or New Agers, Pentecostals or Roman Catholics, Reformed or Arminians, Unitarians or Lutherans. As heretical as it sounds today, it is probably worth telling Americans that you don't need Jesus to have better families, finances, health, or even morality. Coming to the cross means *repentance*—not adding Jesus as a supporting character for an otherwise decent script but throwing away the script in order to be written into God's drama. It is death and resurrection, not coaching and makeovers.

When we try to fit God into our *life movie*, the plot is all wrong—and not just wrong but trivial. When we are pulled out of our own drama and cast as characters in his unfolding plot, we become part of the greatest story ever told. It is through God's Word of judgment (law) and salvation (gospel) that we are transferred from our own pointless scripts and inserted into the grand narrative that revolves around Jesus Christ. In the process, as Dietrich Bonhoeffer reminds us,

> We are uprooted from our own existence and are taken back to the holy history of God on earth. There God has dealt with us, with our needs and our sins, by means of the divine wrath

94

and grace. What is important is not that God is a spectator and participant in our life today, but that we are attentive listeners and participants in God's action in the sacred story, the story of Christ on earth. God is with us today only as long as we are there. Our salvation is "from outside ourselves" (*extra nos*). I find salvation, not in my life story, but only in the story of Jesus Christ. . . . What we call our life, our troubles, and our guilt is by no means the whole of reality; our life, our need, our guilt, and our deliverance are there in the Scriptures.[11]

Jesus knew why he came. It was not to help people find a little more happiness and success in life. In fact, his life was filled with suffering, under the long shadow of Calvary. "For this purpose I have come," he said, referring to the cross (John 12:27). "The Son of Man has come to seek and to save that which was lost" (Luke 19:10 NKJV).

The disciples thought the road to Jerusalem led to victory. Entering as conquerors at the side of the Messiah, they would drive out the Romans and usher in the everlasting reign of God. Each time Jesus reminded them that he was going to Jerusalem to die on a cross and be raised on the third day, they either didn't respond or (especially in Peter's case) reprimanded him for his negative thinking (Matt. 16:21–23; Mark 8:31–38; 10:32–45). Ever since his temptation by Satan, Jesus had been offered glory without a cross, but it was a false promise. That's why Jesus rebuked Peter's attempt to dissuade him from the cross by saying, "Get behind me, Satan. You are a hindrance to me. For you are not setting your mind on the things of God, but on the things of man" (Matt. 16:23). We can be grateful that Jesus embraced the cross and then entered his glory instead of demanding glory first.

Paul regularly picks up on this theme. Familiar to suffering himself, Paul was always joyful not because of his circumstances but because of the gospel's promise that after we suffer for a little while we will share in Christ's resurrection glory. He warned the church of false teachers who deceive "by smooth talk and flattery" (Rom. 16:18).

The health-and-wealth gospel that Osteen preaches cannot deal with suffering. It is a theology of glory: the offer of the kingdoms of the world here and now. For those who take this path, it may well be that they will have their best life now. But even now, there is no place for suffering in this quintessentially American religion—not Christ's suffering for our sins or our suffering for being united to Christ. In a *New York Times* interview, Osteen was asked why there is suffering. Although he is correct that we cannot solve this dilemma philosophically, he offered no suggestion that it is solved in historical terms by Christ's resurrection as the firstfruits of the new creation. "'The answer is I don't know,' Mr. Osteen said. "'We deal every week with someone whose child got killed, or they lost their job. I don't understand it. All you can do is let God comfort you and move on. Part of faith is not understanding.'"[12]

How can God comfort those who mourn apart from the gospel? Even here, Osteen easily skirts the tragic dimension of our existence by burdening believers once again with their duty to *name and claim* prosperity in their life. So much for the more "positive" message of Joel Osteen. He has nothing to say to people who are at the end of their rope except, "It will get better." But what if it will not, at least in this life? Can his message reach someone who is in the final throes of AIDS? Could his message provoke anything but cynicism for a mother holding her dead infant?

At the end of the day, God's favor—measured in temporal terms—depends entirely on our obedience. Osteen says, "I believe one of the main ways that we grow in favor is by declaring. . . . And some of you are doing your best to please the Lord. You are living a holy, consecrated life, but you're not really experiencing God's supernatural favor. And it's simply because you're not declaring it. You've got to give life to your faith by speaking it out."[13]

Thus, to those who are burned out on trying to merit God's favor, Osteen's only answer—though said with a smile—is to *do more*. "Believe more for your miracle and God will turn it around." Is this a kinder, gentler God or a more than slightly sinister tyrant who keeps raising the hoops for us to jump through before he gives us what we want?

Christianity announces the Good News that God in Christ has saved us now from the condemnation of the law, has dethroned the tyranny of sin, and has delivered us from Satan's oppressive regime. But it gets even better: one day this salvation will be consummated in the gift of resurrection, glorification, and everlasting life free of the very presence of sin, pain, evil, and violence. According to America's pop religion, we save ourselves with God's help from feeling guilty and unhappy. Osteen has at least helped us to see just how stark the contrast is between the gospel of Christ and the motivational hype of popular American culture.

C. S. Lewis once observed, "I haven't always been a Christian. I didn't go to religion to make me happy. I always knew a bottle of Port would do that. If you want a religion to make you feel really comfortable, I certainly don't recommend Christianity."[14] In another essay, he wrote,

> We are defending Christianity; not "my religion." . . . The great difficulty is to get modern audiences to realize that you are preaching Christianity solely and simply because you happen to think it *true*; they always suppose you are preaching it because you like it or think it good for society or something of that sort. Now a clearly maintained distinction between what the Faith actually says and what you would like it to have said or what you understand or what you personally find helpful or think probable, forces your audience to realize that you are tied to your data just

as the scientist is tied by the results of the experiments; that you are not just saying what you like. This immediately helps them to realize that what is being discussed is a question about objective fact—not gas about ideals and points of view.[15]

It all depends on whether we start with what we have decided to be our greatest need or with the God in whose presence we discover needs we never knew we had.

If we begin with ourselves and our felt needs, we may have room for a spirituality that assists us in our self-realization and success in life, but the chief question will be how we can justify God in a world so obviously out of whack. If we begin with God—his holiness, justice, and righteousness as well as his love, mercy, and grace—then there will be a very different question: How can I, a sinner, be justified before this God? Describing his own process of conversion, Lewis explains, "I was the object rather than the subject in this affair. I was decided upon. I was glad afterwards at the way it came out, but at the moment what I heard was God saying, 'Put down your gun and we'll talk.' . . . I chose, yet it really did not seem possible to do the opposite."[16]

We do not "put down [our] gun" until we give up even on religion and spirituality as our way of ascending to heaven. We do not know what is relevant or of utmost concern until God's Word addresses us. Discourses on modern man may be occasionally interesting, says Karl Barth.

> But who and what [humanity] is before God, as the one addressed in His Gospel, is something which Narcissus as such cannot discover in any age for all the loving exactitude of his self-analysis, self-appraisal, and self-description, and something which he cannot accept even in his most ruthless sincerity. To know himself as the one who is intended, addressed and known by God in the Gospel, he must first be radically disturbed and interrupted in the work of self-analysis by receiving the Gospel of God.[17]

Through faith in Christ we have the assurance that the last judgment has already been determined in our favor despite our sinfulness even as Christians. In the midst of our suffering, pain, and even death, we can confidently cling to the promise that Paul quotes from Isaiah 64:4, namely that which "no eye has seen, nor ear heard, nor the heart of man imagined, what God has prepared for those who love him" (1 Cor. 2:9).

Where the gospel offers salvation from the guilt and tyranny of sin now and from the presence and effects of sin in the future, Osteen's very American message presents the gospel as salvation from the symptoms of sin now without any clear proclamation of the far greater liberation from God's wrath.

Because he does not face the bad news, Osteen does not really have any good news. To paraphrase Jesus's description of his generation in Luke 7:31–35, Osteen's message teaches us to sing neither the Blues nor the triumphant anthem. It's more like a steady, droning, upbeat hum that we hear on the elevator or at the mall, keeping everything light and undisturbed.

The best news that Osteen has for us in these books is that by following these seven steps he has been given good parking spaces, the best seat in a restaurant, and an unexpected upgrade to first class on the plane. But the gospel tells us that God has taken all of the steps down to us, saving us not from discomfort or the ills that are common to humanity in this present age but from the penalty of sin and death. Clothed in Christ's righteousness, no longer condemned, we are adopted and made alive in Christ, "and if children, then heirs—heirs of God and fellow heirs with Christ, provided we suffer with him in order that we may also be glorified with him" (Rom. 8:17). Chosen by God before creation, redeemed by Christ, justified, renewed, being sanctified, and one day raised bodily in glory—what could be better news than this? Paul adds,

For I consider that the sufferings of this present time are not worth comparing with the glory that is to be revealed in us. For the creation waits with eager longing for the revealing of the sons of God. . . . For we know that the whole creation has been groaning together in the pains of childbirth until now. And not only the creation, but we ourselves, who have the firstfruits of the Spirit, groan inwardly within us as we wait eagerly for adoption as sons, the redemption of our bodies. For in this hope we were saved. Now hope that is seen is not hope. For who hopes for what he sees? But if we hope for what we do not see, we wait for it with patience.

Romans 8:18–20, 22–25

4

How We Turn Good News
into Good Advice

Raising a six-year-old and nearly five-year-old triplets requires all the advice my wife and I can get. James Dob-
son's books have been helpful, but we have also benefited
tremendously from the wisdom of non-Christians, especially my
barber and his wife, whose family has been a huge assistance
in all sorts of ways. Just as people are not likely to get the best
entertainment at church, they may not get the same quality of
daily advice from their pastor that they might get from Dr. Phil
or Dr. Laura. You just don't need the Bible in order to know
that your children need regular sleep patterns, the secret to a
good marriage is "talk, talk, talk," divorce is normally devastating for children, and if you don't rule your credit cards they'll
rule you. Of course the Bible gives us a lot more wisdom than
this, but there are plenty of non-Christian families who actually

do a better job at *doing the right thing* than some Christian families.

It is no wonder that the average person today assumes that all religions basically say the same thing and that singling one out as the only truth is arrogant. After all, who *doesn't* believe in the Golden Rule: "Do unto others as you would have them do unto you"? The moral law that we find in the Bible (especially the Ten Commandments) is quite similar to the codes of other religions and can be found in civilizations that predate the giving of the law at Mount Sinai. Some of its wisdom flows from that special covenantal relationship between God and Israel, but much of it (especially Proverbs) is simply a clear articulation of the way God wired everyone in creation.

If religion is basically ethics—getting people to do the right thing—then why get uptight over the different historical forms, doctrines, rituals, and practices that distinguish one version of morality from another? Let a thousand flowers bloom as long as people are being helped, right?

Reduce Christianity to good advice and it blends in perfectly with the culture of *life coaching*. It might seem relevant, but it is actually lost in the marketplace of moralistic therapies. When we pitch Christianity as the best method of personal improvement, complete with testimonies about how much better we are ever since we "surrendered all," non-Christians can legitimately demand of us, "What right do you have to say that yours is the only source of happiness, meaning, exciting experiences, and moral betterment?" Jesus is clearly not the only effective way to a better life or to being a better me. One can lose weight, stop smoking, improve one's marriage, and become a nicer person without Jesus.

What distinguishes Christianity at its heart is not its moral code but its story—a story of a Creator who, although rejected by those he created in his image, stooped to reconcile them to himself through his Son. This is not a story about the individual's heavenward progress but the recital of historical events of God's incarnation, atonement, resurrection, ascension, and return and the exploration of their rich significance. At its heart, this story is a gospel: the Good News that God has reconciled us to himself in Christ.

In 1 Corinthians, Paul points out that Greeks (basically, Gentiles) do not understand the gospel because they are looking for wisdom. Greek philosophy was obsessed with *the good life*, and there were different schools of thought about how to attain it. So it is surprising that when the apostle to the Gentiles was given a spot at the philosophers' forum in Athens, he did not offer Christ as the best path to "your best life now" but told the story of how God is the Creator who needs nothing from us but has stooped to save us through his Son. Everyone must now repent and turn to Christ, for God has proved the imminence of the final judgment by raising Jesus from the dead (Acts 17).

Paul reminds the Corinthian believers that although foolishness to Greeks and a stumbling block to Jews, "to those whom God has called, both Jews and Greeks, Christ [is] the power of God and the wisdom of God. For the foolishness of God is wiser than man's wisdom, and the weakness of God is stronger than man's strength" (1 Cor. 1:24–25 NIV). The real power and wisdom is not found in principles for our victorious living but in the announcement of God's victory in Christ. In fact, Christ does not just show us wisdom, he "has become our wisdom . . . , righteousness, holiness and redemption" (v. 30). This is exactly the same situation in which we find ourselves today, with the world telling us that it will take our practical advice (of course, weighing it with other spiritual and moral therapies) as long as we stay away from the scandal of Christ and his atoning death for sinners.

103

Of course there is divine wisdom in the Scriptures. The God who justifies us through faith apart from the law also sanctifies us and leads us by his law. However, the principal wisdom of the Bible is Christ's person and work, promised in the law and the prophets and fulfilled in the new covenant. Nothing comes close to the wisdom that God has displayed in the salvation of sinners. J. Gresham Machen's cry, directed at Protestant liberalism, can as easily be addressed to evangelicals today: "What I need first of all is not exhortation, but a gospel, not directions for saving myself but knowledge of how God has saved me. Have you any good news? That is the question that I ask of you. I know your exhortations will not help me. But if anything has been done to save me, will you not tell me the facts?"[1]

Last year I evacuated my family from devastating fires that ravaged Southern California. As I wrote the first draft of this chapter, I was not even sure that our house or the seminary where I teach was still standing. The previous Sunday night we had gone to bed concerned, and I awoke at four Monday morning and turned on the news. Within hours, we were packing up a few valuables and moving the family to safety. My wife and I needed a paradigm shift. It takes a lot to move us from "I can handle this" to "Run for the hills!"

A similar paradigm shift is exactly what we need if we are to flee "the fierceness of [God's] wrath" that is coming upon the world (Rev. 16:19 NKJV). We must be stripped of our fig leaves in order to be clothed with Christ's righteousness so we can stand in the judgment of a holy God. The question is whether the aim of ministry today is to tear off our fig leaves so we can be clothed with Christ or to help us add a few more.

News is a particular kind of communication. It comes to us from the outside, taking us away from our preoccupations to hear about something that has happened. If it is big enough news, it can change us forever. Some readers will remember where they were when they read the headline, "Victory in Europe!" As beneficiaries of the sacrificial work of others on the field of battle, those who received that news were changed by it. Instead of simply walking to work or coming home from school with a dull sense of war, they began dancing with strangers in the street. Of course there is bad news too. Many recall where they were when they heard that John F. Kennedy had been assassinated or when they first saw the pictures of the Twin Towers falling on September 11, 2001. Those who have received the report of their loved one's death or their own incurable disease are never the same afterward. News organizes, disrupts, and rearranges not only our sense of the world around us but the world inside us.

The central message of Christianity is not a worldview, a way of life, or a program for personal and societal change; it is a gospel. From the Greek word for "good news," typically used in the context of announcing a military victory, the *gospel* is the report of an appointed messenger who arrives from the battlefield. That is why the New Testament refers to the offices of apostle (official representative), preacher, and evangelist, describing ministers as heralds, ambassadors, and witnesses. Their job is to get the story right and then report it, ensuring that the message is delivered by word (preaching) and deed (sacrament). And the result is a church, an embassy of the Triune God in the midst of this passing evil age, with the whole people of God giving witness to God's mighty acts of redemption.

It is not incidental, then, that this story of redemption is called *Good News*. If it were merely information or a program for self-improvement, it would be called something else, like *good advice* or *a good idea* or *good enlightenment*. But it's Good News because it is an announcement of something that someone else has already achieved for us.

When we are distracted from this commission, we begin to think of ourselves not as ambassadors of a great King and witnesses to that which someone else has accomplished for us but as the stars of the show. Instead of *reporting* the news, we *become* the news. In fact, today we often hear Christians speak of "living the gospel" and "being the gospel," as if anything we do and are can be considered a supplement to God's victory in Christ Jesus. Instead of ambassadors, heralds, reporters, and witnesses, pastors become entrepreneurs, managers, coaches, therapists, marketing gurus, and communications specialists.

With this transition, the focus necessarily falls on what we do, and Jesus's role is reduced to an example. Books and sermons that offer good advice rank higher on the relevance scale than those offering the Good News. Just visit your local Christian bookstore and compare the number of books on Christ's person and work with the aisles of "Christian" self-help literature. Yet the Bible provides a very different focus. With the exception of a few important passages in which we are told to follow Christ's example of suffering love on behalf of others, the New Testament makes it clear that Jesus is unique in every way: in who he was, what he did, and what he said. Only he could be God incarnate; only he could produce miracles that were signs of his deity and messianic mission; only he could inaugurate the kingdom with his blessings and curses; only he could die as an atoning sacrifice for sinners and be raised as the firstfruits of those who sleep.

When pastors are expected to be coaches sending in the plays and their parishioners are expected to be all-stars to take Jesus's team to victory in the culture wars, the focus must necessarily fall on what we do rather than on what God has done, on our stories and strategies rather than God's. But this means that much of our ministry today is law without gospel, exhortation without news, instructions without an announcement, deeds without creeds, with the accent on "What Would Jesus Do?" rather than "What Has Jesus Done?" None of us is immune to this indictment that we are losing our focus upon, confidence in, and increasingly even our knowledge of the greatest story ever told.

Another way of talking about the difference between law and gospel is the distinction in the Greek language itself between the imperative and indicative moods. An indicative tells us what is in fact the case: for example, *the cat is on the mat*. An imperative tells us to do something: *put the cat on the mat*. "Try harder" is an imperative, not an indicative. The mood itself (easily discerned in the Greek language) tells us that it is law rather than gospel.

I do indeed need to try harder; that's not in dispute. The question is whether exhortations to try harder, and even specific tips on how to do that, hold any possibility of driving me to anything but spiritual death apart from the gospel.

Now, as we go back to God's Word with the distinction between law and gospel in mind, we can accept the full force of his moral will without trying to water it down. We do not love God and our neighbors as God expects. Therefore we are not just failing to be all we can be and missing out on God's best for our life, we are condemned as transgressors of God's holy will. Our righteousness is "filthy rags" (Isa. 64:6 NIV). Through the gospel, however, the Spirit clothes us with Christ's righteousness (justification) and renews us (regeneration), conforming us daily to the image of Christ (sanctification). All along the way, the law tells me what God requires, but only the gospel brings salvation both from the law's just sentence and the dominion of sin and death.

Confusing Law and Gospel: Easy-Listening Legalism

Softening the seriousness of God's law and the fact that we stand before God's judgment as transgressors may seem kinder, but it is not. In fact, it is cruel. Instead of ending all attempts to rise up to God in self-confidence and giving people a Savior who has accomplished everything for our rescue, this easy-listening legalism perpetuates a life of constant anxiety. Once upon a time we knew legalism when we saw it: the old-style evangelist preaching hellfire-and-brimstone as the way of getting people to get in line. Today, however, the charge of legalism hardly seems sensible.

Like the rules of the Pharisees, the older legalism substituted its own regulations for the weighty matters actually commanded by God. Sin was not a condition that corrupted even our best works but the violation of certain taboos. We didn't necessarily have to love God and our neighbor perfectly, but we had to stay out of bars and pool halls. Furthermore, such violations could make us lose jewels in our crown or provoke God's judgment on our life. If we encountered some sort of disaster, a well-meaning brother or sister might ask, "What hidden sin is there in your life?" In more severe versions, we might lose our salvation.

Thanks to the Boomer generation, which blossomed into adulthood (as much as possible) in the sixties and seventies, there seems to have been a reaction in the direction of antinomianism—that is, rebellion against fixed doctrines and norms. Guilt is *out*; upbeat, motivational encouragement is *in*. Instead of losing rewards or salvation, we lose out on God's best for our lives here and now. Francis Schaeffer used to call this *the religion of personal peace and affluence*. The shift from the stern conservatism of our parents' generation was not from guilt to grace or from law to gospel but from sticks to carrots, from ominous threats to a constant nagging to *do better*—always with a smile. (After all, the symbol of the Boomer generation is the smiley face.)

Whether expressed in the more radical politics of the left or the more conservative politics of the right, the goal of evangelism, discipleship, and corporate church life became a softer version of legalism—a constant stream of exhortations to follow the example of Jesus while assuming familiarity with the gospel of Jesus. More recently, the Emergent Church movement, if anything, intensifies the call to discipleship while in some cases even modifying the gospel. Although the politics, vocabulary, style, and ambiance might suggest otherwise, it represents the same emphasis that many of us recall from conservative evangelical upbringing: Do more. Be a leader, not a follower. Accomplish great things for God. Discipleship, not doctrine (as if *disciple*, meaning "student," and *doctrine*, meaning "teaching," were somehow antithetical).

It's important to point out that law and gospel do not simply refer to the Ten Commandments and John 3:16, respectively. Everything in the Bible that reveals God's moral expectations is *law* and everything in the Bible that reveals God's saving purposes and acts is *gospel*. Not everything in God's Word is gospel; there are a lot of exhortations, commands, and imperatives. They are to be followed. However, they are not the gospel. Not everything that we need is *gospel*. We also need to be directed. We need to know God's commands so we will come clean, acknowledge our sins, and flee to Christ and also so they can direct us in grateful obedience. When it comes to doing something, we are answering the law (works); when it comes to believing what has been done for us by Christ, we are answering the gospel (faith). Confused with faith as the means of inheriting God's gift, our "good works" become the most offensive sins against God. But when faith alone receives the gift, it immediately begins to yield the fruit of righteousness. When even good, holy, and proper things become confused with the gospel, it is only a matter of time before we end up with *Christless Christianity*: a story about us instead of a story about the Triune God that sweeps us into the unfolding drama.

The God of fundamentalism may have been too graceless, but the God of contemporary American religion is too trivial to be worth our time. The *old-time religion* may have been legalistic, adding its own rules and regulations to God's law, but at least it recognized that God *commanded* certain things. Today it is less about measuring ourselves against God's holy will than about helping make good people better through good advice. To whatever extent the mood and motives have changed, however, the emphasis still falls on imperatives—things to do. Central Bible Church, Bubbling Brook Community Church, and St. Matthew's Episcopal Church may give you very different things to do, but *doing* is what it is all about. It is amazing what a lot of Christians (including many pastors) seem absolutely certain about and what they regard as up in the air. Although there is not a single passage in the Bible that tells us what Jesus would do on a whole host of personal and social issues of morality, economics, politics, and law, we often hear confident jeremiads and assertions by the same people who express ambiguity (disguised as humility) about matters clearly addressed and treated as matters of great importance in Scripture.

Seeking to find their way back to their roots, many younger evangelicals today are attracted to the Anabaptist legacy. Brian McLaren explains, "Anabaptists see the Christian faith primarily as a way of life," interpreting Paul through the lens of Jesus's Sermon on the Mount rather than vice versa.[2] The emphasis falls on discipleship rather than on doctrine, as if following Jesus's example could be set against following his teaching.

What happens when the Sermon on the Mount is assimilated to a general ethic of love and doctrine is made secondary? Christ himself becomes a mere example to help even adherents of other religions become better. In fact, going beyond most Anabaptists I know, McLaren writes, "I must add, though, that I don't believe making disciples must equal making adherents to the Christian religion. It may be advisable in many (not all!) circumstances to help people become followers of Jesus *and* remain within their Buddhist, Hindu, or Jewish contexts."[3] Of course, this makes sense if Christ's significance lies primarily in the moral example he calls us to imitate. "I don't hope all Jews or Hindus will become members of the Christian religion," McLaren writes. "But I do hope all who feel so called will become Jewish or Hindu followers of Jesus."[4]

It is no wonder, then, that McLaren can say concerning liberal Protestants, "I applaud their desire to live out the meaning of the miracle stories even when they don't believe the stories really happened as written."[5] After all, it's deeds, not creeds. Following Jesus can exist with or without explicit faith in Christ.

There is nothing especially *postmodern* about any of this, of course. Writers like McLaren advocate very little that cannot be found with greater sophistication in German and American divinity faculties at the turn of the twentieth century. If we are allowed to pick and choose whatever we like from the New Testament (again, hardly a uniquely postmodern trend), we will always gravitate toward the contrast drawn by that most modern of all modern thinkers, Immanuel Kant: *pure religion* (morality) as opposed to *ecclesiastical faith* (doctrine). The only difference is that in their day, it was called *modernism*. Hitching our wagon to the spirit of the age, whatever we call it, always leads to one form or another of culture-Christianity—in other words, to our native Pelagianism.

I realize that the Emergent Church movement is doctrinally fluid, and some leaders who appreciate the postmodern emphasis yet are uncomfortable being identified with McLaren and others often prefer the more general label "emerging." Furthermore, I often find myself identifying with many of the criticisms of certain aspects of modern evangelical faith and practice. However, many of these writers (especially McLaren) seem to be reacting against caricatures, real or imagined, of at least fuller forms of evangelical Christianity.

McLaren would no doubt agree with the criticisms in this book of modernity's programmatic, technique-oriented, consumer-driven, and individualistic influence on the church. Having been reared in similar backgrounds, we share a common reaction against mere assertions and slogans and the often unreflective, unquestioning dogmatism that assumes that we have all the answers and everyone else is wrong. I share his interest in the wider horizon of the kingdom of God for our theology and his concern that the gospel is often reduced to a quasi-Gnostic promise of saving the soul (i.e., "going to heaven when we die") rather than ultimately, in the words of the Apostles' Creed, "the resurrection of the body and the life everlasting," which includes the whole creation. This leads to a world-affirming, world-embracing kind of Christianity rather than to a merely negative, reactionary, and reductionistic piety.

However, I encountered this "new" paradigm by stumbling into Reformed Christianity. It was from this tradition that I learned that questions were good and that sometimes "I don't know" is the right answer; that the Bible is not simply about "me and my personal relationship with Jesus" or merely a doctrinal or moral textbook but a story in which we find ourselves—and the whole creation of which we are a part. In addition to being overwhelmed by God's amazing grace, I was also given a new sense of being called into a communion of saints and a new rationale for responsibility in the world—not to save it, but to love and serve my neighbors and to be a steward of a creation that will be renewed rather than to be simply a consumer of a creation that will be destroyed.

However, McLaren seems never to have found an alternative kind of evangelical faith to the more pietistic and legalistic background in which he was raised. When he recoils from the doctrine of Christ's atoning death as bearing God's righteous judgment in our place (i.e., penal substitution), I know the distortion he is reacting against. Yet it was a wise and elderly systematic theologian at the seminary where I now teach who warned us never to present this precious truth as if a vengeful Father was taking out his anger on his Son. Rather, he instructed us from the relevant passages, the Father gave his Son because of his love, and the Son was not a victim but a willing substitute who gave himself in love as well.

Whatever the reasons, McLaren—along with other pastors and writers, like British evangelical Steve Chalke—rebound from a popular caricature of evangelical Christianity into the arms of a different kind of moralism that is often indistinguishable from the moves that were made long ago by Protestant liberalism and more radical versions of various liberation theologies. Chalke describes penal substitution as "divine child abuse" and McLaren expresses the same view in the voice of one of his fictional characters.[6] After offering a caricature of the "conventional view" of Christ's atonement, McLaren offers his alternative "emerging view": "God graciously invites everyone and anyone to turn from his or her current path and follow a new way. This," he says, "is the good news."[7] While in the conventional view, "original sin" is the root problem and God provides salvation from his wrath as "a free gift," the gospel according to the emerging view is that Jesus "inserted into human history a seed of grace, truth and hope that can never be defeated. . . . All who find in Jesus God's hope and truth discover the privilege of participating in his ongoing work of personal and global transformation and liberation from evil and injustice."[8]

Thus, our labors are not simply the fruit of salvation but are part of Christ's "ongoing work." Lost in this view is the uniqueness of Christ's once-and-for-all work *for* us, *apart* from us, *outside* of us, in the past, and the work that only he can do when he returns in glory. Jesus and the community, his work and ours, blend into one saving event.

Radically different from the narcissism and individualism of Joel Osteen's prosperity gospel, McLaren's message nevertheless shares important similarities. It translates sin and judgment into actions and attitudes that we can overcome with the right agenda in order to transform ourselves and the world. Whereas for Osteen the reference point for "sin" and "salvation" shifts from God to the happiness and betterment of the self through moral improvement, for McLaren the frame of reference is global warming, poverty, AIDS, and capitalist greed. In many ways mirroring the Religious Right's confusion of Christ's kingdom of grace with his coming kingdom in glory and the latter with the triumph of a particular agenda already defined by a political party, the emerging Religious Left seems just as prone to enlist Jesus as a mascot for our own programs of national and global redemption.

Osteen speaks of salvation entirely in terms of prosperity here and now, while McLaren speaks of salvation primarily in terms of peace and justice here and now. In both cases, it is up to us to bring about this salvation, which in some sense Christ has made possible by planting a seed in us all. Whether we define the *gospel* as God's invitation to everyone "to turn from his or her current path and follow a new way" (with McLaren) or as "becoming a better you" (with Osteen), we are confusing law and gospel, the command to follow Christ with the announcement from heaven that *he* has defeated death, condemnation, and sin's tyranny, and will come again in power and glory, first to judge and then to make all things new.

Even on the more conservative side of the Emergent (or "Emerging") Church movement, Dan Kimball, pastor of Santa Cruz Bible Church, announces his goal: "Going back to a raw form of vintage Christianity, which unapologetically focuses on kingdom living by disciples of Jesus."[9] Another of the movement's leaders, Mark Oestreicher, adds, "Yup, I still believe salvation comes only through Jesus Christ. But does a little dose of Buddhism thrown into a belief system somehow kill off the Christian part, the Jesus-basics?" Of course, the answer is *no* if Christianity is essentially law rather than gospel. "My Buddhist cousin, except for her unfortunate inability to embrace Jesus, is a better 'Christian' (based on Jesus's description of what a Christian does) than almost every Christian I know. If we were using Matthew 25 as a guide, she'd be a sheep; and almost every Christian I know personally would be a goat."[10]

Unlike McLaren, Kimball is not interested in challenging traditional evangelical doctrines. However, he reflects the widespread assumption that Christians today already understand and believe the gospel but need more calls to serious discipleship. When the focus of mission and ministry is on our *kingdom living* rather than on the one who brought and brings his own kingdom, ushering us and our hearers into it through his gospel, Christ-as-example can just as effectively replace Christ-as-Savior at least in practice.

It is indeed a tragedy when we say one thing and then live in a way that brings reproach to that gospel. There have been Christians whose doctrine of Christ was superb but who supported slavery, racism, materialism, and a host of other lifestyles that are incompatible with God's Word. Younger evangelicals are alert to the inconsistencies and hypocrisy of a movement that professes commitment to Jesus Christ while exhibiting its profound love affair with consumerism, greed, militarism, and apathy toward stewardship of God's creation. Kimball's comments strike home when he quotes Mahatma Gandhi: "I like your Christ, but I do not like your Christians. Your Christians are so unlike your Christ," or when he reminds us of *The Simpsons'* Ned Flanders and his family: "Almost every time Christians are portrayed on television or in the movies, they appear somewhat unintelligent, mindless, even cultish, usually engaging in angry crusades to wipe out the evils of society and convert people to their point of view. Add to all this the public arrest of a pastor or priest for some sexual crime."[11]

Kimball puts his finger on a serious issue. Like much of America, we are suspicious of leaders who appear to have all the answers—with little self-questioning—yet who lead us astray and leave disillusionment in their wake. A lot of us have grown up watching our religious leaders attack pornography and gay rights while employing prostitutes of both genders. But is the answer to "mindless, even cultish . . . crusades to wipe out the evils of society" simply another crusade with a different agenda? The proper preaching of the law and the gospel is the *real* antidote to self-righteousness of every stripe. It is interesting that when the apostle Paul had to write a disciplinary letter to the Corinthian church for its sexual immorality, hypocrisy, strife, and pride, he began by telling them the gospel all over again. He never assumed it. In fact, he assumed that if the church is in a particular mess ethically, it probably did not really get the message yet. Only after once again preaching *Christ and him crucified* would Paul turn to the practical exhortation to live in the light of their high calling in Christ.

Furthermore, younger church leaders seem to overlook the extent to which their movements also exhibit an inordinate attachment to the culture of their own generation rather than reflecting the intergenerational wisdom of the church in all times and places. For many of us who were reared on the "Christian America" hype of the religious right, "emerging" church movements may seem like a major shift, but is it just a change in parties? The sociology is also different: Starbucks and acoustic guitars in dark rooms with candles rather than Wal-Mart and praise bands in brightly lit theaters. Yet in either case, moralism continues to push *Christ crucified* to the margins. We are totally distracted on the right, left, and in the middle!

As I write, these challenges are being recognized by writers like Dan Kimball and Mark Driscoll. Hype eventually leads to burnout, regardless of the ideology, and it can only be hoped that the honesty, vitality, and eagerness for something deeper than another *Seven Steps* to something banal will lead to a rediscovery of the gazillion steps God has made and continues to make toward us in Jesus Christ.

The question for us all is whether we believe the church is the place where the gospel is regularly proclaimed and ratified to Christians as well as non-Christians. Like many Emergent Church leaders, Kimball invokes a famous line from Francis of Assisi that I also heard growing up in conservative evangelicalism: "Preach the gospel at all times. If necessary, use words." Kimball goes on to say, "Our lives will preach better than anything we can say."[12] (We encountered a nearly identical statement from Osteen in the previous chapter.) If so, then this is just more bad news, not only because of the statistics we have already seen, which evidence no real difference between Christians and non-Christians, but because despite my best intentions, I am not an exemplary creature. The best examples and instructions—even the best doctrines—will not relieve me of the battle with indwelling sin until I draw my last breath. Find me on my *best* day—especially if you have access to my hidden motives, thoughts, and attitudes—and I will always provide fodder for the hypocrisy charge and will let down those who would become Christians because they think I and my fellow Christians are the gospel. I am a Christian not because I think that I can walk in Jesus's footsteps but because he is the only one who can carry me. I am not the gospel; Jesus Christ alone is the gospel. *His* story saves me, not only by bringing me justification but by baptizing me into his resurrection life.

Conformity to Christ's image (sanctification) is the process of dying to self (mortification) and living to God (vivification) that results from being regularly immersed in the gospel's story of Christ's life, death, and resurrection. Another way of putting it is *dislocation* (from Adam and the reign of sin and death) and *relocation* (in Christ). That my life is not the gospel is good news both for me and for my neighbors. Because Christ is the Good News, Christians as well as non-Christians can be saved after all. For those who know that they too fall short of the glory that God's law requires—even as Christians who now have a new heart that loves God's law—the Good News is not only enough to create faith but to get us back on our feet, assured of our standing in Christ, ready for another day of successes and failures in our discipleship.

We do not preach ourselves but Christ. The good news—not only for ourselves, but for a world (and church) in desperate need of good news—is that what we *say* preaches better than our lives, at least if what we are saying is *Christ's* person and work rather than our own. The more we talk about Christ as the Bible's unfolding mystery and less about our own transformation, the more likely we are actually to be transformed rather than either self-righteous or despairing. As much as it goes against our grain, the gospel is the power of God unto salvation for justification *and* sanctification. The fruit of faith is real; it's just not the same as the fruit of works-righteousness.

Yes, there is hypocrisy, and because Christians will always be simultaneously saint and sinner, there will always be hypocrisy in every Christian and in every church. The good news is that Christ saves us from hypocrisy too. But hypocrisy is especially generated when the church points to itself and to our own "changed lives" in the promotional materials. Maybe non-Christians would have less relish in pointing out our failures if we testified in word and deed to our need and God's gift for sinners like us. If we identified the visibility of the church with the scene of sinners gathered

118

by grace to confess their sins and their faith in Christ, receiving him with open hands, instead of with our busy efforts to *be the gospel*, we would at least beat non-Christian critics to the punch. We know that we are sinners. We know that we fall short of God's glory. That's exactly why we need Christ. I know that many of these brothers and sisters would affirm that we are still sinners and that we still need Christ, but it sure seems to be drowned out by a human-centered focus on our character and actions.

Kimball writes that the "ultimate goal of discipleship . . . should be measured by what Jesus taught in Matthew 22:37–40: 'Love the Lord with all your heart, mind, and soul.' Are we loving him more? Love others as yourself. Are we loving people more?"[13] I was raised in conservative evangelicalism on this same diet of sermons that ended with a question like this one. A truly radical change in our approach would be to proclaim Christ as the one who fulfilled this law in our place, bore its sentence, and now freely gives us his absolution. Only then, ironically, are we truly liberated to love again. For all of the Emergent Church movement's incisive critiques of the megachurch model, the emphasis still falls on measuring the level of our zeal and activity rather than on immersing people in the greatest story ever told. It may be more earnest, more authentic, and less consumeristic, but how different is this basic message from that of Joel Osteen, for example? Across the board in contemporary American Christianity, that basic message seems to be some form of law (do this) without the gospel (this is what has been done).

From Riches to Rags: Losing the Gospel by Taking It for Granted

The greatest threat to Christ-centered witness even in churches that formally affirm sound teaching is what British evangelical

David Gibson calls "the assumed gospel."[14] The idea is that the gospel is necessary for getting saved, but after we sign on, the rest of the Christian life is all the fine print: conditional forgiveness. It often comes in the form of, "Well, of course, but. . . ." After a month of Sundays with exhortation apart from Good News, one might ask, "But what about the part about *God* persevering in spite of human sin and overcoming it for us at the cross?" "Well, of course! But everybody here already believes that. Now we just need to get on with living it out." We got in by grace but now we need to stay in (or at least become first-class, sold-out, victorious, fully surrendered Christians) by following various steps, lists, and practices. There was this brief and shining moment of grace, but now the rest of the Christian life is about our experience, feelings, commitment, and obedience. We always gravitate back toward ourselves: "Prone to wander, Lord, I feel it; prone to leave the God I love."[15] We wander back toward self-confidence just as easily as into more obvious sins. It is no wonder that many Christians find themselves in the spiritual equivalent of midlife crisis, losing their first love, even wondering perhaps deep down whether it is all just a game.

Tragically, my generation will likely fare no better than the previous one on the hypocrisy test. We too will fall far short of that mandate to love God and our neighbor. What we need, therefore, is a gospel that is sufficient to save even unfaithful Christians. We can never take the gospel for granted. It is always the surprising announcement that fills our sails with faith for an active life of good works.

This is not an invitation to moral apathy but to godly sanity. The bad news is far worse than occasionally failing to live up to my potential. The smallest sin in my eyes—not only what I've done, but what I've failed to do; not only what my hands have done, but what I've conceived in my heart—is sufficient to banish me from God's holy and joyful presence forever. But the good news is far greater than the bad news is bad. The good news is far greater than "just try harder next time." In fact, that is not good news at all because I know that God does not grade on a curve and he has not asked me to try harder. He demands perfect righteousness, not good intentions. The harder I try to cover up my nakedness in God's presence, the more I hate God, fleeing in self-deceit from his terrifying presence. Left to myself, I will always accuse God and excuse myself—even using religion to hide my ineradicable guilt.

The good news is that Christ's righteousness is greater than my sin. Fully absolved in Christ, I am free to confess my sins, receive the assurance of pardon, and go on in my imperfect yet Spirit-led obedience.

Across the entire spectrum from conservative to liberal, we are being told that we need to focus on deeds, not creeds. Of course Christ's person and work are important, but we already believe that, right? That's *doctrine*, we are told, not helping people *where they live*. Now we have to save America and the world through our holy actions. We all get the doctrine; we're just not living it. These are the assumptions I hear across the theological and denominational spectrum. But do we really get it? Not according to the statistics we have already encountered. The gospel is so odd, even to us Christians, that we have to get it again and again. That is why God has graciously created different avenues for getting it to us: he proclaims it by the mouth of another in Christ's name, bathes me in it with water, and puts it in my hand through bread and wine.

For all of their rivalry, Protestant liberalism actually grew out of pietism and, especially in the United States, Protestant modernism grew partly out of revivalism. Machen writes, "Here is found the most fundamental difference between liberalism and Christianity—liberalism is altogether in the imperative mood, while Christianity begins with a triumphant indicative.

Liberalism appeals to man's will, while Christianity announces, first, a gracious act of God. . . . Liberalism regards Christ as an Example and Guide; Christianity as a Savior. Liberalism makes Him an example for faith; Christianity, the object of faith." Liberalism proceeds on the basis of religious experience, while Christianity is attentive to God's Word, which comes to us from the outside.[16] In every generation, our natural tendency to put the focus back on ourselves—our inner life, piety, community, and actions—withers the very root of faith that yields love and service.

The worst thing that can happen to the church is to confuse law and gospel. When we soften the law, we never give up on our own attempts to offer our rags of "righteousness" to God. When we turn the gospel into demands, it is no longer the saving Word of redemption in Jesus Christ alone.

According to the Scriptures, there are two ways of inheriting God's blessings. After the fall, God's everlasting blessings can only be secured through the forgiveness of sins in Jesus Christ. This promise to provide a Savior was a unilateral pledge to Adam and Eve after the fall, to Abraham and Sarah, and to David; it also appears in the new covenant prophesied in Jeremiah 31 and elsewhere. Then there were the temporal land promises that God made to Israel, based on the nation's pledge, "All this we will do." As Paul says, "These are two covenants": a covenant of grace leading to eternal life and a covenant of law leading to bondage (Gal. 4:24–25). The problem with the Jews of Paul's day was that they had confused the conditional inheritance of an earthly land with the unconditional election and redemption of sinners through faith in Christ. Confusing law and gospel is the natural tendency of the fallen heart. Every religion—including *Christless Christianity*, which is no Christianity at all—assumes some form of redemption by self-effort. It is always surprising, counterintuitive, and even offensive for human beings to hear that salvation does not depend on human decision or effort but on God who shows mercy (Rom. 9:16). We naturally think that if you want people to do the right thing, you just need to tell them what to do and exhort them to do it with sufficient passion and effective methods. This, however, avoids both the law and the gospel. If we really come to grips with God's righteous will, we are undone. The law unmasks our pretensions, showing us that we deserve God's judgment for the pride clinging to our best works and intentions—never mind the obvious sins (Isa. 64:6). The law commands, but it does not give us any power to fulfill its conditions. On its own, more advice (law, commands, exhortations) will only lead us to either self-righteousness or despair. Yet the more Christ is held up before us as sufficient for our justification and sanctification, the more we begin to die to ourselves and live to God.

No longer threatened with hell or comforted with heaven, the new legalism is the upbeat and cheerful hum playing in the background. It's still a form of works-righteousness, with its carrots and sticks. Follow my advice and you'll really "connect" with God's best for your life. If you are not happy, perhaps you have fallen out of God's favor and blessing. Only those who are "completely surrendered" can be confident that they are in God's Plan A. Now here are the steps to living the victorious Christian life. Are you following the steps? Do you have enough faith? Are you praying enough, reading the Bible enough, witnessing enough, serving in the church enough, loving enough? This diet of imperatives becomes just as burdensome and human-centered as the older legalism; it's just *Legalism Lite*. And when we burn out on one program, there is always another best-seller, movement, or plan around the corner.

Even if more recent generations are recovering some of the weightier matters of the law, such as loving and serving our neighbor, the law is not the gospel. Once we realize the difference, we can finally give each its due. Let the law be law and let the gospel be gospel.

Distinguishing Law and Gospel

We need the law and the gospel, but each does different things. When we confuse law and gospel, we avoid both the trauma of God's holiness and the liberating power of his grace. We begin to speak about *living* the gospel, *doing* the gospel, even *being* the gospel, as if the Good News were a message about us and our works instead of about Christ and his works. The proper response is neither to dispense with the law nor to soften it from demand to helpful advice. Rather, it is to recognize the difference between law and gospel. We are not called to live the gospel but to believe the gospel and to follow the law in view of God's mercies. Turning the gospel into law is a very easy thing for us to do; it comes naturally. That is why we can never take the Good News for granted.

Any form of *doing* the gospel is a confusion of categories. The *law* tells us what to do; the *gospel* tells us what God has done for us in Christ. When it comes to the question about how we relate to God, *doing* is the wrong answer. Paul explains, "Now to the one who works, his wages are not counted as a gift but as his due. And to the one who does not work but believes in him who justifies the ungodly, his faith is counted as righteousness" (Rom. 4:4–5). It is not just some deeds on our part that are excluded here, but our works of any kind. "But if it is by grace, it is no longer on the basis of works; otherwise grace would no longer be grace" (Rom. 11:6).

Principles for living, practical advice, secrets of victorious living, calls to discipleship, and instruction all fall under the category of law, whether they are offered sternly or gently, whether they are God's commands or our own. The point is not to jettison these words, but (a) to make sure they are God's words rather than our own, and (b) to recognize that even when they are God's, they are different from God's word of gospel: the good news that although we have not done any of the things we said we would do, Christ has been made our "righteousness, holiness and redemption" (1 Cor. 1:30 NIV). The law tells us what God expects of us; the gospel tells us what God has done for us.

So law and gospel are not inherently opposed, but when it comes to how we are saved, these two principles could not be more antithetical. And since our faith in every moment is threatened by our natural tendency to be distracted from its object—Christ—we need the gospel placarded before us not just at the beginning but throughout the Christian life. The gospel is for Christians too. We need to be evangelized every week. It is not by following Christ's example but by actually being inserted into Christ, clothed with Christ, united to Christ—as the Spirit creates faith through the gospel—that we are not only justified but sanctified as well.

Why Law Makes Sense and the Gospel Sounds Strange

Paul's argument in Romans 1–3 is that Gentiles are guilty before God on the basis of the law as it is written on their conscience. God's existence and attributes "have been clearly perceived, ever since the creation of the world, in the things that have been made. So they [Gentiles] are without excuse" (Rom. 1:20). Created in God's image, in perfect holiness and righteousness, Adam was to lead all of creation into the everlasting Sabbath rest. Just as God completed his work and then entered his enthronement over creation, his lieutenant was to follow in his train as the representative head of humanity.

Endowed with glory, beauty, goodness, and justice, we were suitably equipped for the task that lay before us. Then, out of nowhere, Adam abused his freedom, bringing himself, his wife, and his posterity—in fact all of creation—under the curse of God's law.

Paul says this moral sense—the awareness of God's existence and our accountability to his law—is innate in each of us (Rom. 1:32; 2:12–16). I just came across an interview with Prince Hassan bin Talal of Jordan (brother of the late King Hussein), who is trying to strike up conversations between the various religions in the Middle East. "I keep saying that if we all observed the Ten Commandments, we would not have succumbed to so much grief in the first place," says Prince Hassan. "Whether it is the Golden Law, the Straight Path, or the Ten Commandments, we recognize that we do not need to reinvent the code of conduct."[17]

There is a lot of consensus on the law: "Do unto others as you would have them do unto you" is not a precept unique to Christianity. And here we should be eager to find agreements on our conduct in a world rife with conflict. In a recent *Los Angeles Times* story, staff writer Steve Padilla pointed out that even well-known atheist Sam Harris had once written that "there is clearly a sacred dimension to our existence, and coming to terms with it could well be the highest purpose of human life." Harris added that he is "interested in spiritual experience. . . . There is such a thing as profoundly transformative, meaningful experience that can be very hard won. You might have to go into a cave for a month or a year to have certain experiences. The whole contemplative literature is something I read and I take very seriously. The problem is it is also riddled with religious superstition and dogma, [so] that you have to be a selective consumer of this literature."[18] Referring to Christian colleagues in the sciences, biologist and zealous atheist Richard Dawkins says that he is "baffled, not so much by their belief in a cosmic lawgiver of some kind, as by their belief in the details of the Christian religion: resurrection, the forgiveness of sins and all."[19] Enlightenment philosopher Immanuel Kant related that the older he grew the more convinced he was of "the starry heavens above and the moral law within." That's why "pure religion" (morality) is universal and useful, while "ecclesiastical faiths" are superstitious and divisive. Treat religion as private therapy to improve our lives and make us better people and it has its important place; treat it as public truth—Good News to the whole world—and it provokes tremendous offense. Moral and spiritual enlightenment is one thing; redemption by a one-sided divine rescue operation is another.

Yet, like a murderer fleeing the scene of the crime, we run from the voice that calls out, "Adam, where are you?" We cover ourselves, as Adam and Eve did, with fig leaves. We like morality and spirituality but not *dogmas* about sin, judgment, atonement, and grace. As long as we are in control (or at least think we are), using "the sacred dimension" for our own ends, even an atheist can express some interest. However, the moment we are put back in the position of being arraigned before God in his courtroom, our spin factory operates at full capacity. "For the wrath of God is revealed from heaven against all ungodliness and unrighteousness of men, who by their unrighteousness suppress the truth" (Rom. 1:18).

Although God took the Jewish people under his special care and gave them a written version of this law, they too demonstrated that they were transgressors, like the rest of us descendants of Adam (Romans 5). "Like Adam, they have broken the covenant" (Hosea 6:7 NIV). After the fall, no one can be saved by their own righteousness. Rather, the law arraigns all of humanity, Gentile and Jew alike, "so that every mouth may be stopped, and the whole world may be held accountable to God. For by works of the law no human being will be justified in his sight, since through the law comes knowledge of sin" (Rom. 3:19–20). Just as a mirror exposes our dirty faces but cannot clean them, the law reveals God's moral will but gives no power to fulfill it.

Only when another word was spoken were Adam and Eve stopped in their tracks and surprised by good news of a coming redeemer. Stripped of their fig leaves, they were clothed by God in animal skins (Gen. 3:15–16, 20–21) prefiguring the Lamb of God (John 1:29). It is that good news that Paul turns to immediately in the next verses: "But now the righteousness of God has been manifested apart from the law, although the Law and the Prophets bear witness to it—the righteousness of God through faith in Jesus Christ for all who believe" (Rom. 3:21–22). So the law reveals the righteousness that God *is*, by which we are judged (and therefore condemned); the gospel reveals the righteousness that God freely *gives* to sinners through faith in Jesus Christ. Over the next three chapters, Paul unpacks the surprising good news that God justifies the wicked. Salvation, from start to finish, is his work for us, not a matter of saving ourselves or even of cooperating with him. It is a divine rescue operation. Even our sanctification is grounded in God's act of justifying us and uniting us, by his Spirit, to Christ's death and life (Romans 6).

So there are really only two religions in the world: a religion of human striving to ascend to God through pious works, feelings, attitudes, and experiences and the Good News of God's merciful descent to us in his Son. The religions, philosophies, ideologies, and spiritualities of the world only differ on the details. Whether we are talking about the Dalai Lama or Dr. Phil, Islam or Oprah, liberals or conservatives, the most intuitive conviction is that we are good people who need good advice, not helpless sinners who need the Good News.

Proper Preaching of the Law

The law is good, but I am not, Paul reminds us (Rom. 7:7–24). It is the abiding standard of God's perfect holiness and the revelation of his holy will for our lives. First of all, it comes to kill us—not to improve us, but to end our life *in Adam*, exposing us for what we really are. "The very commandment that promised life proved to be death to me" (Rom. 7:10; cf. 2 Corinthians 3). Second, the law guides those who are justified apart from it. Since it can no longer condemn the believer, and in fact must recognize the believer as righteous because of his or her justification in Christ, the law is now a friend. As Paul says in Romans 7, he now loves the law even when he disobeys it. Non-Christians do not recognize themselves in Paul's struggle. Concerned with bad habits that might lead to obesity, alcoholism, broken relationships, losing their job, or disappointment with failing to reach their personal goals, unbelievers nevertheless do not wrestle with the paradox of their love for God and his moral will on one hand and their ongoing sinfulness on the other. Talk of saving the family or saving the earth from environmental catastrophe will resonate with non-Christians. But the speech and actions to which the church witnesses—God's judgment and justification of sinners through Christ—is strange.

So the law functions first of all to kill me, to end my self-creation—all attempts to write my own life movie and reinvent my character. The gospel inserts me into a new script: "alive in Christ." And now the law gives me concrete direction as to what it means to live out this life in love toward my brothers and sisters as well as neighbors and coworkers. The law cannot sanctify any more than it could justify. Although it can no longer condemn me, the law still cannot produce in me the desire to keep it; it can only tell me what God requires.

Even as a Christian, my faith will actually be weakened when it is assumed that I already know the gospel and now I just need a steady diet of instructions. I will naturally revert to my moralistic impulse and conclude either that I am *fully surrendered* or that I cannot pull this off and might as well stop trying. When my conscience leads me to despair, the exhortation to try harder will only deepen either my self-righteousness or my spiritual depression. In other words, it will draw me away from my location in Christ and gradually bring me back to that place where I am turned in on myself. If the conscience is to find peace with God, there can be no help from the law; in fact, it is the law that arouses my conscience to my utter sinfulness.

It is therefore critical to bear in mind that the law is innate and intuitive, while the gospel is an external announcement. The command to love is not surprising, disorienting, or strange; it is familiar to us. We know what we should do by nature. Like the "Greeks" who "look for wisdom," as Paul explained, most of our fellow Americans are not looking for salvation from God's coming judgment but for help in their moral dilemmas. No one will be offended if we tell them that they are good people who could be a little better. The offense comes when we tell them that they—and we—are ungodly people who cannot impress God or escape his tribunal. Until our preaching of the law has exposed our hearts and God's holiness at that profound level, our hearers will never flee to Christ alone for safety even if they come to us for advice.

As the Good News about God's decision to save human beings after they had sinned and therefore had no reason to expect anything but judgment, the *gospel* is not only outside our consciousness but runs against the grain of our common way of thinking. We would know right from wrong even if we never read the Bible. What Paul calls "the righteousness that is by works" (in contrast to "the righteousness that is by faith in Christ") is natural to us (Rom. 10:5–6 NIV). Even lifelong

Christians gravitate toward doing something to save ourselves rather than receive a salvation that has been accomplished for us by someone else.

Our default setting is law rather than gospel, imperatives (things to do or feel) rather than indicatives (things to believe). It is the law, not the gospel, that is a "Well, of course, but . . ." Everyone assumes the law. It is the gospel that is a surprising announcement that none of us had a right to expect. As such, it has to be told—again and again. And the only people who can tell it are those who have themselves heard the story, sung the story, and can herald it to others.

To those who thought of themselves as pretty nice people, Jesus held up the mirror of genuine love of God and neighbor, leaving his hearers to dismiss either him or their own righteousness in favor of being clothed with Christ's obedience. Paul the Pharisee realized this fork in the road and, although his external obedience to the Mosaic code was impeccable by human standards, he said that he now counted as "dung" (KJV) all of this accumulated achievement "in order that he might gain Christ and be found in him, not having a righteousness of his own that comes from the law, but that which comes through faith in Christ, the righteousness from God that depends on faith" (Phil. 3:8–9). He took his place with the bartender in Jesus's parable rather than with the Pharisee, and he went home justified (Luke 18:13–14).

Far from being a kinder, gentler Moses, Jesus exposed the inner impulse of the law. People could perhaps keep from sleeping with each other's spouses, but making lust equivalent to adultery was, as they say, "over the top." Once again we are reminded of Jesus's point that when John the Baptist came with the seriousness of the law and judgment, the religious leaders didn't mourn their lost condition, and when the Son of Man came with the joy of the gospel, they did not dance (Matt. 11:17).

131

In my experience, this is where a lot of Christians are living today: not quite accosted by the death sentence of the law, they are also not regularly hearing the liberating Good News of the gospel. Our intuition tells us that if we just hear more *practical* preaching (that is, moving exhortations to follow Jesus), we will improve. When this becomes the main diet, however, we do not find ourselves improving. We neither mourn nor dance. But bring me into the chamber of a holy God, where I am completely undone, and tell me about what God has done in Christ to save me; tell me about the marvelous indicatives of the gospel—God's surprising interventions of salvation on the stage of history despite human rebellion—and the flickering candle of faith is inflamed, giving light to others.

The law *guides*, but it does not *give*. For all who seek to be acceptable to God by their obedience, love, holiness, and service, the call to obedience only condemns. It shows us what we have *not* done, and the more we hear it properly, the more we actually lose our moral self-confidence and cling to Christ. It stops our inner spin machine that creates a false view of God and ourselves.

In this preaching of the law, sin is recognized as a condition that yields certain acts, not vice versa. The goal of such preaching is to lead us to the sort of confession that we find expressed in the Heidelberg Catechism:

> Even though my conscience accuses me of having grievously sinned against all God's commandments and of never having kept any one of them, and even though I am still inclined toward all evil, nevertheless, without my deserving it at all, out of sheer grace, God grants and credits to me the perfect satisfaction, righteousness, and holiness of Christ, as if I had never sinned nor been a sinner, as if I had been as perfectly obedient as Christ was obedient for me.[20]

The proper preaching of the law will lead us to despair of ourselves, but only so that we may finally look outside ourselves and look to Christ.

"The righteousness that is by faith" Paul sets against "the righteousness that is by law." When it comes to how one is justified—accepted as righteous before God—nothing could be more opposed than the law and the gospel. The law doesn't offer assistance to wayward souls, but it assures certain and just condemnation. It came not to encourage, edify, or coach a keep-your–chin-up strategy for victory but to kill—to end the domain of sin at its very core, namely, the pride of self-rule and self-confidence. Once despairing of any hope from good advice and moral improvement, one then flees to Christ for safety.

I am always annoyed by my annual medical checkup, primarily because the nurse weighs me, and each time the result is about ten pounds more depressing than when I weigh myself. At home I can tinker a bit with the scales, but the nurse at the doctor's office won't even let me empty my pockets. When she weighs me, it goes down in a chart. I offer a rationalization; she smiles as if she has heard it a thousand times before, but she makes no adjustments in her calculation.

We are brilliant at rationalizing and manipulating the evidence. We "suppress the truth" (Rom. 2:18). We are spiritual spin doctors. Unlike the pious advice of others or the standards we set for ourselves, God's law is the true scales that we cannot tamper with, weighing us in comparison with God's holiness, not with the neighbor next door. But how often are we weighed in God's scales, undressed in his presence, laid bare and left with no excuses?

The Gospel of Love

We've gone from the caricature of Dana Carvey's *Saturday Night Live* character, Church Lady, with her air of moral superiority and scolding disapproval, to the sentimental and therapeutic caricature of Al Franken's Stuart Smalley on the same show. Each monologue of psychobabble closed with Smalley leading the audience to repeat after him, "I'm good enough, I'm smart enough, and doggone it, people like me." Many people think this represents a refreshing shift from legalism to a more positive spirituality. But is it just another version of imperative-driven religion, a watered-down version of the law? And if the world ridicules this therapeutic moralism, who are we trying to impress?

While on the road recently, I surfed the television channels looking for some news and happened upon Joyce Meyer, a popular prosperity evangelist. Much like Joel Osteen, Meyer reflects the antipathy of Boomers toward their strict upbringing. After railing against the rule-driven religion of her past, Meyer said, "I finally realized that the gospel is not about rules; it's about loving God and each other. So what have you done this week to help out someone you know?" We have already encountered a similar theme in Joel Osteen: Christianity isn't a bunch of rules; its essence is loving God and others. This sentiment is expressed across the spectrum, as we have seen, from conservative to liberal, traditional to megachurch to Emergent Church.

Not long ago, I also came across a passage in John Calvin's work where he observed that many of his Roman Catholic friends were also reacting against the rules and regulations of their youth by saying that we just need to love each other. "As if that were *easier*!" Calvin exclaimed.

Like Meyer, what Calvin's contemporaries failed to realize is that love is actually the summary of the law. God's commands stipulate what love of God and neighbor means. In the Bible, the law simply nails down what it means to love God and our neighbor. Long before Jesus summed up the law in this way (Matt. 22:39), it was delivered by the hand of Moses (Lev. 19:18, 34), and Paul reiterated the point (Rom. 13:8–10). I may be able to keep from stealing my neighbor's wife and car, but do I give my neighbor what I owe? Have I sold everything I have and given it to the poor? This is how Jesus defined the law and forced people (like the rich young ruler) to realize that they have not kept all these things from their youth (Matt. 19:20).

It is always amazing to me when people suggest that the God of the Old Testament (and perhaps their fundamentalist upbringing) is rule-oriented and judgmental, while the God of the New Testament is loving and lenient. It is even more amazing when they appeal to Jesus's Sermon on the Mount. Not only sleeping with your neighbor's wife, but lusting in your heart; not only killing someone, but hating your neighbor; not only stealing, but depriving your neighbor of your own material resources: that is what Jesus says the law truly requires of us. So it is hardly good news when people tell us that God required a bunch of rules but now tells us just to love him and each other.

Defined in this way, loving God and neighbor is a lot *harder* than following a few rules. When Jesus defines the law of love—even more than that, embodies it in his very person and actions—I am undone. Before singing "What a Friend We Have in Jesus," I find myself, with Peter, saying, "Depart from me, for I am a sinful man" (Luke 5:8). And Peter did not feel this only once, when he first met Jesus. His journey with Jesus fluctuated from high points, such as his confession of Jesus as the Christ, to the low point of denying Christ three times, back to the high point of being martyred for his testimony to his Savior. Like Peter, our Christian life is a roller coaster of faithfulness and unfaithfulness. Since we always drift back to self-confident triumphalism (remember Peter's protest, "I will never deny you!" just before he did), we need to hear God's verdict on our righteousness through the law and his assurance of pardon in the gospel. Jesus's example is not good news but a terrifying burden unless he is first of all the one who saves me from my inability to follow it.

Those who think they can wrap themselves in the fig leaves of their loving intentions and actions toward God and neighbor are in for a big surprise. "Just love God and people" is not the gospel; it is precisely that holy demand of the law that we have grievously failed to keep. Where much of the preaching today (illustrated by Joyce Meyer's comment above) offers a false distinction between law and love, the biblical distinction is between law and gospel. Our love toward God and neighbor is the essence of the law; God's love toward us in Jesus Christ is the essence of the gospel. "In this is love, not that we have loved God but that he loved us and sent his Son to be the propitiation for our sins" (1 John 4:10).

Commandments, Not Suggestions

What we all need today is a fresh encounter with God's law in its full force. When the Israelites heard God speak his law at Mount Sinai, even Moses trembled with fear (Heb. 12:21). The people were terrified and said to Moses, "You speak to us, and we will listen; but do not let God speak to us, lest we die" (Exod. 20:19). Why such a reaction? We are told that it was "because they could not bear what was commanded" (Heb. 12:20 NIV).

God's law is not a list of suggestions. Nor is the principal reason for the law our happiness, although we were created in God's image and therefore were designed to find our deepest fulfillment in glorifying and enjoying God. The law is an expression of *God's* own glory—his moral character. Furthermore, the covenant of law sworn by Israel at Mount Sinai was not, "We will try really hard to have our best life now," but, "All this we will do." To confirm their oath, Moses splashed blood on the people, visually ratifying their commitment to personally and perfectly fulfill the terms of the covenant. It is no wonder that the Israelites, terrified by God's commanding voice, begged Moses to be their mediator. Yet when Moses was absent from the congregation, receiving this law from God on the mountain, the people decided to construct a more user-friendly representation of God—the golden calf—which, instead of inspiring awe and fear, encouraged them to a lighter form of worship: "The people sat down to eat and drink and rose up to play" (Exod. 32:6).

If God's voice of law does not de-center us, throw us off balance, and judge our best efforts as having fallen short of God's glory, we will never flee to Christ as our Mediator greater than Moses. Instead, we will come up with our own representations of God—the golden calves of our own forms of worship—gentle suggestions for life, and helpful advice that lulls us into thinking at last we have a friendly God who does not provoke the cry, "God, be merciful to me, a sinner!" (Luke 18:13).

There is no *balance* here between law and gospel. The law tells us what we must do; the gospel tells us what God has done for us. These are two distinct words; each must be heard on its own terms, in the full force of its judgment and absolution. In justifying sinners, God does not relax his righteousness that is revealed in his law but imputes Christ's righteousness to every believer. In this way, God's justice is not sacrificed to his love; rather, his love *and* his justice are mutually satisfied. We are saved by works—in fact, by perfect love and obedience. However, it is Christ's works rather than ours that serve as the basis for our confidence: "Therefore, there is now no condemnation for those who are in Christ Jesus" (Rom. 8:1 NIV). The good news is that, "But now, apart from law, the righteousness of God has been disclosed, and is attested by the law and the prophets, the righteousness of God through faith in Jesus Christ for all who believe," since sinners "are now justified by his grace as a gift, through the redemption that is in Christ Jesus, whom God put forward as a sacrifice of atonement by his blood, effective through faith" (Rom. 3:21–25 NRSV).

When Secondary Questions Become Primary

Why did Jesus come? What was his mission? Jesus himself said, "The Son of Man came . . . to give his life a ransom for many" (Matt. 20:28 NKJV). When he was rebuked by his disciples for raining on their parade by talking about the cross, Jesus said, "It was *for this very reason* I came to this hour" (John 12:27 NIV; emphasis added). When Philip asked Jesus to *show them* the way to the Father, Jesus said that he *is* the Way (John 14:8–14).

Similarly, Paul told the Corinthians that he was not only single-mindedly determined to preach Christ alone, but "Christ *crucified*," although it is "a stumbling block to Jews and foolishness to Gentiles," since it is the only Good News capable of saving either (1 Cor. 1:23 NIV; see 1 Cor. 1:18–2:1–2). Paul knew that preachers could even use the name of Jesus, but too often it was used as something or someone other than the vicarious sacrifice for sinners (2 Cor. 11:4–6).

The Pharisees quizzed Jesus about marriage and divorce, adultery, and taxes, and they criticized him for picking grain on the Sabbath and eating and drinking with publicans and sinners (Matt. 11:19). Focused on ushering in God's kingdom by strictly observing the rules of the elders—and trying to trap Jesus on legal questions—they were sidetracked from the real mission of the Messiah. Looking at themselves when they should have been looking to Christ as "the Lamb of God, who takes away the sin of the world" (John 1:29), they were distracted. So too were the disciples themselves, who routinely changed the subject whenever Jesus spoke of the cross as they neared Jerusalem. They were thinking inauguration day, with the last judgment and the consummation of the kingdom in all of its glory. Jesus knew, however, that the only route to glory down the road was the cross up ahead.

Jesus contrasts the false piety of the Pharisee with the genuine faith and repentance of the citizen of his kingdom in his famous parable in Luke 18:

> Two men went up to the temple to pray, one a Pharisee and the other a tax collector. The Pharisee, standing by himself, was praying thus: "God, I thank you that I am not like other people: thieves, rogues, adulterers, or even like this tax collector. I fast twice a week; I give a tenth of all my income." But the tax collector, standing far off, would not even look up to heaven, but was beating his breast and saying, "God, be merciful to me, a sinner!" I tell you, this man went down to his home justified rather than the other; for all who exalt themselves will be humbled, but all who humble themselves will be exalted.
>
> Luke 18:10–14 NRSV

Jesus told the Pharisees, "You are those who justify yourselves in the sight of others, but God knows your hearts; for what is prized by human beings is an abomination in the sight of God" (Luke 16:15 NRSV). While Jesus basically seems to ignore the Sadducees, since they probably viewed each other as irrelevant, he warns repeatedly of "the yeast of the Pharisees," which is "their hypocrisy" (Luke 12:1 NRSV).

In the parable that Jesus tells, the Pharisee even prays, "I thank you that I am not like . . . this tax collector." The only thing worse than his self-righteousness is that he pretends to give God a little credit for it. We have all witnessed awards ceremonies in

139

which recipients acknowledged the many people without whom such success could not have been possible. This is quite different, however, from being the beneficiary of the estate of someone who, at the very moment of drafting the bequest, was treated as an enemy by the heir. So all of the questions that the religious leaders put to Jesus were *law* questions: What do you do in situation *x* or *y*? What is the one thing I need to do to obtain eternal life—in addition to all of the commandments in the law, which I've kept?

Jesus pushes these questioners (like the rich young ruler) to recognize that they have not actually kept the law. Similarly, Paul challenged the Galatians: "For all who rely on works of the law are under a curse; for it is written, 'Cursed be everyone who does not abide by *all* things written in the Book of the Law, and do them.' Now it is evident that no one is justified before God by the law, for 'The righteous shall live by faith'" (Gal. 3:10–11; emphasis added). Those are the terms! No grading on a curve; no time off for good behavior or good intentions. That should drive us to our knees in confession of our utter helplessness, but instead it often arouses our self-righteousness. If the latter, we will avoid the law's noble work of driving us out of ourselves to Christ. Good principles commanded by God himself actually become a distraction rather than a schoolmaster to lead us to Christ. The *good* news, Paul adds, is that "Christ redeemed us from the curse of the law by becoming a curse for us" (v. 13). The Jews, Paul says, stumble over Christ. He is the rock of offense; he is in the way of our "transformational" activism.

The Gentiles love wisdom, so show them a Jesus who is smarter at solving the conundrums of daily living and the church will throng with supporters. Paul says that his Jewish contemporaries love signs and wonders. So tell people that Jesus can help them have their best life now, or bring in the kingdom of glory, or drive out the Romans and prove their integrity before the pagans, and Jesus will be laureled with praise. Give them some moral wisdom from your own *faith tradition* that might help them be better parents and spouses, and they might listen—as long as you provide suggestions and not commands on the basis of which God will judge on the last day. But proclaim Christ as the Suffering Servant who laid down his life and took it back up again, and everybody wonders who changed the subject.

The church exists in order to change the subject from us and our deeds to God and his deeds of salvation, from our various missions to save the world to Christ's mission that has already accomplished redemption. He sends us into the world, to be sure, but not to save it. Rather, he sends us into the world to witness to Christ as the only Savior and to love and serve our neighbor in our secular vocations. Evil lies not outside us but inside; it is salvation that comes from outside ourselves.

Nothing the church does extends, completes, or fulfills Christ's all-sufficient, once-and-for-all, completed work of living, dying, and rising for sinners. So enough about us! We are the sinners he saves, not the redeemers he inspires. *That* is the content of our witness, which is why we are heralds of the Good News rather than mere purveyors of good advice. And even in terms of evangelistic impact, I am confident that this orientation is more effective with non-Christians. They may not like our message anyway, but at least they might be relieved that we have stopped holding ourselves up as the way, the truth, and the life.

If the message the church proclaims makes sense without conversion, if it does not offend even lifelong believers from time to time so that they too need to die more to themselves and live more to Christ, then it is not the gospel. When Christ is talked about, a lot of things can happen, none of which necessarily have any lasting impact. When Christ is proclaimed in his saving office, the church becomes a theater of death and resurrection.

Missing the Point: Turning the Bible into *Life's Instruction Manual*

Is it possible to be a Bible-believing fundamentalist and miss the point that Christ is the sum and substance of its message?

The Pharisees were the guardians of Scripture, so concerned about following it strictly that they even devised numerous hedges to protect its commands. If the law commanded you to rest from your ordinary labors on the Sabbath, these religious leaders insisted that a poor person could not pick grain on the Sabbath even for survival. In fact, just after Jesus was rebuked by the Pharisees for letting his disciples do this very thing, he told them, "You search the scriptures because you think that in them you have eternal life; and it is they that testify on my behalf. Yet you refuse to come to me to have life" (John 5:39–40 NRSV). The Scriptures he had in mind were what we call the Old Testament. They were zealously committed to the Bible, but they missed the point.

After his resurrection, Jesus met up with some of his depressed disciples along the Emmaus road and cheered them up by reminding them of what their Scriptures said: "'Was it not necessary that the Messiah should suffer these things and then enter into his glory?' Then beginning with Moses and all the prophets, he interpreted to them the things about himself in all the scriptures" (Luke 24:26–27 NRSV). No wonder their hearts burned within them as he opened up the Scriptures (v. 32).

Apart from Christ, the Bible is a closed book. Read with him at the center, it is the greatest story ever told. The Bible is trivialized when it is reduced to *life's instruction manual*. What is the point of the historical books, the Psalms, the wisdom literature, and the Prophets? According to the apostles—and Jesus himself— the Bible is an unfolding drama with Jesus Christ as its central character. As the narratives themselves make plain enough, the

Old Testament saints were not heroes of faith and obedience but sinners who, despite their own wavering, were given the faith to cling to God's promise. According to the apostle Paul, the Old Testament itself proclaimed this gospel of free justification in Christ alone through faith alone: "But now a righteousness from God, apart from law, has been made known, to which the Law and the Prophets testify" (Rom. 3:21 NIV).

In his first letter, the apostle Peter reminds believers of the "indescribable and glorious joy" resulting from the fact that they are "receiving the outcome of your faith, the salvation of your souls." Then he adds,

> Concerning this salvation, the prophets who prophesied of the grace that was to be yours made careful search and inquiry, inquiring about the person or time that the Spirit of Christ within them indicated when it testified in advance to the sufferings destined for Christ and the subsequent glory. It was revealed to them that they were serving not themselves but you, in regard to the things that have now been announced to you through those who brought you good news by the Holy Spirit sent from heaven—things into which angels long to look!
>
> 1 Peter 1:8–12 NRSV

Isn't it amazing that, according to Jesus, the whole Bible is about him and Peter says that the angels long to understand the Good News that is (or should be) brought weekly by heralds, but we decide that someone or something else should be the focus of our sermon and worship this week? "Yes, but we already understand all of that," I hear someone saying. Do we? Not if we are by nature self-righteous and self-confident, answering the law with the oath of the Israelites at Mount Sinai, "All this we will do."

It is just as easy to lose Christ by distraction as it is by denial. We keep expecting the ball to be fumbled by the liberals, when conservative churches are often as likely to be interested in someone or something other than *Christ crucified* this week. A woman who was struggling in her marriage told a pastor friend of mine that she decided to visit his church because her home church was going through a series on "How to Have a Better Marriage." "What I need to hear most right now is who God is and what Christ has done for me even though I'm a wreck. My marriage needs a lot of things, but that more than anything else." She was right.

Christless Christianity does not mean religion or spirituality devoid of the words *Jesus*, *Christ*, *Lord*, or even *Savior*. What it means is that the way those names and titles are employed will be removed from their specific location in an unfolding historical plot of human rebellion and divine rescue and from such practices as baptism and communion. Jesus as life coach, therapist, buddy, significant other, founder of Western civilization, political messiah, example of radical living, and countless other images can distract us from the stumbling block and foolishness of "Christ and him crucified." This gospel may even be tacked on to the end of sermons. The question, however, is whether we are preaching the Word from Genesis to Revelation as a testimony to Christ or as a resource for writing our own story.

In other words, the drift toward Christless Christianity can happen through addition as well as subtraction. In C. S. Lewis's *Screwtape Letters*, the devil, Screwtape, instructs his minion, Wormwood, to keep the Christians distracted from Christ as Redeemer from God's wrath. Rather than clumsily announce his presence by direct attacks, Wormwood should try to get the churches to become interested in *Christianity and . . .* : Christianity *and* the War, Christianity *and* Poverty, Christianity *and* Morality, and so on.

I hear someone saying, "But we have to make Jesus and the gospel relevant to people in our own time and place." But what does it say about Jesus Christ if the relevance of his person and work cannot stand on its own? Sure, Christ came as "the Lamb of God, who takes away the sin of the world" (John 1:29), but can he help me get that promotion at work or relieve my stress? Can he keep my kids' attention so they will stay off drugs? "Christianity and . . ." already assumes that Christianity itself is uninteresting. But as an adjective for other things (Christian aerobics, Christian values, Christian music, etc.), it is just a valuable trademark. As counterintuitive as it may seem, being grounded in the gospel of Christ relieves stress in deeper places than we even knew we had inside ourselves, and I have witnessed countless examples of young people liberated from boredom-induced addictions and sinful patterns by becoming captivated with God's amazing grace in his Son. Nobody had to tell them that drugs were wrong; they knew that. And all the banal lectures on self-esteem and emotional summer camp calls to "surrender all" only made them more cynical. Genuine preaching of the law diagnoses the sinful condition—the root, not just the fruit—and the gospel is its radical solution.

Often in popular preaching today it seems that the goal is to get through the interpretation of the passage in order to arrive at the *contemporary application*, which typically evidences the preacher's own hobbyhorses and recent diet of reading or movies. Usually, *application* equals *law*—to-do lists—rather than using the passage to actually absolve sinners of their guilt and rescript them in their new roles as those who have been transferred from the covenantal headship of Adam to Christ.

Of course I am not denying any more than Lewis that Christians should have an interest in pressing issues of the day or that there is an important place for applying biblical teaching to our conduct in the world. But with Lewis I am concerned that when the church's basic message is less about who Christ is and what he has accomplished once and for all for us and more about who we are and what we have to do in order to make his life (and ours) relevant to the culture, the religion that is made "relevant" is no longer Christianity. However frequently his name is invoked, a religion that turns on "What Would Jesus Do?" is not the Christian faith. Not thinking that "Christ crucified" is as relevant as "Christ and Family Values" or "Christ and America" or "Christ and World Hunger," we end up assimilating the gospel to law.

When people ask for more *practical* preaching, for a more *relevant* message than Christ and him crucified, what they are falling back on is law rather than gospel. Another way of saying it is that we always prefer giving God a supporting role in our life movie—our own glory story—rather than being recast in his unfolding drama of redemption. How can God fix my marriage? How can he make me a more effective leader? How can I overcome stress and manage my time and finances better? These are not bad questions. In fact, the Scriptures do bring sound wisdom to bear on these issues. But they are not the major questions, not even for lifelong Christians.

Unless Christ is *publicly exhibited as crucified*—placarded before us week after week in Word and sacrament—we will, like the Galatians, drift toward the view that we begin with Christ and his Spirit and then end up striving for our own righteousness before God (Gal. 3:1–3). Since even Christians remain simultaneously justified and sinful, we will always gravitate back toward ourselves: that which happens within us, that which we can measure and control, that which we can see and feel.

Wherever God's Word addresses our world, we must witness to his command as well as his promise. Nevertheless, ministers are not trained to be experts in economics, business, law, and politics. People may get a lot better financial, marital, and child-rearing advice from wise uncles and aunts or even non-Christian neighbors than from their pastor. Rather, ministers are trained to be wise in the Scriptures, which center on the drama of redemption. They are not sent on their own mission but are ambassadors and heralds sent from God to a world of sin and death. They are called to proclaim the most important and relevant announcement, which cannot be heard anywhere else.

Once liberated by the gospel from the condemnation of the law, our hearts are filled with gratitude. The law not only drives us to Christ, it tells gospel-created faith what to do. Early in my marriage, it was very important to me to buy my wife Christmas and birthday presents that *I* wanted her to have. It bothered me when she spoiled the surprise by telling me what she really wanted. "Why can't I be spontaneous?" I asked her, "so that it's really *my* gift?" It took me a while to realize that I was actually being selfish. Similarly, God's law tells us what God approves—what his heart delights in. He does not ask us to be spontaneous, creative, or self-willed but to do the things that he regards as righteous, holy, true, and good.

Even when so much of the preaching and popular Christian literature today focuses on imperatives, it is often our clever suggestions (disguised as "applications") rather than the clear implications of a given passage. So we need renewed attention to God's Word not only to properly proclaim and receive the gospel, but in order to properly direct our obedience to his commands.

Even this preaching of the law as the rule of Christian gratitude cannot have the last word, though. We have probably all heard sermons that, after laying out God's expectations or the example of someone in the Bible, concluded, "Does this describe you?" If you judge me by the righteousness that God requires, I cannot truthfully answer *yes* in those moments. The good news is that because Christ's righteousness has been credited to me, it does describe me. Although I am also being renewed according to Christ's likeness, this sanctification (unlike justification) remains unfinished, partial, and often ambiguous to me and to others. That means that I'm going to have to decide this one based on God's promise and not on my experience. I do not see myself as a *conqueror*, but *God says* that in spite of our suffering and continuing struggles with indwelling sin, "We are more than conquerors through him who loved us" (Rom. 8:37). I am a recipient of Christ's victory over the guilt and tyranny of sin. Tell me who I am in Christ (the indicative), and now suddenly, in view of "the mercies of God," the commands (imperatives) become my "reasonable service" (Rom. 12:1 NKJV). Why should I want to be conformed any longer to this world's pattern of thinking when I have been written into God's script as a coheir with Christ of the kingdom of heaven (vv. 2–21)?

When the gospel of Christ as *Savior* is taken for granted, we are no longer being constantly converted—not only from our immorality, greed, and selfishness but from our spiritual pride, hypocrisy, and self-trust—to that faith in Christ which alone can yield the fruit of the Spirit that blesses the communion of saints and goes out in loving service to our neighbors.

Dare to Be a Daniel!

So the Bible is not an instruction manual for daily living. Of course it reveals God's moral will for our lives, but it's the story of redemption that is central.

How often have we heard the Old Testament interpreted as a collection of pious stories that we can use for our daily life? From Genesis, we might have any number of heroes to imitate and villains to shun. I never knew growing up in evangelicalism that the Old Testament was about Christ. I thought it was about Bible heroes whose character I was to emulate. Be faithful like Abraham, devoted like Moses, and so on. Joshua's life could be mined for leadership principles, and we all dared to be a Daniel.

What were the five smooth stones I could find in my bag to slay the Goliaths of my life as did David?

The Bible is nothing like Aesop's fables: a collection of brief stories that end with a moral principle. Abraham was in many ways a moral failure: sleeping with his servant when God had promised the heir through his wife, Sarah, lying to a king by telling him that Sarah was his sister in order to get himself out of a bind, and so forth. Even his willingness to sacrifice Isaac was not an example for us but an occasion for God to foreshadow Christ as the ram caught in the thicket so that Isaac—and the rest of us—could go free. Jacob was a schemer, but God had chosen him and, in spite of the fact that he continued to commit terrible sins throughout the course of his life, God kept his gracious promise. Joshua is not a source for leadership principles, unless we're planning on leading a campaign of destruction against idolatrous nations in order to establish righteousness in God's holy land. Yet read in the light of the history of redemption, Joshua and his ministry point forward to Christ's person and work.

David can only ambiguously be held up as a heroic example; his main role in the story is to presage his greater Son who assumed the everlasting throne that God promised unconditionally to David's heirs. Though described as "a man after God's own heart," David committed adultery and covered up his crime by having the victim's husband—one of David's loyal soldiers—sent to certain death in battle. He was not allowed to build the temple because of the violence of his reign, and his family yielded one ghastly king after another. Nevertheless, God kept his unilateral promise to preserve a Davidic king on Judah's throne forever. God, not David, was the hero, and Christ as the royal Son of David, not my imitation of David, is the point.

Countless other examples can be adduced. Even the so-called "Hall of Heroes" in Hebrews 11 is misnamed. The writer consistently mentions that they overcame by faith in Christ, not by their works. In fact, God overcame their sins to further his redemptive purposes, working through their folly as well as their faithfulness. The whole point is to demonstrate that God's foolishness is wiser than human wisdom and God's weakness is greater than human strength. Furthermore, the examples selected in that chapter are precisely like David: in each case, saint and sinner simultaneously. In fact, Paul appeals to Abraham and David in Romans 4 as examples for us, to be sure, but as sinners who were justified through faith alone in Christ alone.

Given the moralistic expectations often assumed, it is no wonder that people find the Old Testament boring and much of the New Testament incomprehensible. Contrast this approach to Luther's interpretation of the story of David and Goliath, for example:

> When David overcame the great Goliath, there came among the Jewish people the good report and encouraging news that their terrible enemy had been struck down and that they had been rescued and given joy and peace; and they sang and danced and were glad for it (1 Sam. 18:6). Thus this gospel of God or New Testament is a good story and report, sounded forth into all the world by the apostles, telling of a true David who strove with sin, death, and the devil, and overcame them, and thereby rescued all those who were captive in sin, afflicted with death, and overpowered by the devil.[21]

As Graeme Goldsworthy comments,

> The important point to note is that Luther has made the link between the saving acts of God through David and the saving acts of God through Christ. Once we see that connection, it is impossible to use David as a mere model for Christian living since his victory was vicarious and the Israelites could only rejoice in what was won for them. In terms of our interpretative principles,

150

we see David's victory as a salvation event in that the existence
of the people of God in the promised land was at stake.[22]

Instead of drawing a straight line of application from the narrative to us, which typically moralizes or allegorizes the story,
we are taught by Jesus himself to understand these passages in
the light of their place in the unfolding drama of redemption
that leads to Christ.

Regardless of the official theology held on paper, moralistic
preaching (the bane of conservatives and liberals alike) assumes
that we are not really helpless sinners who need to be rescued
but decent folks who need good examples, exhortations, and
instructions. Unbelievers certainly need to be saved, but believers
need to be prodded with good examples. However, Goldsworthy
continues,

> We are not saved by our changed lives. The changed life is the
> result of being saved and not the basis of it. The basis of salva-
> tion is the perfection in the life and death of Christ presented
> in our place. . . .
>
> By reverting to either allegorical interpretation on the one
> hand, or to prophetic literalism on the other, some evangelicals
> have thrown away the hermeneutical gains of the Reformers in
> favour of a medieval approach to the Bible. . . . Evangelicals have
> had a reputation for taking the Bible seriously. But even they have
> traditionally propagated the idea of the short devotional reading
> from which a "blessing from the Lord" must be wrested.[23]

Once again, everything depends on whether we use the Bible to
fix our own inner problems or hear God addressing us through his
Word, calling us outside ourselves to our Redeemer in history.

No matter what we hold on paper as sound evangelical doctrine, a steady diet of moralistic preaching, youth ministry,
Sunday school, devotional literature, and outreach will always

produce churches filled with practicing Pelagians. Goldsworthy calls attention to this difference:

> The pivotal point of turning in evangelical thinking which demands close attention is the change that has taken place from the Protestant emphasis upon the objective facts of the gospel in history, to the medieval emphasis on the inner life. The evangelical who sees the inward transforming work of the Spirit as the key element of Christianity will soon lose contact with the historic faith and the historic gospel. . . . Inner-directed Christianity, which reduces the gospel to the level of every other religion of the inner man, might well use a text from the Apocrypha to serve as its own epitaph for the Reformers: "There are others who are remembered; they are dead, and it is as though they never existed" (ben Sirah 44:9).[24]

It will always go against our grain to be driven outside ourselves by God's Word, but it is only through this gracious intrusion of a sovereign God that we will receive and then express true faith, hope, and love.

Not only in its *content*, but in its *form*, the gospel is not about us and what we have done but about God and his success story. After all, it is *news*. I recently watched a PBS conversation between retired television news anchors. One interesting point that all three participants made was that journalism (especially on television) has shifted from an older slogan like, "All the news you need to know," to "All the news that you can use." Even news has been turned into therapy and entertainment. By definition, however, news is something you don't already know and you may not already think it is all that useful. You have to be told what has happened. Furthermore, you hear the news. In other words, you are a recipient. You did not make the news, but if the news is significant enough, it can make you.

Creeds and Deeds: Doctrine, Doxology, and Duty

Romans is the Bible's most systematic presentation of the Christian faith. Paul has told us the bad news: everyone, Jew and Gentile alike, is *in Adam* and under the condemnation of the law. Yet this merely sets the stage for the Good News that everyone who has faith in Christ is justified. After holding up this shimmering, many-faceted gem to our wondering eyes, Paul meets the objection that this gospel of free grace has always met: namely, that it will lead to moral license. Yet even here, the answer is not to reign in grace as if it were too much of a good thing but to explain how Christ is the answer to the power as well as the penalty of sin.

> Moreover whom He predestined, these He also called; whom He called, these He also justified; and whom He justified, these He also glorified.
>
> What then shall we say to these things? If God is for us, who can be against us? He who did not spare His own Son, but delivered Him up for us all, how shall He not with Him also freely give us all things? . . . Who is he who condemns? It is Christ who died, and furthermore is also risen, who is even at the right hand of God, who also makes intercession for us. Who shall separate us from the love of Christ?
>
> Romans 8:30–35

What can separate us from Christ's love? Nothing. Absolutely nothing. Each ascent leads us to ever-higher vistas, all the way through the purposes of God's electing grace in chapters 9–11, until Paul reaches his summit:

> Oh, the depth of the riches both of the wisdom and knowledge of God! How unsearchable are His judgments and His ways past finding out!

"For who has known the mind of the LORD?
Or who has become His counselor?"
"Or who has first given to Him
And it shall be repaid to him?"

For of Him and to Him and through Him are all things,
     to whom be glory forever. Amen.

Romans 11:33–36 NKJV

We have moved from doctrine to doxology, and only after this do we meet Paul's transition to application.

Notice how Paul's call to discipleship feeds off an explicit and constant focus on the doctrine that he has explained for the previous eleven chapters: "Therefore, I urge you, brothers, *in view of God's mercy*, to offer your bodies as living sacrifices, holy and pleasing to God—this is your spiritual act of worship" (Rom. 12:1 NIV, emphasis added). Furthermore, in the next sentence he urges us on to deeper transformation, not simply by greater moral resolve, but by first changing our thinking: "Do not conform any longer to the pattern of this world, but be transformed by the renewing of your mind" (v. 2 NIV). The creed leads to deeds; doctrine fuels doxology, generating love and service to the saints as well as to our unbelieving neighbors (vv. 6–15).

Paul makes the same point in 2 Corinthians 9, where he says that the generosity of those who serve Christ's body materially as well as spiritually "will produce thanksgiving to God." Such service "will glorify God because of your submission *flowing from your confession of the gospel of Christ*." It will witness to "the surpassing grace of God upon you" and the apostle can only conclude with the exclamation, "Thanks be to *God* for *his* inexpressible gift!" (vv. 11–15; emphasis added). Gifts come from God to us and through us to others, while thanksgiving rises up to God.

154

It is no wonder that the Heidelberg Catechism moves through three sections: guilt, grace, and gratitude. This is the movement that we find in the Psalms and in Paul's letters. Those who are forgiven much love much (Luke 7:47). There is nothing wrong with being deeply moved emotionally by truth. In fact, Good News generates doxology, so if we are not affected by the doctrine or motivated by it to love our neighbors, then we have probably misunderstood something. Psalm 45 begins, "My heart is stirred by a noble theme" (v. 1 NIV), and then recites that theme: the triumphs of God's Messiah in the earth.

The psalms typically follow this pattern: telling the story of God's triumphs despite his people's unfaithfulness, leading to praise for God's character and finally to the response of grateful obedience. I have often noticed that in settings where praise choruses are even taken from the psalms, it is a snippet and almost always excerpted from the second or third section without the first. Instead of starting with the Good News of God's mighty acts, we start with our response: "I will praise you," "I love you, Lord," "I will serve you," "I bow down and worship you," etc. But this means that we are encouraging faith in faith, confidence in our own experience and praise, rather than faith in Christ as the *amen* to God's promises. In other words, the part of the psalm that such examples illustrate is the *reasonable service* without the *in view of God's mercies*. Rehearsing God's deeds takes a back seat to expressing our zeal and commitment. This is to have the law without the gospel, lifting the *reasonable service* out of its native habitat of the story of redemption. For Paul, however, the service is now reasonable because it is the sensible response to the news we have heard.

If you are subjected week after week to a diet of "do *more*," "be *more* authentic," "live *more* transparently," and "feel *more*," you will eventually become like a prisoner who is forced into hard labor without adequate food. If you are regularly treated to the feast of God's works and the zeal that consumed our Savior in the service of our redemption, the exhortations will no longer be an unreasonable burden but a guide to expressions of thanksgiving in which our gracious God delights.

What a relief it is when we are liberated from thinking that we are called to *be* the gospel! Now we can simply receive it and draw upon it daily for the confidence to look up to God in faith and out to our neighbor in love. Now the law can guide and direct us, no longer out of fear of judgment, but out of genuine thanksgiving for God's grace.

The gospel *changes* lives; it is not *our* changed life. "We do not preach ourselves, but Jesus Christ as Lord" (2 Cor. 4:5 NIV).

As has been frequently pointed out, Paul often moves from doctrine to application in all of his epistles. In fact, he is pretty obvious about it. In 1 Corinthians he moves back and forth between diagnosis and cure—from division, strife, sexual immorality, lawsuits, and mistreatment of the poor to God's faithfulness, justification, sanctification, and the unity of the saints in union with Christ, especially as engendered by the Lord's Supper. Galatians, Ephesians, Colossians, and Romans exhibit an even clearer pattern. In each case, the first half or more of the letter expounds the riches of our inheritance in Christ by grace alone through faith alone, and then specific exhortations are given to realize the impact of these truths in the concrete relationships of believers between each other, in their homes, and in their relationships with non-Christians as neighbors, coworkers, citizens, and so forth. Peter's epistles also follow a similar pattern.

The apostles would have considered it inconceivable that a church might have its doctrine right but be uninterested in missions, evangelism, prayer, and works of service and charity to those in need or, conversely, that a church might be faithful in life apart from sound doctrine. Orthodoxy (correct doctrine) and orthopraxy (correct practice) were inseparable and mutually dependent elements of their message. Therefore, deeds without creeds means law without gospel; but we have seen that the biblical pattern is to move from doctrine to doxology to service, "bearing fruit in every good work and increasing in the knowledge of God" (Col. 1:10).

People are looking for authenticity, but this includes acknowledgment of our sin and self-righteousness and our need for Christ. What could be less authentic and honest than assuming that our lives can preach better than the gospel? According to George Barna, our witness points unbelievers to our own lifestyle. "What they are looking for is a better life." Barna assumes, however, that the unchurched already know what they really need: a good example, good resources, and good advice. He continues, "Can you lead them to a place or to a group of people that will deliver the building blocks of a better life? Do not propose Christianity as a system of rules but as a relationship with the One who leads by way of example. Then seek proven ways to achieve meaning and success."[25] Barna not only confuses the gospel (Christ's work) with the law (our work), he assumes that moral betterment can be defined apart from the law that God actually established. Clearly affirming neither God's law nor gospel, such advice substitutes our own principles of better living.

In the parable of the sower, Jesus refers to four different *hearers* of the gospel: The first reject it. The second "receive it with joy" at first, but the seed has "no root," and when suffering comes, it cannot endure. The third is choked by pleasure and prosperity. Only in the fourth does it take root and produce an abundant crop. Jesus concludes, "Take care then how you hear" (Luke 8:11–15, 18). We have to be hearers of the gospel before we are doers of the law. Otherwise, when the initial emotion and zeal wear off, we will be tumbleweeds blown in every direction—away from God's garden of grace.

5
_____

Your Own Personal Jesus

C iting examples from television, pop music, and best-selling
books, an article in *Entertainment Weekly* noted,

> Pop culture is going gaga for spirituality. . . . [However,] seek-
> ers of the day are apt to peel away the tough theological stuff and
> pluck out the most dulcet elements of faith, coming up with a
> soothing sampler of Judeo-Christian imagery . . . , Eastern medi-
> tation, self-help lingo, a vaguely conservative craving for "virtue,"
> and a loopy New Age pursuit of "peace." This happy free-for-all,
> appealing to Baptists and stargazers alike, comes off more like
> Forrest Gump's ubiquitous "boxa chocolits" than like any real
> system of belief. You never know what you're gonna get.[1]

The *search for the sacred* has become a recurring cover story
for national news magazines for some time now. Although this
search is often identified as an encouraging sign of interest in God,
it may be more dangerous than atheism. At least atheism makes

arguments and shows an interest in a world external to the feelings of the inner self. Furthermore, after each round of this quest for the holy grail, evangelicalism itself looks more and more indistinguishable from the ooze of pop spirituality more generally.

Not only historians and sociologists but novelists are writing about the Gnostic character of the soup that we call *spirituality* in the United States today. In an article in *Harper's*, Curtis White describes our situation quite well. When we assert, "This is my *belief*," says White, we are invoking our right to have our own private conviction, no matter how ridiculous, not only tolerated politically but *respected* by others. "It says, 'I've invested a lot of emotional energy in this belief, and in a way I've staked the credibility of my life on it. So if you ridicule it, you can expect a fight.'" In this kind of culture, "Yahweh and Baal—my God and yours—stroll arm-in-arm, as if to do so were the model of virtue itself."

> What we require of belief is not that it make sense but that it be sincere. This is so even for our more secular convictions. . . . Clearly, this is not the spirituality of a centralized orthodoxy. It is a sort of workshop spirituality that you can get with a cereal-box top and five dollars. And yet in our culture, to suggest that such belief is not deserving of respect makes people anxious, an anxiety that expresses itself in the desperate sincerity with which we deliver life's little lessons. . . . There is an obvious problem with this form of spirituality: it takes place in isolation. Each of us sits at our computer terminal tapping out our convictions. . . . Consequently, it's difficult to avoid the conclusion that our truest belief is the credo of heresy itself. It is heresy without an orthodoxy. It is heresy *as* an orthodoxy.[2]

When the political freedom of religion has been broadened to the dogma that "everyone is free to believe whatever she likes," says White, "there is no real shared conviction at all, and hence no church and certainly no community. Strangely, our freedom to believe has achieved the condition that Nietzsche called nihilism, but by a route he never imagined." While European nihilism just denied God, "American nihilism is something different. Our nihilism is our capacity to believe in everything and anything all at once. It's all good!"[3]

Combining this view of personal truth with free-market capitalism, even our beliefs become commodities—"content," just as books are now "sales units."

> Our religious content becomes indistinguishable from our financial content and our entertainment content and our sports content, just as the sections of your local newspaper attest. In short, belief becomes a culture-commodity. We shop among competing options for our belief. Once reduced to the status of a commodity, our anything-goes, do-it-yourself spirituality cannot have very much to say about the more directly nihilistic conviction that we should all be free to *do* whatever we like as well, each of us pursuing our right to our isolated happiness.[4]

Like Nietzsche himself, who said that truth is made rather than discovered and was described by Karl Barth as "the man of azure isolation," Americans just want to be left alone to create their own private Idaho. While evangelicals talk a lot about truth, their witness, worship, and spirituality seem in many ways more like their Mormon, New Age, and liberal nemeses than anything like historical Christianity.

White poignantly concludes his essay:

> We would prefer to be left alone, warmed by our beliefs-that-make-no-sense, whether they are the quotidian platitudes of ordinary Americans, the magical thinking of evangelicals, the mystical thinking of New Age Gnostics, the teary-eyed patriotism of social conservatives, or the perfervid loyalty of the rich

to their free-market Mammon. We are thus the congregation of the Church of the Infinitely Fractured, splendidly alone together. And apparently that's how we like it. Our pluralism of belief says both to ourselves and to others, "Keep your distance." And yet isn't this all strangely familiar? Aren't these all the false gods that Isaiah and Jeremiah confronted, the cults of the "hot air gods"? The gods that couldn't scare birds from a cucumber patch? Belief of every kind and cult, self-indulgence and self-aggrandizement of every degree, all flourish. And yet God is abandoned.[5]

So the search for the sacred is really another round of American heresy-as-orthodoxy—the flight of the lonely soul from nowhere to nowhere. We are prisoners of our own subjectivity, confined to the tiny cell of our own limited experiences, expectations, and felt needs.

As far back as the early eighteenth century, the French commentator Alexis de Tocqueville observed the distinctly American craving "to escape from imposed systems" and "to seek by themselves and in themselves for the only reason for things, looking to results without getting entangled in the means toward them. . . . So each man is narrowly shut up in himself, and from that basis makes the pretension to judge the world." Americans do not need books or any other external authorities in order to find the truth, "having found it in themselves."[6] In his famous Harvard Divinity School address, transcendentalist Ralph Waldo Emerson (1803–1882) announced that "whatever hold the public worship held on us is gone or going," prophesying the day when Americans would recognize that they are "part and parcel of God," requiring no Mediator or ecclesiastical means of grace. Walt Whitman's "Song of Myself" captured the unabashed narcissism of American romanticism that plagues our culture from talk shows to church.

During this same period, the message and methods of American churches also felt the impact of this romantic narcissism. It can be recognized in a host of sermons and hymns from the period, such as C. Austin Miles's hymn, "In the Garden":

> I come to the garden alone, while the dew is still on the
> roses;
> And the voice I hear, falling on my ear, the Son of God
> discloses.
> And He walks with me, and He talks with me, and He
> tells me I am His own,
> And the joy we share as we tarry there, none other has
> ever known.[7]

The focus of such piety is on a personal relationship with Jesus that is individualistic, inward, and immediate. One comes alone and experiences a joy that "none other has ever known." How can any external orthodoxy tell me I'm wrong? My personal relationship with Jesus is *mine*. I do not share it with the church. Creeds, confessions, pastors, and teachers—perhaps not even the Bible—can shake my confidence in the unique experiences that I have alone with Jesus.

A Perfect Storm

If moralism represents a drift toward the Pelagian (or at least semi-Pelagian) heresy, *enthusiasm* is an expression of the heresy known as Gnosticism. A second-century movement that seriously threatened the ancient churches, Gnosticism tried to blend Greek philosophy and Christianity. The result was an eclectic spirituality that regarded the material world as the prison house of divine spirits and the creation of an evil god (Yahweh). Their goal was to return to the spiritual, heavenly, and divine unity of which their inner self was a spark, away from the realm of earthly time, space, and bodies. (Gnostics would have applauded

163

many of Joel Osteen's emphases, particularly the thesis of *faith teachers* that we have divine DNA.)

Identifying sinfulness with creation as such, some Gnostic sects were extremely ascetic and rule oriented, while others were a free-for-all of orgies and mystical ecstasy. With little interest in questions of history or doctrine, the Gnostics set off on a quest to ascend the ladder of mysticism. They were all in agreement that the institutional church, with its ordained ministry, creeds, preaching, sacraments, and discipline, was alienating—like the body, it was the prison house of the individual soul.

Pelagianism and Gnosticism are different versions of what Gerhard Forde called the "glory story." Following Luther's Heidelberg Disputation, which followed Romans 10 and 1 Corinthians 1, the Reformer contrasts the theology of glory with the theology of the cross. As Forde explains,

> The most common overarching story we tell about ourselves is what we will call the glory story. We came from glory and are bound for glory. Of course, in between we seem somehow to have gotten derailed—whether by design or accident we don't quite know—but that is only a temporary inconvenience to be fixed by proper religious effort. What we need is to get back on "the glory road." The story is told in countless variations. Usually the subject of the story is "the soul." . . . The basic scheme is what Paul Ricoeur has called "the myth of the exiled soul."[8]

In neither version does one need to be rescued. Assisted, directed, enlightened perhaps, but not rescued—at least not through a bloody cross.

Both versions of the glory story drive us deeper into ourselves, identifying God with the inner self instead of calling us outside ourselves. In the 1930s, Yale's H. Richard Niebuhr offered a scolding description of Protestant liberalism's message: "A God without wrath brought men without sin into a world without judgment through the ministrations of a Christ without a cross."⁹ The *cross story* and the *glory story* represent not merely different emphases but entirely different religions, as J. Gresham Machen points out in his controversial book, *Christianity and Liberalism*.

The glory story is our natural religion, woven throughout the world's religions, philosophies, spiritualities, and moralities. It makes sense to us. As we are wired for law, we are also wired for glory. God set before Adam a covenant of life by which he would attain everlasting life for himself and his posterity. All of us are still created in God's image, naturally recognizing this sense of a divine commission. We come into the world ready for action. The only difference since the fall is that we've gone AWOL, using all of these gifts of our creation against the Creator and making a mess of things. We need the cross, but we think we just need to find our way back to the glory road to resume our upward march.

Since the fall, our natural wiring for fulfilling a task in order to attain everlasting blessedness with God has been corrupted into a tyrannical march across the landscape of creation, building empires of oppression, injustice, and pride. Religion is just another way of turning our native awareness of God into our own attempts to take heaven by storm and bring it under our control. Pelagianism does this by practical works, and Gnosticism ascends the ladder of mystical spirituality. No longer a sovereign God who reigns over us and is completely different from us, the God of Gnosticism is always friendly and familiar precisely because our own inner self is itself divine.

Pelagianism leads to Christless Christianity because we do not need a Savior but a good example. Gnosticism's route to Christless Christianity is by turning the story of a good Creator, a fall into sin, and redemption through the incarnation, bloody death, and bodily resurrection of the Son into a myth of an evil creator, a fall into matter, and redemption by inner enlightenment. While the gospel calls us to look outside ourselves for salvation, Pelagianism and Gnosticism combine to keep us looking to ourselves and within ourselves. Together, they have created the perfect storm: the *American religion*. No one has to teach us a gospel of salvation by inner enlightenment and moral self-improvement; rather, the Word of God has to *break* our addiction to this glory story by telling us the truth about what God's law really demands and his gospel really gives.

In his description of the theology of glory, Luther speaks of the different ladders that we vainly try to climb to ascend to God: rational speculation, mystical experience, and moral striving. All three are as abundantly evident today as part of the American captivity of the church as they were in Luther's day. These are fairly sweeping accusations, so I will try to make the case that we are caught up today in the throes of this perfect storm.

Gnosticism as the American Religion?

Contemporary descriptions in news periodicals and polling data consistently reveal that the ever-popular *search for the sacred* in American culture shares a lot of similarities with Gnosticism. Of course in the most popular versions there may be no explicit awareness of this connection or any direct dependence on such sources.

There is an explicit revival of Gnosticism in our day, in both the academy and popular culture, from Harvard Divinity School seminars to Dan Brown's *The Da Vinci Code*. The Gnosticism aisle in the typical bookstore chain (next to religion and spirituality) is evidence of renewed interest in pagan spiritualities. But from a Christian perspective, perhaps the greatest motivation for such widespread interest is that Gnosticism deflects accountability for sin and evil to the Creator rather than to the creature, allowing us to suppress the truth, locking within ourselves to create out of our own imagination an idol that we can manipulate and control—one who, like Israel's golden calf, will no longer terrify with disturbing words. Matthew Fox, repeating the warning of self-described Gnostic psychologist Carl Jüng, expresses this sentiment well: "One way to kill the soul is to worship a God outside you."[10] That was the message also of the American transcendentalists, such as Henry David Thoreau, Ralph Waldo Emerson, and Walt Whitman.

Some scholars and religious leaders are attracted to Gnosticism today because it offers spirituality without any particular creed—certainly without being nailed down to the particularity of Jesus Christ and his exclusive claims. Although the so-called Gnostic Gospels were written much later than the canonical Gospels of the New Testament, they are often celebrated as the expression of an alternative Christianity that was more tolerant and open to paganism than the official church that tried to silence them. In some of the Gnostic texts there is a celebration of the goddess, who is androgynous and engages in lesbian practices.[11] Others see Gnosticism as a way of blending various mystical traditions of East and West: Jewish, Christian, Islamic, Buddhist, Hindu, and new religions. In addition to these motives, Gnosticism is seen as a way of blending science and magic. "By integrating magic and science, art and technology," writes Marilyn Ferguson, "it will succeed where all the king's horses and all the king's men have failed."[12]

As we participate in an increasingly diverse culture, younger Christians are especially vulnerable to syncretism (that is, blending Christian and non-Christian beliefs and practices) if they have been less immersed in the Scriptures than in the culture's religious pluralism. Just as likely as their parents to defend their personal faith in the spirit of moralistic, therapeutic deism, as

Christian Smith documents, this generation is even more uncomfortable with exclusive truth claims and even more unlikely to know the basics of Christian doctrine.

Other Christian writers have concentrated on the revival of Gnosticism in its explicit forms.[13] I am more concerned here, however, with the more general and unwitting *Gnosticism Lite* that has pervaded American spirituality for some time, including evangelicalism. This version does not require any explicit awareness of, much less attachment to, Gnosticism's esoteric myth of creation and redemption by enlightenment. But the opposition between inner divinity, enlightenment, and redemption and an external God, the external Word, an external redemption in Christ and an institutional church offers a striking parallel to America's search for the sacred.

In American religion, as in ancient Gnosticism, there is almost no sense of God's difference from us—in other words, his majesty, sovereignty, self-existence, and holiness. God is my buddy, my inmost experience, or the power source for my living my best life now. God is not strange (that is, holy), and he is certainly not a judge. He does not evoke fear, awe, or a sense of terrifying and disorienting beauty. Furthermore, all the focus on making atonement through a bloody sacrifice seems crude and unspiritual to Gnostics when, after all, the point of salvation is to escape the physical realm. All of this is too "Jewish," according to Gnostics from Marcion to Scheiermacher to the Re-Imagining Conference of mainline Protestant leaders (especially radical feminists), who explicitly appeal to Gnosticism in their screeds against Christ's atoning sacrifice. The God of Gnosticism is not the one before whom Isaiah said, "Woe is me, for I am undone!" (Isa. 6:5 NKJV), or Peter said, "Depart from me, for I am a sinful man" (Luke 5:8). Whether in its explicit or implicit expressions, Gnosticism exchanges the strange and often troubling God of Israel for an idol that never really judges and therefore never really forgives.

168

Instead of God's free decision to make his home with us in the world he created, Gnostics believe we are at home with God already, in the stillness of our inner self and away from all entanglements in space and time. As the second-century church father Irenaeus pointed out, Gnostics simply do not care about the unfolding plan of redemption in history because they do not care about history. Time and space are alien to the innermost divine self. It is not surprising news that God loves us. After all, God is always our friend, never our enemy. God cannot help but like us—both because of who he is (Love) and because of who we are (lovely). Luther and Calvin say that this was the essence of "enthusiasm" (literally, *God-within-ism*). As Luther puts it, this is the attempt to ascend the ladder from matter and history to spirit and the eternal vision of the *naked God*. Yet, apart from the incarnate Word, this dazzling god we encounter at the top of that ladder is really the devil, who "disguises himself as an angel of light" (2 Cor. 11:14).

This characteristically American approach to religion, in which the direct relationship of the soul to God generates an almost romantic encounter with the sacred, makes inner experience the measure of spiritual genuineness. Instead of being concerned that our spiritual leaders faithfully interpret Scripture and are sent by Christ through the official ordination of his church, we are more concerned that they exude *vulnerability, authenticity,* and the familiar *spontaneity* that tells us that they have a personal relationship with Jesus. Everything perceived as external to the self—the church, the gospel, the Word and sacraments, the world, and even God—must either be marginalized or, in more radical versions, rejected as that which would alienate the soul from its immediacy to the divine.

When push comes to shove, many Christians today justify their beliefs and practices on the basis of their own experience. Regardless of what the church teaches—or perhaps even what is taught in Scripture—the one unassailable authority in the American religion is the self's inner experience. This means, however, that it is not only one's relationship with Jesus but Jesus himself who becomes a wax figure to be molded according to whatever experiences, feelings, and felt needs one has decided to be most decisive. No longer constrained by creeds and confessions, sermons and catechism, baptism and Eucharist in the covenant assembly, the romantic self aspires to a unique and spontaneous experience. As the hymn cited earlier has it, "I come to the garden *alone*. . . . And the joy we share as we tarry there, *none other has ever known*" (emphasis added).

It is therefore not surprising that today the *search for the sacred* continues to generate a proliferation of sects. In fact, sociologist Robert Bellah has coined the term *Sheilaism* to describe American spirituality, based on one interview in which a woman named Sheila said she just follows her own inner voice.[14] Your own "Personal Jesus," as the title of a Depeche Mode song parody,[15] seems to be the informal but very intense spirituality of many American Christians as well.

Philip Lee's *Against the Protestant Gnostics* (Oxford, 1987) and Harold Bloom's *The American Religion* (Simon and Schuster, 1992) point out the connections between this popular spirituality and Gnosticism with great insight. It is especially worth pondering Harold Bloom's learned ruminations here because, as he himself observes, Philip Lee *laments* the Gnosticism of American religion while Bloom *celebrates* it.[16]

Hailed as America's most distinguished literary critic, Bloom (whose fascinating seminar on Shakespeare I had the pleasure of taking) displays a sophisticated grasp of the varieties of ancient Gnosticism as well as its successive eruptions in the West, through radical forms of Jewish and Christian mysticism (especially Kabbalah), Joachim of Fiore, and Meister Eckhart, to the Anabaptists, millennial enthusiasts, *inner light* sects, all the way to American transcendentalism (Whitman, Thoreau, and Emerson), Mormonism, and the New Age movement.

First of all, says Bloom, "Freedom, in the context of the American Religion, means being alone with God or with Jesus, the American God or the American Christ." This unwritten creed is as evident in the history of American evangelicalism as it is in Emerson. "As a religious critic," Bloom says, "I remain startled by and obsessed with the revivalistic element in our religious experience. Revivalism, in America, tends to be the perpetual shock of the individual discovering yet again what she and he always have known, which is that God loves her and him on an absolutely personal and indeed intimate basis."[17]

Second, as extreme as it at first appears, Bloom suggests that whatever the stated doctrinal positions evangelicalism shares with historic Christianity,

> Mormons and Southern Baptists call themselves Christians, but like most Americans they are closer to ancient Gnostics than to early Christians. . . . The American Religion is pervasive and overwhelming, however it is masked, and even our secularists, indeed even our professed atheists, are more Gnostic than humanist in their ultimate presuppositions. We are a religiously made culture, furiously searching for the spirit, but each of us is subject and object of the one quest, which must be for the original self, a spark or breath in us that we are convinced goes back to before the Creation.[18]

"The Christ of the twentieth century" is no longer really even a distinct historical person but "has become a personal experience for the American Christian, quite clearly for the Evangelicals."[19] In this scheme, history is no longer the sphere of Christianity. The focus of faith and practice is not so much Christ's objective person and work for us, outside of us, as it is a *personal relationship* that is defined chiefly in terms of inner experience.

Although he may at times overstate his thesis, Bloom draws on numerous primary and secondary sources from the history of particular movements to build his case. In one chapter, for example, titled "Cane Ridge through Billy Graham," Bloom explores the enthusiastic revivalism of Barton Stone, who broke away from Presbyterianism to found what he regarded as the finally and fully restored apostolic church: the Church of Christ (Disciples). In his *Memoirs*, Stone wrote, "Calvinism is among the heaviest clogs on Christianity in the world," even from the very beginning of its assumptions, "its first link is total depravity."[20]

Later Bloom states,

A full generation before Emerson came to his spiritual maturity, the frontier people experienced their giant epiphany of Gnosis at Cane Ridge. Their ecstasy was no more communal than the rapture at Woodstock; each barking Kentuckian or prancing yippie barked and pranced for himself alone. . . . American ecstasy is solitary, even when it requires the presence of others for the self's glory.[21]

Bloom adds,

What was missing in all this quite private luminosity, was simply most of historic Christianity. . . . I hasten to add that I am celebrating, not deploring, when I make that observation. . . . Jesus is not so much an event in history for the American Religionist as he is a knower of the secrets of God who in return can be known by the individual. Hidden in this process is a sense that depravity is only a lack of saving knowledge.[22]

This intuitive, direct, and immediate knowledge is set over against the historically mediated forms of knowledge. What an American knows in his or her heart is more certain than the law of gravity.

So the *deeds, not creeds* orientation of American revivalism is driven not only by a preference for works over faith (Pelagianism) but by the Gnostic preference for a private, mystical, and inward *personal relationship with Jesus* in opposition to everything public, doctrinal, and external to the individual soul. Religion is formal, ordered, corporate, and visible; spirituality is informal, spontaneous, individual, and invisible.

As sweeping as it may first appear, there are clear similarities between fundamentalism and Pentecostalism on one hand and Protestant liberalism on the other. In fact, one reason that these forms of religion have survived modernity, against all expectations to the contrary, is that they not only can accommodate modernity's privatization of faith as an inner experience but can thrive in this atmosphere. As I observed especially in relation to the Pelagian emphases of Finney and his legacy, the seeds of liberalism were already sown by a revivalistic heritage that is shared by many conservative evangelicals. Repeatedly in the last few centuries we have seen how easily an inner-directed pietism turns to the vinegar of liberalism. One example is a statement by Wilhelm Herrmann, a liberal Pietist whose statement early in the twentieth century could be heard in many evangelical circles then as now: "To fix doctrines . . . into a system is the last thing the Christian Church should undertake. . . . But if, on the other hand, we keep our attention fixed on what God is producing in the Christian's inner life, then the manifoldness of the thoughts which spring from faith will not confuse us, but give us cause for joy."[23]

For liberals, Christian morality, piety, and experience could survive the abandonment of Christian doctrine and even the formal, public, corporate service of Word and sacrament. The inner light was not extinguished by abandoning creedal Christianity because one could still have a stirring personal relationship with Jesus within the heart even if he was not raised bodily in history.

Evangelicals are obviously not liberals, but the dominant orientation seems to put them perpetually on that trajectory.

It is not surprising, then, that today's fundamentalists eventually become tomorrow's liberals, in recurring cycles that pass through stages of intense controversy. Bloom follows a similar narrative in relation to Gnosticism. For example, although he overestimates the influence of E. Y. Mullins, as if he single-handedly shaped the Southern Baptist denomination, Bloom points out that Mullins's core assumptions were basically the same as those of Ralph Waldo Emerson and William James. The Gnostic impulse is evident, for example, in the doctrine of *soul competency*, which became prominent especially through Mullins.

While Luther, Calvin, and their heirs sought to reform the church, the more radical Protestant movements have sought an immediate, inner gnosis. Where the Reformers pointed to the external ministry of the church, centering on Word and sacrament, as the place where God promised to meet his people, *enthusiasm* (the Reformers' term for radical Protestant groups) was suspicious of everything external. Similarly, Emerson resigned his Unitarian pulpit at least in part because he was unwilling to celebrate the Lord's Supper (although it is unclear to me why Unitarians would retain the rite anyway). His reason was that he could abide nothing external, creaturely, or physical violating the immediacy of his divine soul with the Divine Spirit. His arguments were not that far from that of the Quakers in their rejection of baptism and the Lord's Supper by appealing to the doctrine of the inner light.

Although evangelicals typically retain the sacraments, like everything else, they are made a vehicle of individual experience—a personal relationship—that does not depend on such practices. Everything turns on the self-reliant soul of the individual to experience a direct and unmediated relationship with

Jesus. If baptism or the Lord's Supper can facilitate a direct experience with the "naked God," we will add them to the list of useful rungs on our ladder. They may be acceptable as long as they are our means of ascent, but calling them "means of grace" (that is, a ladder from God to us rather than from us to God) provokes controversy. In the history of American (and to some extent British) evangelicalism, the fear of sacraments (as opposed to ordinances) was expressed as a legitimate response to the perpetual threat of Romanism.

In all likelihood, however, the real source of unease was that evangelicalism has listed toward Gnosticism: nothing can be allowed to get in the way of my personal and utterly unique relationship with Jesus. E. Y. Mullins was not saying anything that was not already elaborated by American transcendentalists when he wrote, "That which we know most indubitably are the facts of inner experience."[2²] "A thorough pragmatist, deeply influenced by William James, Mullins grounded his faith upon 'experience' in James's sense."[25] The individual believer, alone with his or her Bible, was all that was necessary for a vital Christian experience.

Bloom quotes Mullins's axiom, "Religion is a personal matter between the soul and God."[26] This may be the most agreed-upon dogma in the United States today.

With great insight (and affirmation), Bloom points out how writers like Mullins simply translated the Bible into a uniquely American language. According to Mullins, William James "explains the fact of regeneration in terms which are quite in harmony with those of the Pauline epistles." Therefore, Bloom concludes, "Pragmatic, experiential, and American as he was, Mullins almost involuntarily translated Paul into Jamesian terms. The primacy of human feeling is not the dynamic of Paul's work, but it is of James's and of Mullins's."[27] Furthermore, Bloom observes, triumphalism—the inability to face the depravity of the inner self even at its best—marks the Gnostic spirit.[28]

175

Other than in the East and the esoteric sects of the West, where but in the United States could an entire religion emerge in the nineteenth century that denies the reality of the body, illness, and death. According to Mary Baker Eddy, the founder of Christian Science, "Sin, illness, and death itself . . . had come into the world because of 'the belief that Spirit materialized into a body, infinity became finity, or man, and the eternal entered the temporal.'"[29] Notice that her description of the source of our fall is Christianity's description of the source of our redemption: namely, the incarnation, life, death, and resurrection of God the Son in the flesh. Gnostics are allergic to any talk about the reality of sin and death. Substituting the idea of *passing away* for *death*, Baker Eddy made a considerable—and, from a Christian point of view, considerably unfortunate—contribution to the English language.

For Bloom, two outstanding exceptions to this Gnostic trajectory are Karl Barth and J. Gresham Machen. "Barth knows the difference between the Reformed faith and Gnosis," says Bloom, pointing out the critical divergence: the subjective experience of the self over God's objective word and work. Where Barth was confident in a transcendent God and deeply suspicious of human experience, morality, or religion as a way of scaling the wall separating Creator and creature, pietism and liberalism were locked in victory mode.[30]

The other anti-Gnostic figure, an American, is J. Gresham Machen. What we call fundamentalists, says Bloom, are really Gnostics of an anti-intellectual variety. If there were a possibility of an anti-Gnostic version of fundamentalism, says Bloom, such proponents "would find their archetype in the formidable J. Gresham Machen, a remarkable Presbyterian New Testament scholar at Princeton, who published a vehement defense of traditional Christianity in 1923, with the aggressive title *Christianity and Liberalism.*" Bloom adds, "I have just read my way through

this, with distaste and discomfort but with reluctant and growing admiration for Machen's mind. I have never seen a stronger
case made for the argument that institutional Christianity must
regard cultural liberalism as an enemy to faith." In contrast to
this defense of traditional Christianity, those who came to be
called fundamentalists are more like "the Spanish Fascism of
Franco, . . . heirs of Franco's crusade against the mind, and not
the legatees of Machen."[31]

In short, "The Calvinist deity, first brought to America by the
Puritans, has remarkably little in common with the versions of
God now apprehended by what calls itself Protestantism in the
United States." Again, as Bloom himself points out, Philip Lee's
Against the Protestant Gnostics makes almost the same argu-
ments, with many of the same historical examples. What makes
Bloom's account a little more interesting is that he champions the
American religion and hopes for even greater gains for Gnosticism
in the future. A "revival of Continental Reformed Protestantism
is precisely what we do not need," according to Bloom.[32]

Sociological analyses of contemporary American spirituality,
especially those of Wade Clark Roof, Robert Wuthnow, Robert
Bellah, Marsha Witten, Anne Douglas, and James D. Hunter,
have documented the dominant characteristics that seem to me
to justify the comparisons that Bloom has highlighted.

Although Roof does not mention the ancient heresy, his description of contemporary American spirituality picks up Gnosticism's main characteristics: a religion that "celebrates experience
rather than doctrine; the personal rather than the institutional;
the mythic and dreamlike over the cognitive; people's religion
over official religion; soft, caring images of deity," which can
even be described as "feminine and androgynous," over images
of God as Creator, Redeemer, Lord, and Judge.[33]

According to Hunter, "The spiritual aspects of evangelical
life are increasingly approached by means of and interpreted in

terms of 'principles,' 'rules,' 'steps,' 'laws,' 'codes,' 'guidelines,' and the like."[34] Roof adds, "Salvation as a theological doctrine . . . becomes reduced to simple steps, easy procedures, and formulas for psychological rewards. The approach to religious truth changes—away from any objective grounds on which it must be judged, to a more subjective, more instrumental understanding of what it does for the believer, and how it can do what it does most efficiently."[35]

Like ancient Gnosticism, contemporary American approaches to spirituality—however different conservative and liberal versions may appear on the surface—typically underscore the inner spirit as the locus of a personal relationship. As conservative Calvary Chapel founder Chuck Smith expresses it, "We meet God in the realm of our spirit."[36] This view is so commonplace that it seems odd to hear it challenged.

Philip Lee's contrast between Gnosticism and Calvinism can be just as accurately documented from a wide variety of Christians through the ages: "Whereas classical Calvinism had held that the Christian's assurance of salvation was guaranteed only through Christ and his Church, with his means of grace, now assurance could be found only in the personal experience of having been born again. This was a radical shift, for Calvin had considered any attempt to put 'conversion in the power of man himself' to be gross popery."[37] In fact, for the Reformers, adds Lee, the new birth was the opposite of "rebirth into a new and more acceptable self"; it was the death of the old self and its rebirth in Christ.[38]

Like ancient Gnosticism, American spirituality uses God or the divine as something akin to an energy source. Through various formulas, steps, procedures, or techniques, one may *access* this source on one's own. Such spiritual technology could be employed without any need for the office of preaching, administering baptism or the Lord's Supper, or membership in a visible church, submitting to its communal admonitions, encouragements, teaching, and practices.

According to Roof's studies, "The distinction between 'spirit' and 'institution' is of major importance" to spiritual seekers today. "Spirit is the inner, experiential aspect of religion; institution is the outer, established form of religion." He adds, "Direct experience is always more trustworthy, if for no other reason than because of its 'inwardness' and 'withinness'—two qualities that have come to be much appreciated in a highly expressive, narcissistic culture."[39]

Again, these studies point up the fact that evangelical pietism and revivalism are uniquely equipped to thrive in American culture. Even the popular Keswick "Higher Life" movement in British and American evangelicalism, which profoundly shaped evangelical piety in the nineteenth century, was criticized early on by B. B. Warfield and more recently by J. I. Packer as advancing an almost magical view of faith, *using* God like electricity for one's own ends and will.[40] Like a mighty river, the Spirit can be harnessed by our spiritual technology. The way many evangelicals today speak of *accessing* God and *connecting* with him underscores this point.

Just as there were legalistic and antinomian versions of ancient Gnosticism, contemporary spirituality can take fundamentalist and liberal forms. Yet they all give precedence to inner experience over external norms, the individual over the communion of saints, the immaterial over the material; the immediate, spontaneous, ever-new, and ever-unique personal experiences over the ordinary means of grace that God has provided for our maturity together in the body of Christ. Profoundly aware of our difference from God, not only as creatures but also as sinners, biblical faith underscores the need for mediation. God finds us by using his own creation as his "mask" behind which he hides so he can serve us. The Gnostic, by contrast, needs no mediation. God is not external to the self; in fact, the human spirit and the divine Spirit are already a unity.

The net effect of this pervasive American spirituality has been to assimilate God to our own experience, felt needs, and aspirations. As the architects of modern atheism such as Feuerbach, Marx, Nietzsche, and Freud saw with tremendous insight, religion is easily reduced to anthropology—or even psychology. It is not a matter of actually being surprised by the voice of a stranger, calling us outside ourselves, as we are stripped of our pretensions and stand naked before a holy God. Rather, it is a projection of the self's own longings for comfort in the face of a vast and foreboding cosmos teeming with dangers and disasters. The line between religion and magic, faith in God and using God, becomes virtually indistinguishable.

To the extent that churches in America today feel compelled to accommodate their message and methods to these dominant forms of spirituality, they lend credence to the thesis that Christianity is not news based on historical events but just another form of therapy. If this were the only path of true religion, the argument of modern atheism would offer the best explanation of the whole phenomenon. We never really meet God—someone who is different from us, who stands over against us in judgment and grace—but only ourselves in the mirror of our own utterly unique, private, and extraordinary experience. Measured by this Gnostic sentiment, Protestant liberalism in the line of Schleiermacher and Protestant evangelicalism in the line of pietism and revivalism differ perhaps in degree but not in their basic religious outlook.

The New Testament and Gnosticism

Scholars are still debating the exact relationship between the New Testament and Gnosticism. While Gnosticism became a loosely organized movement with various sects only in the second century, incipient forms were already emerging in Jewish and Christian circles in the apostolic era. The apostle Paul spoke of the super-apostles as those who are "puffed up with conceit" and are "depraved in mind and deprived of the truth, imagining that godliness is a means of gain" (1 Tim. 6:4–5). Such a person "teaches a different doctrine and does not agree with the sound words of our Lord Jesus Christ and teaching that accords with godliness" (v. 3). Paul warns Timothy to "flee these things," teaching believers to be content with God's provisions.

> Fight the good fight of the faith. Take hold of the eternal life to which you were called and about which you made the good confession in the presence of many witnesses. . . . O Timothy, guard the deposit entrusted to you. Avoid the irreverent babble and contradictions of what is falsely called "knowledge" [*gnosis*], for by professing it some have swerved from the faith. Grace be with you.
>
> 1 Timothy 6:12, 20–21

Paul's counsel in Romans 16 is equally pertinent:

> I appeal to you, brothers, to watch out for those who cause divisions and create obstacles *contrary to the doctrine that you have been taught*; avoid them. For such persons do not serve our Lord Christ, but their own appetites, and *by smooth talk and flattery they deceive the hearts of the naive*. For your obedience is known to all, so that I rejoice over you, but I want you to be wise as to what is good and innocent as to what is evil. The God of peace will soon crush Satan under your feet. The grace of our Lord Jesus Christ be with you.
>
> Romans 16:17–20; emphasis added

Plagued by sectarian strife, the Corinthian church had apparently been infected with the teaching that the body is either evil or inconsequential, leading to extremes of both legalistic proscriptions against sexual intercourse or antinomian license—since the acts done in the body could not taint the purity of the inner spirit (1 Cor. 5; 6:12–7:40). Paul answers both by declaring, "The body is not meant for sexual immorality, but for the Lord, and the Lord for the body. And God raised the Lord and will also raise us up by his power. Do you not know that your bodies are members of Christ?" (1 Cor. 6:13–15). Paul's emphasis on the Lord's Supper and defense of bodily resurrection against false teachers (chap. 15) testify further to the existence of this proto-gnostic circle and its influence. He also counters an ascetic form of this heresy in Colossians 2. John directly challenges "the spirit of the antichrist," the denial that Jesus has come in the flesh (1 John 4:1–3, 6).

It is not surprising that John's Gospel emphasizes not only Christ's deity, but the marvelous—and scandalous—truth that "the Word became flesh" (John 1:14). Not a universal spiritual or moral idea, but a particular human person who lived, suffered, died, rose again, and will come again in the flesh.

Evangelicals, of course, have courageously defended the historicity of Christ's bodily resurrection and return in glory against the dogmatic anti-supernaturalism of liberalism. At the same time, when it comes to popular piety, both evangelicals and liberals (to the extent that they share a common heritage in pietism) often emphasize the immediacy of Jesus to our experience more than the reality of his bodily resurrection, ascension, and return. Whenever this happens, however important these dogmas may be for defending Christ's deity, his humanity seems to play a minor role. For example, why should we long for Jesus Christ's appearing in the flesh when he already lives in our heart? As one gospel song puts it, "You ask me how I know he lives? He lives within my heart," but this is a sentiment that could just as easily warm the heart of any liberal Protestant. It makes no difference whether Jesus rose from the dead in the flesh two thousand years ago, as long as he is somehow "still with us" in our personal experience today.

In sharp contrast, Paul defended the resurrection in the flesh as a datable event with eyewitnesses. John begins his letter of warning about the "antichrists" who deny that Christ has come in the flesh by immediately stating, "That which was from the beginning, which we have heard, which we have seen with our eyes, which we have looked upon and have touched with our hands, concerning the word of life—the life was made manifest, and we have seen it, and testify to it" (1 John 1:1–2). Similarly, Peter testifies, "For we did not follow cleverly devised myths when we made known to you the power and coming of our Lord Jesus Christ, but we were eyewitnesses of his majesty" (2 Peter 1:16). It is significant that for the apostles, offering their testimony meant witnessing to the concrete person and work of Christ in history, where for us today it usually means witnessing to our personal experience and moral improvement.

Because the Spirit is sent to testify concerning Christ, give us faith in Christ, unite us to Christ, and keep us in Christ, the Spirit's indwelling of every believer as a first installment on our final salvation establishes the most vital and intimate link between the Head and his members. Nevertheless, it is the Spirit, not Jesus, who lives within us. Jesus is in heaven, exalted in his flesh at the Father's right hand, to return in the flesh at the end of the age, raising us up in the flesh to life everlasting as his coheirs. When the Spirit is turned into an abstract principle rather than a concrete person of the Trinity or his person and work are regarded as a distraction from rather than mediation of Christ's person and work, our faith—regardless of whatever official dogmas to which we yield our assent—loses its connection to the Jesus of history who has come and will come again in the flesh.

It is the Spirit who convicts us inwardly of our sin and drives us outside of ourselves to Christ, not only in the message of the gospel to which he testifies but in the creaturely, public, and external means that he employs to do so. In this way, Christ and his saving work not only remain outside of us but penetrate our hearts so deeply that we are truly transformed and continually transformed by his grace. Therefore, intimacy and personal fellowship with Christ by his Spirit through the means of grace are not eliminated but secured—but without simply collapsing Jesus into our inner experience. It is not in a private inner garden where we walk and talk with Jesus and he tells us that we are his own, but in a public garden with visible means of grace. There he forms a people, not just a person, by consecrating ordinary human speech as his Word, ordinary water as his baptism, and ordinary bread and wine as his Communion. The one who assumed our flesh by the power of the Spirit continues to work in us that faith and repentance through physical means in the power of the same Spirit.

Even now, the new birth is not the emancipation of a supposedly truer *inner self* from the external reality of history and the body, but the pledge (*arrobōn*) of the consummation for which the whole creation waits eagerly (Rom. 8:18–25). Unable to bring final liberation of humanity apart from leaving everything creaturely behind, Gnosticism loses the joy of the Christian gospel that leaves nothing behind but sin and death.

Gnosticism's success in the ancient church was due largely to its attempt to blend Greek wisdom with vaguely Christian concepts, but the result was a scheme that was in fact the very opposite of Christianity. Instead of accommodating the biblical story to pagan philosophy, as the super-apostles were doing, Paul told the Corinthians:

For the word of the cross is folly to those who are perishing, but to us who are being saved, it is the power of God. For it is written, "I will destroy the wisdom of the wise, and the discernment of the discerning I will thwart." Where is the one who is wise? Where is the scribe? Where is the debater of this age? Has not God made foolish the wisdom of the world? For since, in the wisdom of God, the world did not know God through wisdom, it pleased God through the folly of what we preach to save those who believe. For Jews demand signs and Greeks seek wisdom, but we preach Christ crucified, a stumbling block to Jews and folly to Gentiles, but to those who are called, both Jews and Greeks, Christ the power of God and the wisdom of God. . . . And I, when I came to you, brothers, did not come proclaiming to you the testimony of God with lofty speech or wisdom. For I decided to know nothing among you except Jesus Christ and him crucified.

1 Corinthians 1:18–24; 2:1–2

The Flight of the Lonely Soul

Longing for Christ's return, the Christian is world-weary because this age lies under the power of sin and death. But even now there is a new power set loose in the world—the penetration of this present evil age with the powers of the age to come. So the Christian is longing for the final liberation *of* creation, not *from* creation. Precisely because the believer is rooted in the age to come, of which the Spirit's indwelling presence is the down payment, there is a simultaneous groaning in the face of the status quo and confidence in God's promise to make all things new.

By contrast, the Gnostic self is rootless, restless, weary of the world not because of its bondage to sin but because it is *worldly*, longing not for its sharing in the liberation of the children of God but in its freedom at last from creation's company. Not the transformation of our times and places, but the transcendence of all times and places is the goal of Gnostic flight. "Taking no root," wrote nineteenth-century American novelist Nathaniel Hawthorne, "I soon weary of any soil in which I may be temporarily deposited. The same impatience I feel, or conceive of, as regards this earthly life."[41] Add to this philosophical orientation the practical transience of contemporary life that keeps us blowing like a tumbleweed across the desert, and Gnosticism can be easily seen to jibe with our everyday experience. Uprooted, we rarely live anywhere long enough even to be transplanted. Flitting like a bumblebee from flower to flower of religious, spiritual, moral, psychic, and even familial and sexual identities, our generation actually finds it plausible that there can be genuine communities on the Internet.

Gnosticism identified God with the inner self, but Christianity has focused all of its resources on God outside of us, who creates, rules, judges, and saves us in our complete personal and corporate existence. It stands to reason that in the Gnostic scheme the inner self could stand above (even over against) not only the external church but its external ministry of preaching and sacrament, discipline and order, catechesis and communion. After all, it is not the public, historical, visible, and messy world that concerns Gnostics but the private, spiritual, invisible, and manageable world of the inner spirit.

With Bishop C. FitzSimons Allison, I confess my own natural attraction to the glory story over the story of the cross:

> As an example of a sinful view of doctrine, I myself feel a great gravitational tug toward Gnostic distortions. I do not like suffering. I would like a religion that saved me from my own and other people's suffering. The whole incarnational theme in Christianity opens me up to the vulnerability of suffering. Yet in spite of my natural proclivities much of the grace I have known has been in that very suffering the gospel has drawn me into, the fellowship of Christ's passion. . . . I also have a heart for that aspect of Arianism that needs no rescuer and for Nestorianism that panders

to my natural Pelagian self-righteousness, that poisonous aspect of my natural self-centeredness that precludes any compassion for sinners and makes me anything but a winsome example of a disciple of Christ.[42]

But the glory story is not all it's cracked up to be. Jean-Paul Sartre recognized that "we are condemned to be free," living like Atlas with the world on our shoulders. That is the glory story, whatever its version. Yet Jesus promises, "You shall know the truth, and the truth shall make you free" (John 8:32 NKJV). That is because the truth that Jesus proclaims—and the Truth that Jesus *is*—remains for all ages, even for Americans, "the power of God for salvation for everyone who believes" (Rom. 1:16).

6

Delivering Christ

The Message and the Medium

I magine two scenarios of church life. In the first, God gathers his people together in a covenantal event to judge and to justify, to kill and to make alive. The emphasis is on God's work for us—the Father's gracious plan, the Son's saving life, death, and resurrection, and the Spirit's work of bringing life to the valley of dry bones through the proclamation of Christ. The preaching focuses on God's work in the history of redemption from Genesis through Revelation, and sinners are swept into this unfolding drama. Trained and ordained to mine the riches of Scripture for the benefit of God's people, ministers try to push their own agendas, opinions, and personalities to the background so that God's Word will be clearly proclaimed. In this preaching, the people once again are simply receivers—recipients of grace. Similarly, in baptism, they do not baptize themselves; they *are baptized*. In the Lord's Supper, they do not prepare and cook the meal; they do not contribute to the fare; but they are guests who simply enjoy the bread of heaven. As this gospel creates, deepens, and inflames faith, a profound sense of praise and thanksgiving fills hearts, leading to good works among the saints and in the world throughout the week. Having been served by God in the public assembly, the people are then servants of each other and their neighbors in the world. Pursuing their callings in the world with vigor and dedication, they win the respect of outsiders. Because they have been served well themselves—especially by pastors, teachers, elders, and deacons—they are able to share the Good News of Christ in well-informed and natural ways. And because they have been relieved of numerous burdens to spend all of their energy on church-related ministries throughout the week, they have more time to serve their families, neighbors, and coworkers in the world.

In the second scenario, the church is its own subculture, an alternative community not only for weekly dying and rising in Christ but for one's entire circle of friends, electricians, and neighbors. In this scenario, the people assume that they come to church primarily to do something. The emphasis is on their work for God. The preaching concentrates on principles and steps to living a better life, with a constant stream of exhortations: Be more committed. Read your Bible more. Pray more. Witness more. Give more. Get involved in this cause or that movement to save the world. Their calling by God to secular vocations is made secondary to *finding their ministry* in the church. Often malnourished because of a ministry defined by personal charisma and motivational skills rather than by knowledge and godliness, these same sheep are expected to be shepherds themselves. Always serving, they are rarely served. Ill-informed about the grand narrative of God's work in redemptive history, they do not really know what to say to a non-Christian except to talk about their own experiences and perhaps repeat some slogans or formulas that they might be hard-pressed to explain. Furthermore, because they are expected to be so heavily involved in church-related activities (often considered more important even than the public services on Sunday), they do not have the time, energy, or opportunity to develop significant relationships outside the church. And if they were to bring a friend to church, they could not be sure that he or she would hear the gospel.

The second scenario has captivated churches across the spectrum. The denominational label or conservative-liberal divide matter little on this score. Everybody seems to think that we come to church mostly to give rather than to receive. For Roman Catholics, the Second Vatican Council defined the Mass as "the work of the people," and this assumption seems to prevail across the ecclesiastical landscape today. Many of us were raised in conservative evangelical contexts in which preaching was chiefly an exhortation to do more, baptism was our act of commitment rather than God's, the Lord's Supper was a means of our remembering rather than a means of God's grace, and many of the songs were expressions of our piety more than a recounting of God's marvelous mercies in the history of redemption. The expectation that God was actually visiting his people to apply the benefits of Christ's victory to sinners—both believers and unbelievers—was less obvious than the sense that we were primarily regrouping to get our marching orders. Of course we do receive exhortations in Scripture, and therefore this must be part of public worship. Law without gospel, however, is death (2 Cor. 3:5–18). Calls to action apart from the announcement of God's action—including its regular delivery and confirmation through the Lord's Supper—gradually de-evangelizes the church. Well-known megachurch pastor Rick Warren has issued a repeated call over the last few years for a second Reformation: this time, a reformation of "deeds, not creeds."[1] Yet in the experience of many of us, "deeds, not creeds," "life, not doctrine," and more

191

commitment rather than more Christ-centered ministry is the emphasis. By the way, my friends reared in mainline Protestant and Roman Catholic backgrounds tell the same story. The list of deeds may be different, but the paradigm is the same.

When it comes to more recent movements that have sought to distance themselves from more traditional evangelical approaches, the apple has not fallen far from the tree. Despite obvious cosmetic differences, the emphasis is the same. A few examples will suffice in making this point.

In 2007 the Willow Creek Community Church provoked media attention when it published the results of its marketing analysis that led its leaders to conclude that its widely influential model of church growth was flawed. Senior pastor Bill Hybels responded to the research by saying that it "did not shine brightly on our church. . . . Among the findings," he writes, "one out of every four people at Willow Creek were stalled in their spiritual growth or dissatisfied with the church—and many of them were considering leaving." Furthermore, the highest percentage of the dissatisfied were the most highly committed Christians. The report "has revolutionized the way I look at the role of the local church, . . . causing me to see clearly that the church and its myriad of programs have taken on too much of the responsibility for people's spiritual growth."[2]

So why would the *most active* participants ("Christ-centered") be the *most dissatisfied* with the church and their own spiritual progress? That was the question that puzzled the church's leadership. "The quick answer: Because God 'wired' us first and foremost to be in growing relationship with him—not with the church." Their conclusion was that God meant for his people to move from dependence on the ministry of the church to "personal spiritual practices," which include "prayer, journaling, solitude, studying Scripture—things that individuals do on their own to grow in their relationship with Christ." As believers mature, they should shift their interest from the church to their own private activities. "The research strongly suggests that the church declines in influence as people grow spiritually." Those who are *fully surrendered* are likened to young adults who no longer need the parenting of the church and can now fend for themselves. "Our people need to learn to feed themselves through personal spiritual practices that allow them to deepen their relationship with Christ. . . . We want to transition the role of the church from spiritual parent to spiritual coach." The authors suggest the analogy of a trainer at the gym who provides a "personalized workout plan."

What I find remarkable is that those who identified themselves as "stalled" said, "I believe in Christ, but I haven't grown much lately," and the dissatisfied said, "My faith is central to my life and I'm trying to grow, but my church is letting me down." These highly committed respondents even said they "desire much more challenge and depth from the services" and "60 percent would like to see 'more in-depth Bible teaching.'" The take-away for the authors, however, was not that Willow Creek should provide a richer ministry but that the sheep must learn to fend for themselves—to become "self-feeders" who need to be more engaged in private spiritual practices.

It is significant that in this report spirituality is measured by how much people do. The church's mission is to provide "opportunities to connect with others," "small group opportunities," and "basic personal spiritual practices." Those who are "close to Christ" (level 3) need "advanced personal spiritual practices," and "Christ-centered" members (level 4) require "a wide range of serving and mentoring opportunities." Although Christ is the referent, all of the measurements are commitments that could as easily be applied to any organization or cause that is interested in spiritual activities. There is no mention of anyone needing to hear the Word of Christ, be baptized, or receive Christ in the Lord's Supper. Although each level is identified in relation to Christ, all of the emphasis is on their practices and serving rather than on God's activity in serving his people. Obviously, if church is all about providing opportunities for the sheep to do something, they can do it by themselves.

In spite of having defined itself largely in antithesis to the megachurch movement, the Emergent Church movement is currently becoming friendlier to its rival, as the recent participation of Brian McLaren at a Willow Creek conference attests. Like McLaren and other Emergent leaders, Doug Pagitt encourages us to think of ourselves and the lives we lead as the gospel.[3] The Bible, says McLaren, is "part of a conversation, not a dead book from which I extract truth."[4] God's Word does not come to us from outside; believers "have the truth of God within them," writes Pagitt. In fact, "Every person has experience, understanding, and perspective; there is no one who is totally devoid of truth."[5]

At stake in this loss of *sola scriptura* (by Scripture alone) are the corollaries: *solo Christo* (by Christ alone), *sola gratia* (by grace alone), *sola fide* (through faith alone), and *soli Deo gloria* (to God alone be glory). These stakes are not too high for Brian McLaren, for example, who scolds Reformed Christians for "their love-affair for the Latin word '*sola*.'"[6]

According to Dan Kimball, the church is not a *place*. "The church is the people of God who gather together with a sense of mission (Acts 14:27). We can't go to church because *we are* the church."[7] From this Kimball draws the familiar contrast between evangelism (mission) and the marks of the church (means of grace). Appealing to Darrell Guder's *The Missional Church*, Kimball thinks things went wrong at the Reformation.

> The Reformers, in their effort to raise the authority of the Bible and ensure sound doctrine, defined the marks of a true church: a place where the gospel is rightly preached, the sacraments are

rightly administered, and church discipline is exercised. However, over time these marks narrowed the definition of the church itself as a "place where" instead of a "people who are" reality. The word church became defined as "a place where certain things happen," such as preaching and communion.[8]

In this way, however, the work of the people displaces the work of God.

The gospel is Good News. The message determines the medium. There is a clear logic to Paul's argument in Romans 10, where he contrasts "the righteousness that is by works" and "the righteousness that is through faith" (Rom. 10:5–6 NIV). We were redeemed by Christ's actions, not ours; the Spirit applies this redemption to us here and now so that we are justified through faith apart from works; even this faith is given to us through the proclamation of Christ. Since this gospel is a report to be believed rather than a task for us to fulfill, it needs heralds, ambassadors, and witnesses.

The method of delivery is suited to its content. If the central message of Christianity were how to have your best life now or become a better you, then rather than heralds we would need life coaches, spiritual directors, and motivational speakers. Good advice requires a person with a plan; Good News requires a person with a message. This is not to say that we do not also need good advice or plans but that the source of the church's existence and mission in this world is this announcement of God's victory in Jesus Christ.

Coaches can send themselves with their own suggestions, but an ambassador has to be sent with an authorized announcement. If the goal is to get people to go and find Christ, then the methods will be whatever we find pragmatically successful; if it's all about Christ finding sinners, then the methods are already determined. Simply quoting Romans 10:13–15 reveals the logical chain of Paul's argument: "'Everyone who calls on the name of the Lord will be saved.' How, then, will they call on him in whom they have not believed? And how are they to believe in him of whom they have never heard? And how are they to hear without someone preaching? And how are they to preach unless they are sent?" The evangel defines evangelism; the content determines the methods of delivery; the marks of the church (preaching and sacrament) define its mission (evangelizing, baptizing, teaching, and communing).

To help identify this connection between the message (covered in the previous chapters) and the mission and methods of delivering Christ, I offer the following table:

Law-Lite	The Gospel
God as Life Coach	God as Judge and Justifier
Good Advice (Doing)	Good News (Done)
Christ as Example	Christ as Savior
The Bible as Instruction Manual	The Bible as Unfolding Mystery of Christ
Sacraments as Means of Commitment	Sacraments as Means of Grace
The Church as Self-Help Resource (focus on our service/ministry)	The Church as Embassy of Grace (focus on God's service/ministry)
We Ascend to God	God Descends to Us
We Send Ourselves	God Sends Us

Reversing the Flow: Transforming God's Work into Our Work

To repeat, these marks of the church focus on what God does for us rather than on what we do for God. God was not just the Savior once upon a time; he is here and now as he delivers Christ and all of his benefits to us week after week. The mission of the church is to bear those marks.

This orientation challenges not only the tendency of revivalistic movements to zeal without knowledge, but the temptation of confessional churches toward confidence in knowledge without zeal. In his Pentecost sermon, Peter announced, "The promise is for you and for your children and for all who are far off, everyone whom the Lord our God calls to himself" (Acts 2:39). Neglecting a covenantal ecclesiology, evangelicalism exhibits a zeal for mission unhinged from the marks of the church. After all, if the gospel is about our experience and activity in personal and social transformation rather than how we can be regular recipients of God's gifts, the means of grace are beside the point. What we really need are means of commitment and action. However, this "missional" activism unhinged from the methods God has prescribed has not only failed to lead to an upswing in professions of faith among "all who are far off," but has led to burnout, instability, and dropout among believers and their children.

Our temptation as Reformed Christians, however, is to pride ourselves on bearing the marks of a true church regardless of whether people are actually being added to the church. After all, we reason, we have the right confession, we administer the sacraments according to Christ's institution, and we have a sound church order. But we can easily forget that all of this exists for the purpose of mission, not so we can celebrate our purity. "The promise is for you and your children," we quite properly emphasize, but what about "all who are far off"? The dichotomy between the marks and mission of the church or teaching the reached and reaching the lost would have been completely foreign to the apostles.

The best way of reintegrating the marks and mission is to start with the gospel itself. I have to say that, at least in my experience, traditionalists and radicals both emphasize our activity over God's. We come to church primarily to do something. We come to serve rather than to be served. Many traditionalists oppose seeker-driven approaches to mission by insisting that what matters in the service is not what we get out of it but what we put into it. God is the audience (receiving our worship) and we are the actors, according to many advocates of traditional worship. Seeker churches typically view themselves as resources for personal improvement, and the Emergent Church movement considers the church a community of world-transforming disciples. *For all of their differences, each of these models practically ignores the central point that God's mission is to serve us through the marks of preaching and sacrament and that the body will be built up in Christ together and bring its witness and good works to its neighbors in the world.*

Even before we come to worship God, we are first of all served by God as he distributes his gifts that provoke our praise and joy. Here Christ wraps the towel around his waist and washes our feet. Like Peter, we may bristle at this strange role reversal, but Jesus said that he "came not to be served but to serve, and to give his life as a ransom for many" (Matt. 20:28). Of course Christ's service to us evokes our praise and makes us fruitful in good works, but the means of grace come before the means of service. Officers—pastors, elders, and deacons—serve the rest of the body in Christ's name. The primary theater for the service of the people is the *world* rather than *service ministries* in the church.

Luther nicely captures the point I'm making here by saying, "God does not need your good works; your neighbor does." God serves us through his means of grace, creating faith and repentance that yield the fruit of the Spirit so that God can then serve our neighbors through our various callings in the world. By contrast, "the righteousness that is by works" (Rom. 10:5 NIV) strives to ascend to God, offering our works of service *to him* so that *we* will be blessed. As the Reformers pointed out, this does not really help anybody since God is not impressed, we are not saved, and our neighbor is not served.

Gifts do not go up to God but come down from the God who does not need anything and cannot be given anything that would obligate a return (Acts 17:24–25; Rom. 11:35–36). God gives us salvation through the gospel and provides temporal goods to our neighbors through our callings even as he makes us witnesses to Christ in our ordinary relationships—which we can have now, since we are not spending all of our time in church-related activities! Everyone has what is needed: God is served by Christ's perfect satisfaction, we are served by his gospel, and our neighbor is served by our witness, love, and diligence in our vocations.

The tendency of contemporary evangelicalism, however, is to reverse this flow of gifts. I surveyed a number of recent systematic theologies by evangelicals, both conservative and progressive, and they all referred to baptism and the Lord's Supper as "means of commitment" rather than "means of grace," adding that there is no reason to limit these to two ordinances. Is this really any different from the Second Vatican Council's definition of the Mass as "the work of the people"?

As Paul makes clear, it is our natural tendency even as Christians to prefer being actors rather than receivers of salvation. Even if we do not change the message in a Pelagianizing direction, we can transform the methods into a form of self-salvation. At least Charles Finney was consistent in this respect.

Since the gospel is a call to moral improvement, the only criterion for the methods employed is pragmatic success. Where the Heidelberg Catechism reminds us that "the Holy Spirit creates faith in our hearts by the preaching of the holy gospel and confirms it by the use of the holy sacraments," Finney was convinced that faith and repentance could be "induced" by "the most efficient means" that our pragmatic minds could conceive. Finney's "new measures" replaced the means of grace. Christians, he said, must be "frequently converted," which means there must always be "new excitements" to move people to ever higher levels of commitment and activism.[9]

"Now the great business of the church is to reform the world—to put away every kind of sin," Finney insisted. "The church of Christ was originally organized to be a body of reformers . . . to reform individuals, communities, and governments."[10] Both personal and social conversion depend on "moral [per]suasion." "Law, rewards, and punishments—these things and such as these are the very heart and soul of moral suasion." If church bodies, colleges, and seminaries will not take up this task, they will be left behind, he argues.[11]

However, Finney's "excitements" and "new measures" led to cycles of enthusiasm and burnout, as historian Whitney R. Cross observes:

> The revival engineers had to exercise increasing ingenuity to find even more sensational means to replace those worn out by overuse. In all of these ways the protracted meeting, though only a form within which the measures operated, helped the measures themselves grow even more intense, until the increasing zeal, boiled up inside of orthodoxy, overflowed into heresy.[12]

Burned out on the perpetual craving for ever-new experiences through ever-new methods, many one-time converts of Finney's revivals simply dropped out of the church altogether. During this time a minister, Albert Dodd, complained, "It is now generally understood that the numerous converts of the new measures have been, in most cases, like the morning cloud and the early dew. In some places, not a half, a fifth, or even a tenth part of them remain."[13]

This is precisely the logic of "the righteousness that is by works" to which Paul refers in Romans 10:5—striving to bring Christ down from heaven or up from the dead, as if he were not as near as the gospel that he proclaims to us. If salvation is

200

in our hands, then the means are as well. Finney says the Great Commission just said, "Go." *"It did not prescribe any forms.* It did not admit any. . . . And [the disciples'] object was to make known the gospel in the *most effectual way* . . . so as to obtain attention and secure obedience of the greatest number possible. No person can find any *form* of doing this laid down in the Bible" (emphasis added).[14] Defining the church as "a society of moral transformers," Finney consistently related what he regarded as the mark of the true church to its mission. Where Reformation Christianity identifies the true church with *God's* activity through his means of grace, Finney identifies the true church with *our* agency, whose methods were determined by what we consider most effective.

Many evangelicals—and certainly Reformed people—will not want to be as consistent as Finney. In his own day, Presbyterians were divided over whether they could be Calvinists in theory and semi-Pelagian in practice. Eventually, the New School Presbyterians alleviated this anxiety by simply becoming Arminians in both. The apostle Paul and Charles Finney offered a stark contrast, but both were utterly consistent. We simply cannot adopt a biblical view of the church's marks and a semi-Pelagian (or Pelagian) view of the church's methods and mission.

Self-Feeders: Who Needs the Church When You Have an iPod?

Like the recent Willow Creek study, George Barna concludes that what individual believers do on their own is more important than what the church does for them. But Barna takes Finney's legacy to the next logical step. A leading marketing consultant to megachurches as well as the Disney Corporation, he has recently gone so far as to suggest that the days of the institutional church are over. Barna celebrates a rising demographic of what he calls "Revolutionaries": "millions of believers" who "have moved beyond the established church and chosen to be the church instead."[15] Since *being the church* is a matter of individual choice and effort, all people need are resources for their own work of personal and social transformation. "Based on our research," Barna relates, "I have projected that by the year 2010, 10 to 20 percent of Americans will derive all their spiritual input (and output) through the Internet."[16] Who needs the church when you have an iPod?

Like any service provider, the church needs to figure out what business it's in, says Barna. "Ours is not the business of organized religion, corporate worship, or Bible teaching. If we dedicate ourselves to such a business we will be left by the wayside as the culture moves forward. Those are fragments of a larger purpose to which we have been called by God's Word. We are in the business of life transformation."[17]

Of course Barna does not believe Christians should abandon all religious practices, but the only ones he still thinks are essential are those that can be done by individuals in private, or at most in families or informal public gatherings. By eliminating the public means of grace, however, Barna (like Willow Creek) directs us away from God's lavish feast to a self-serve buffet.

Addressing his readers in terms similar to the conclusions of the Willow Creek study cited earlier, Barna writes, "Whether you choose to remain involved in the congregational mold or to venture into the spiritual unknown, to experience the competing dynamics of independence and responsibility, move ahead boldly. God's perspective is that the structures and routines you engage with matter much less than the character and commitments that define you." Believers need not find a good church, but they should "get a good coach." If the gospel is good advice rather than Good News, obviously the church is simply "a resource" for our personal development, as Barna suggests.[18]

If the local church is to survive, says Barna, authority must shift from being centralized to decentralized; leadership from "pastor-driven" to "lay-driven," which means the sheep are primarily servers rather than served by the ministry. Further ministry must shift from "resistance" to change to "acceptance," from "tradition and order" to "mission and vision," from an "all-purpose" to a "specialized" approach to ministry, from "tradition bound" to "relevance bound," from a view of the people's role as receivers to actors, from "knowledge" to "transformation."[19]

"In just a few years," Barna predicts, "we will see that millions of people will never travel physically to a church, but will instead roam the Internet in search of meaningful spiritual experiences."[20] After all, he adds, the heart of Jesus's ministry was "the development of people's character." "If we rise to the challenge," says Barna, Americans will witness a "moral resurgence" and new leadership, and the Christian message "will regain respect" in our culture. Intimate worship, says Barna, does "not require a 'worship service,'" just a personal commitment to the Bible, prayer, and discipleship. His book concludes with the warning of the last judgment. "What report of your commitment to practical, holy, life-transforming service will you be able to give Him?" The Revolutionaries have found that in order to pursue an authentic faith, they had to abandon the church.[21]

This is finally where American spirituality leaves us: alone, surfing the Internet, casting about for coaches and teammates, trying to save ourselves from captivity to this present age by finding those *excitements* that will induce a transformed life. Increasingly, the examples I have referred to are what people mean by the adjective *missional*.

Like Finney, George Barna asserts that the Bible offers "almost no restrictions on structures and methods" for the church.[22] In fact, as we have seen, he does not even think the visible church itself is divinely established. Nature abhors a vacuum and where Barna imagines that the Bible prescribes no particular structures or methods, the invisible hand of the market fills the void. He even recognizes that the shift from the institutional church to "alternative faith communities" is largely due to market forces: "Whether you examine the changes in broadcasting, clothing, music, investing, or automobiles, producers of such consumables realize that Americans want control over their lives. The result has been the 'niching' of America—creating highly refined categories that serve smaller numbers of people, but can command greater loyalty (and profits)." The same thing is happening to the church, Barna notes, as if it were a fate to be embraced rather than an apostasy to be resisted.[23] The logic of individualism and moralism has finally reached its consummation in the theory that "self-feeders" and "transformers" do not need the church and the means of grace. God's downward descent to us in grace reversed by our upward ascent in pragmatic enthusiasm, we are increasingly becoming sheep without a Shepherd—and all in the name of mission. Instead of churching the unchurched, we are well on our way to even unchurching the churched. It's worth noting that Barna may have the statistics on his side. According to a recent report listing actions that Americans still consider "sins," "not attending church or religious services regularly" came in next-to-last (18 percent).[24]

However thin, there is a theology behind Barna's interpretation of Jesus as the paradigmatic Revolutionary, and it is basically that of the nineteenth-century revivalist Charles Finney. "So if you are a Revolutionary," says Barna, "it is because you have sensed and responded to God's calling to be such an imitator of Christ. It is not a church's responsibility to make you into this mold. . . . The choice to become a Revolutionary—and it is a choice—is a covenant you make with God alone."[25]

Gospel-Driven Mission

The biblical covenant originates in God's gracious decision, redeeming work, and effectual calling through the gospel, placing us in a family of siblings we did not choose based on our own affinities, hobbies, musical preferences, or political views. The American covenant originates in the individual's choice, moral transformation, and contract with God to be an imitator of Christ.

Where Christ is not King, he is neither Prophet nor Priest. Christ rules his church—instituting its structure and methods—*precisely so that he can effectively deliver his good gifts to the world*.

At the same time, as I have suggested, in my own confessional circles one can discern an obsession with the marks without a corresponding missional orientation. The faithful ministry of Word, sacrament, and discipline *is* the mission (Matt. 28:18–20). A church that is not outward looking, eager to bring the Good News to the ends of the earth, is not really bringing it to those already gathered into Christ's flock. A genuinely *evangelical* church will be an *evangelistic* church: a place where the gospel is delivered through Word and sacrament and a people who witness to it in the world. It will be a place where believers and unbelievers alike will be recipients of God's Good News. We come to receive God's Word, both law and gospel, and to be buried and raised with Christ. We surrender our trivial scripts in order to be written into God's unfolding drama. And then we go out into the world to live out our new role in this play.

Those who are forgiven much love much (Luke 7:47). Only as recipients of Christ and all of his gifts can we become part of God's new creation: witnesses to Christ and servants of our neighbors. Without the marks, the mission is blind; without the mission, the marks are dead. As Lesslie Newbigin has emphasized, the church does not *engage* in mission; it *is* a mission—but *God's* mission, not our own. This theme runs throughout Newbigin's writings, especially *The Gospel in a Pluralistic Society* (Grand Rapids, Eerdmans, 1989).

"Glory, Glory, Hallelujah": Christ as Mascot in the Culture Wars

In the Washington National Cathedral service following the terrorist attacks on September 11, 2001, followed by the parade of the honor guard of the armed forces to the "The Battle Hymn of the Republic," President George W. Bush declared that it was the cause of the United States to "rid the world of evil." A senator announced that the events since 9/11 have reinforced the view that America is a "sacred nation." On the other hand, precisely because of its sacred covenant, according to Jerry Falwell and Pat Robertson, the horrible tragedy was God's judgment on his nation for tolerating abortion and homosexuality.

More recently, in a book titled *God's Judgments: Interpreting History and the Christian Faith*, another evangelical, Steven J. Keillor, explains why he thinks 9/11 was God's judgment for America's greed, free trade policies, and militarism.[26] It is not the *deeds, not creeds* emphasis that is new in evangelicalism but the particular deeds one has in mind. Similarly, Jim Wallis's *God's Politics* simply mirrors on the Religious Left the confusion of the gospel with a partisan agenda that dominated the Religious Right.

Over the last year or so the media has focused on the broadening of the evangelical movement in its political loyalties. No longer stereotyped as the Republican Party at prayer, evangelicalism reflects greater interest in issues such as poverty, the environment, and AIDS. The deeper question, however, is whether the church's mission is to serve the interests of any party or political ideology. Does it really make any difference whether the drumbeat is abortion and gay marriage or global warming and famine if our programs and activities subtly (and not so subtly) replace Christ's? Does it really matter whether a Democrat or a Republican delivers a stump speech from a Christian pulpit? Or does either example reveal where we think the real power lies?

There's even talk now of an "evangelical center," reminiscent of the center-left/center-right parties of Europe (especially the Christian Democrats, a powerful party in Germany). At the risk of offending, I have to say that for the good of the church and the common good, I am more than a little nervous about an evangelical center, an evangelical left, and an evangelical right. Political callings (ranging from voting to holding office) are honorable, neighbor-serving, godly vocations. But "evangelical" means "that which is of the gospel," and the gospel is an announcement that we have to deliver, not an agenda that we have to negotiate with our fellow citizens. Not everything that is important in this time between Christ's two comings is related to delivering this gospel. Christians have other callings besides being members of Christ's visible body. But please, let's stop using "gospel" and "evangelical" for anything and everything we think is best in achieving the common good!

Even where Scripture addresses these important issues and responsibilities, it does so from a completely different perspective (the age to come) and with completely different means (the liberating power of the Spirit through the gospel rather than the coercive arm of the state). We need good churches and good government, but they do different things, with different mandates and means, and with different canons or constitutions. The Bible is the constitution for God's covenant people, not a textbook of general principles. Regardless of whether we think as American citizens that Democratic policies are better for our neighbors, it is not *countercultural* to advocate such policies in the place of Christ's grand narrative of redemption. It is just a different side of the culture wars.

I have argued for some time in books and articles that we should be more pro-life—not just on abortion and euthanasia, but in our concern for stewardship of creation and care for those who get left behind in our cult of individual health, wealth, and happiness. Scripture gives us ample warrant for inculcating such an outlook. But the church as an institution cannot prescribe any particular political agenda for achieving these goals. Believers who care about these matters will differ as much among themselves as with non-Christian neighbors as to how best to approximate the social good. Unlike the various vocations of Christians in the world, the institutional church exists not to fix the world's temporal problems (which inevitably divides Christ's body over policy agendas) but to administer Christ's own service of reconciling sinners to himself, caring for his flock in body (through the diaconate) as well as in soul (through the ministers and elders). Having been first ministered to in these ways, the members love and serve each other according to their particular needs and then carry this service out to their non-Christian neighbors. The Scriptures alone are the church's constitution, and the church has no legitimate authority or power to speak or act beyond this divine Word. However convinced we are in our own minds about how to vote, ministers are Christ's ambassadors, completely restricted by his words. They abuse their authority when they use this office to endorse candidates, parties, and policies.

It is not *radical discipleship* to switch from one party to another or to broaden the church's political to-do list. Radical discipleship means bringing to the world—including Christians—the wonderful, surprising, and offensive news of the gospel.

Nothing we have done, are doing, or can do is radical. It is the same old story of human striving. But in the public assembly of his people, God is at work raising the dead. Through Word and sacrament, Christ's kingdom is breaking into this present age in the power of the Spirit. This in-breaking is not propping up this present evil age, but it is sowing the seeds of the age to come. It comes not to improve people or societies but to kill and make alive in Christ. Whatever we might need in society, the church doesn't need a cultural shift; it needs a paradigm shift from our agenda to God's.

It is God's ordinary providence that keeps this present age from being as bad as it could be, giving us a confidence in our secular callings to love and serve our neighbors even in ways that are not ultimately redemptive. I can work, vote, and dialogue side-by-side with non-Christian neighbors on a host of issues related to improving our neighborhoods, society, and the world. We do not need more *Christian* service organizations but more churches that serve the sheep and send them out to love and serve their neighbors alongside non-Christians as employees, employers, volunteers, friends, and family members. Since we all share the awareness of God's law in our conscience (however we might suppress it), and the Spirit works through common grace as well as saving grace, the church-as-institution does not have to do, prescribe, or dictate everything we do as citizens in the culture. We do not need more Christian art, philosophy, politics, and business; we need more Christian proclamation and the genuinely transformed thinking and living that arise from it.

The church as *people*—scattered as salt and light throughout the week—has many different callings, but the church as *place* (gathered publicly by God's summons each Lord's Day) has one calling: to deliver (and receive) Christ through preaching and sacrament. On this day, we are not Republicans or Democrats with an agenda but sinners in fellowship around a common

Savior. We are not Builders, Boomers, Busters, or emergent but a communion of saints. "There is one body and one Spirit—just as you were called to the one hope that belongs to your call—one Lord, one faith, one baptism, one God and Father of all, who is over all and through all and in all" (Eph. 4:4–6). On *this* day, the sheep are not called to make the world a greener pasture but are led into the luxuriant pastures planned, purchased, and prepared by the Triune God. This is the day of the week that participates in the everlasting Sabbath that will characterize every day in the age to come. It is into this day that we long to bring our family, friends, and coworkers. On this day we do not come to create a story for ourselves or to build a kingdom; we come as those who are "grateful for *receiving* a kingdom that cannot be shaken" and therefore offering "to God acceptable worship, with reverence and awe" (Heb. 12:28; emphasis added). As I have already pointed out, this movement from doctrine (God's deeds) to doxology (our thankful worship) to duties (our reasonable service) is the direction that God's Word typically takes. "Therefore, as you received Christ Jesus the Lord, so walk in him, rooted and built up in him and established in the faith, just as you were taught, abounding in thanksgiving" (Col. 2:6–7).

I recently heard a sermon that ended with the appeal, "Are you going to accomplish great things for God?" It is easy for believers with a sensitive conscience to come away from the average spiritual diet in church thinking they must be a Paul in evangelism, a Wilberforce in culture, and a Thomas à Kempis in spiritual disciplines. *Radical discipleship* in this triumphalistic vein seems rather far from Jesus's invitation, "Come to me, all who labor and are heavy laden, and I will give you rest. Take my yoke upon you, and learn from me, for I am gentle and lowly in heart, and you will find rest for your souls. For my yoke is easy and my burden is light" (Matt. 11:28–30).

Calling us to accomplish great things for God is part of the hype that constantly burns out millions of professing Christians. Telling us about the great things God has accomplished—and, more than that, actually delivering his achievement to sinners—is the real mission of church. And it might even put wind in the sails of those among us whom God *has* called to extraordinary achievements! But it will be enough if it puts wind in the sails of those whom God has called to ordinary and fruitful lives. On Monday, a congregation once again assured of God's amazing grace to sinners, will be scattered into the world as salt and light. If we think the main mission of the church is to improve life *in Adam* and add a little moral strength to this fading evil age, we have not yet understood the radical condition for which Christ is such a radical solution.

If the Triune God is the only agent of salvation, the church will first of all be a society of receivers—recipients of that salvation. If salvation is in our hands, however, we need to find the best means of transportation for attaining it. Finney was at least consistent with his theology when he said that the church was originally established to be a body of moral reformers.

While Finney's social agenda reflects positions that would be identified with both conservative and liberal politics today, more recently it has split into Republican and Democratic factions. For all their ideological differences, however, the fundamental vision of the church as a sociopolitical movement—activists more than recipients—remains a constant. Jerry Falwell and Jim Wallis both identify Charles Finney as one of their heroes.

Although one could find similar examples from other denominations, imitating Marsha Witten's sampling cited in a previous chapter, I examined recent resolutions on public policy issues by a mainline denomination, the Presbyterian Church (USA), and the more conservative Southern Baptist Convention. The PC(USA) *Book of Order* states that the church's mandate

for "doing justice" requires "working for fair laws and just ad-
ministration of the law."[27] As a consequence, in the last two
years alone there are numerous General Assembly resolutions
on everything from the Israeli-Palestinian conflict to farm policy.
In 2004 the General Assembly created a "Resolution Calling for
a Comprehensive Legalization Program for Immigrants Living
and Working in the US," and two years later they adopted an
immigration policy with fine print that obliged the conscience
of millions of Presbyterians to minute specifics concerning this
complicated issue. In fact, the report calls upon the denomination
to "encourage Presbyterian legislators serving in the House and
Senate to actively work across party lines to defeat this proposed
legislation while actively working across party lines to achieve
more amicable legislation that resolves the conflicts surrounding
immigration policy issues."[28]

While there is a noble history of Presbyterian laypeople serving in public office, the denomination was historically committed to limiting its authority to Christ's commission. In fact,
Presbyterianism arose in the Church of England primarily in
protest of the view that the church or the state could command
the conscience apart from Scripture. Where its King has not
spoken, the church does not speak—its members are free to
use their own wisdom to arrive at conclusions concerning their
conduct and political views.

All of this has changed—on both sides of the culture wars.
Conservative Presbyterian bodies have also pronounced on issues
such as women in combat. The mainline Presbyterian Church
(USA) has also weighed in on NAFTA and CAFTA, oppos-
ing free trade in principle, and has called for specific policy
regarding farm bills. The theologically broad World Alliance
of Reformed Churches, of which the PC(USA) is a member,
decided recently "that working to create a more just economy
is *essential to the integrity of Christian faith*. We believe that

the integrity of our faith is at stake if we remain silent or refuse to act in the face cf the current system of neoliberal economic globalization."[29]

In this perspect_ve, not only is it tolerable for church bodies to issue verdicts on behalf of their membership on domestic and foreign policy; failure to do so places the integrity of the Christian faith in jeopardy. It is remarkable that the PC(USA), like many other Protestant denominations rapidly losing their memberships, refuses to enforce the ecumenical creeds or its Confession of Faith when ministers transgress their ordination vows, yet it obliges the whole body to endorse specific domestic and foreign policy objectives for the United States at the risk of sacrificing the integrity of its faith.

Not to be outdone by the left-leaning denominations, the Southern Baptist Convention has offered resolutions of this kind as well on the other side of the political aisle. In "On the Liberation of Iraq" (June 2003), we read,

> Whereas we believe Operation Iraqi Freedom was a warranted action based upon historical principles of just war; now, therefore, be it resolved, that the messengers to the Southern Baptist Convention meeting in Phoenix, Arizona, June 17–18, 2003, affirm President George W. Bush, the United States Congress, and our armed forces for their leadership in the successful execution of Operation Iraqi Freedom. . . . We call on the United States government and the international community to ensure that the Iraqi people enjoy all the blessings of liberty, including economic, politica., and religious freedom.[30]

In 1988 the Convention included a resolution condemning U.S. government suppor- of international markets for alcohol and tobacco: "Be it resolved, that we encourage the United States Government to cease to assist these industries via trade talks; and . . . Southern Baptists . . . declare their opposition to these hypocritical practices by the United States Government on behalf of the alcohol and tobacco industries."[31]

In 2007 the same body issued a resolution "On Global Warming." After listing no fewer than nineteen reasons for contesting the warning that global warming constitutes a "catastrophic human-induced" challenge, the messengers passed the following resolution:

> Resolved, that we consider proposals to regulate CO_2 and other greenhouse gas emissions based on a maximum acceptable global temperature goal to be very dangerous. . . . Resolved, that we urge Congress and the president to only support cost-effective measures to reduce CO_2 and other greenhouse gas emissions and to reject government-mandated reductions in greenhouse gas emissions.[32]

Since any number of secular NGOs (nongovernmental organizations) currently exist to lobby for precisely the same policies, why do churches believe it is within their area of expertise, much less their official mandate, to offer pronouncements in God's name on these issues? Why not allow their members to pursue the general human calling to public justice through these *common grace* institutions alongside non-Christians? Why must denominations commit their entire membership to very specific policies while often leaving matters of doctrine and worship more ambiguous and open-ended?

Surely the abolition of the slave trade was a noble work, yet it is interesting that in Britain it was not the church as an institution that abolished it but Christians who had been shaped by the church's ministry and held public office in the state. When William Wilberforce came to John Newton for advice on whether he should enter the ministry, Newton encouraged his friend to pursue politics instead. It was as a member of Parliament that Wilberforce loved and served his neighbor, benefiting from the ordinary means of grace that Newton ministered to him. The church preached God's transcendent law and gospel, and her children pursued their cultural mandate in their secular vocations. Thank God that Newton was a pastor and Wilberforce was not!

I often wonder how American history might have turned out differently if the *churches* in the South had disciplined members who held slaves. In other words, if the churches had simply followed their own mandate of preaching the Word, administering the sacraments, and exercising discipline and care for the well-being of their flock. Would not the institution have lost its moral credibility even outside of the church? Both Northern and Southern churches had reduced slavery merely to a political issue when they should have done what only churches *can* do: proclaim God's judgment upon the kidnapping and forced labor of fellow humans and excommunicate members who refused to repent of the practice. At the same time, church members could have exercised their moral conscience in deciding for themselves how best to abolish the institution in courts and legislatures.

These questions are especially pertinent in the light of the comparatively swift dismantling of apartheid in South Africa. According to Allen Boesak, John de Gruchy, F. W. de Klerk, and Nelson Mandela, the turning point was not the sanctions imposed on the apartheid government but the announcement in the late 1980s by the Dutch Reformed Church that "apartheid is a heresy." Invoking the now popular maxim that churches grow more quickly when they consist of the same racial and socioeconomic groups, according to John de Gruchy, the Pietists and revivalists overturned the policy of mixed churches that had been in place since the Synod of Dort (1618–1619).[33] Only when the most influential white church, ejected by the worldwide community of Reformed churches, came to realize that it had falsely interpreted Scripture to justify apartheid did the institution lose its moral legitimacy.

The church as an institution appointed by Christ has a narrow mandate with global significance. Individual Christians, however, have as many mandates as they do callings: as parents, children, extended relatives, neighbors, coworkers, and so on. In addition to loving and serving each other in the fellowship of saints, believers are enjoined "to aspire to live quietly, and to mind your own affairs, and to work with your hands, as we instructed you, so that you may walk properly before outsiders and be dependent on no one" (1 Thess. 4:11–12). It may not sound as grand as creating a global trading policy or ushering in the kingdom by driving out the "Romans" (whether Democrats or Republicans) in the next election, but it is the proper kind of discipleship for this phase of Christ's rule: the kingdom of grace, which only at Christ's return will be a kingdom of glory.

So getting the church to mind its own business and get its own house in order is not a call to passivity in the face of injustice, unrighteousness, and oppression. Especially when dominant churches have succumbed to civil religion, their repentance has enormous significance in the wider society. Even where it does not have that kind of effect, however, the church's repentance is always God's call. Christians can always have a broader impact in their callings than the church as an institution with its restricted mandate. Even so, a church that fully exercises its commission is a potent source of genuine transformation, forming a new society within the secular city that is nevertheless completely distinct from it.

The church desperately needs a second Reformation, to be sure, but one that—like the first one—returns the church's focus to Christ and his work. Neither the Republican nor the Democratic Party is entrusted with this commission. If Christian morality is becoming a distant memory in the culture, it is because it is increasingly the church itself that is in moral chaos. And beneath these symptoms is the real disease: "There arose another generation after them who did not know the LORD or the work that he had done for Israel" (Judg. 2:10). America has never been a Christian nation, but the real crisis with which the church is always faced is whether it will de-Christianize its own message, ministry, and mission. In an interview with Billy Graham's *Decision* magazine, C. S. Lewis was asked, "Do you feel, then, that modern culture is being de-Christianized?" Lewis responded,

> I cannot speak to the political aspects of the question, but I have some definite views about the de-Christianizing of the church. I believe that there are many accommodating preachers, and too many practitioners in the church who are not believers. Jesus Christ did not say, "Go into all the world and tell the world that it is quite right." The Gospel is something completely different. In fact, it is directly opposed to the world.[34]

As Athanasius realized, the church must stand *against* the world *for* the world, and this includes supposedly *Christian nations*.

Gospel Logic and the Mission of the Church

In contrast with both Pelagian and Gnostic attempts to scale heavenly heights, the gospel of Christ creates its own delivery system. As we have already seen, Paul bears this out in Romans 10, lamenting that his contemporaries were trying to save themselves by their efforts. "I bear them witness that they have a zeal for God," he affirmed, "but not according to knowledge" (v. 2). And it was not knowledge in general of which they were fatally ignorant but knowledge of a specific truth: "For, being ignorant of the righteousness that comes from God, and seeking to establish their own, they have not submitted to God's righteousness. For Christ is the end of the law so that there may be righteousness for everyone who believes" (vv. 3–4 NRSV). Paul continues: works-righteousness requires perfect obedience. "But the righteousness based on faith says, 'Do not say in your heart, "Who will ascend into heaven?"' (that is, to bring Christ down) or '"Who will descend into the abyss?"' (that is, to bring Christ up from the dead)" (vv. 6–7).

In other words, works-righteousness calls for moral ascent, zealously climbing the ladder to heaven rung by rung. It is as if Christ were far away and it is up to us to find him, or perhaps he is still lying in the grave waiting for us to bring him up by our earnestness. But the "righteousness that is by faith" recognizes that God has descended to us in mercy, not only long ago when the Word became flesh, but even now, as "the word of faith that we proclaim" is brought to us (Rom. 10:6, 8). We cannot climb up to God, but God has climbed down to us. He is as near as the gospel of Christ that is preached to us. "So faith comes from hearing, and hearing through the word of Christ" (v. 17).

Preaching is central, not because we value the intellect to the exclusion of the emotions and the will, but because it is God's action rather than our own. The God who accomplished our salvation now delivers it to us. So the argument that an emphasis on preaching tilts toward intellectualism is wide of the mark. The real issue is not whether we give priority to a particular human faculty (intellect, will, or emotion) but whether we give priority to God's action over ours. In preaching, we are *addressed*—we are not in charge but are seated to be judged and justified. In baptism, too, we are passive receivers—we do not baptize ourselves but *are baptized*. In the Lord's Supper, Christ gives himself to us as our food and drink for eternal life; it is a banquet set for us—the meal has already been prepared, and Christ even serves it to us through his ministers. We *are fed*; our filthy rags removed, we are bathed and clothed with Christ and fed for our pilgrimage to the City of God.

In *The Lion, the Witch, and the Wardrobe*, C. S. Lewis creates a marvelous scene in which three of the four children are introduced to Aslan, who declares, "Let the feast be prepared!" Commanding his servants to "take these daughters of Eve to the pavilion and minister to them," Aslan says to Peter (the firstborn), "Come, son of Adam, and I shall show you a far-off sight of the castle where you are to be King."[35] In this scene, Lewis vividly captures the character of the relationship Christ establishes with his people through the banquet that he sets. Ministers are simply God's waiters at the feast.

In Romans 10, Paul is telling us not only that Christ's work in the past is sufficient for our redemption, but Christ himself says, in effect, "Just stay put. I'll give you myself and all of my riches. I have made the trip before, and I will continue bringing you the gift through my ambassadors whom I send." Christ delivers himself to us through the preaching of the gospel (Rom. 10:6–8), baptism (Acts 2:38; 22:16; Rom. 6:3–4; 1 Cor. 12:13; Col. 2:12; 1 Peter 3:21), and the Lord's Supper. "The cup of blessing that we bless," Paul asks, "is it not a participation in the blood of Christ? The bread that we break, is it not a participation in the body of Christ?" (1 Cor. 10:16). We do not simply remember Christ or rededicate ourselves to Christ in this meal; rather, Christ gives himself to us as the Bread of Life. Beyond our powers to comprehend, the Spirit communicates Christ to us through these creaturely means of preaching and sacrament so that the ascended Head will not be without his body. "Because there is one bread, we who are many are one body, for we all partake of the one bread" (1 Cor. 10:17). These are all means that convey God's saving grace rather than methods of our own striving. Before we serve, we are served. Before we do anything, something is done to and for us.

Yet once even these means of God's grace are transformed into our means of ascending to God, it will then be easy to conclude that there are many other means than these for our accomplishing this feat. When this happens, we will naturally see the visible church and its public ministry as something we can take or leave. If we can find good *advice* on the Internet, with a group of Christian friends over coffee, on television, in conferences, by listening to Christian music, or through private reading and spiritual disciplines, who needs the church? That defines *church* exclusively as the sum total of converted activists rather than as the place where *God* is at work, delivering his Son by his Spirit to the ungodly.

There is a direct correlation, then, between a theology of self-salvation and the church chiefly as a center of human rather than divine activism. No longer do we need formally trained ministers of the Word but charismatic and entrepreneurial leaders who can inspire activistic movements.

According to Scripture, however, the church is the creation of the Word. Like the first creation, the new creation arises from God's activity, not from its own inherent possibilities. Furthermore, the gospel is a particular kind of Word, as we have seen: Good News. And it creates its own community, making strangers into a family. Far greater than any natural affinity, the event of Christ—and the reporting of this event—forges a new community in the Spirit that is different from any circle of friends we would have naturally chosen for ourselves!

The Reformers emphasized that when one presumes to sit in a corner by oneself, there is no telling what *spirits* he or she will receive, but God has pledged his Spirit's presence wherever the Word is proclaimed. When Luther said that "the church is not a pen-house but a mouth-house"[36] and the Westminster divines confessed that the Spirit blesses "the reading but especially the preaching of the Word" as a means of grace,[37] they were asserting that faithful, meditative, and prayerful reading of Scripture in private or family devotions was subordinate to the public ministry of the Word in the common life of the church. Just as the Word creates the community, it can only be truly heard, received, and followed in the concrete covenantal exchanges within that community.

Writing as a self-professed Jewish Gnostic, Harold Bloom has approvingly characterized American religion generally as Gnostic: an *inner* word, spirit, and church set over against an *external* Word, Spirit, and church.[38] Evangelical pietism began as a renewal movement in the churches of the Reformation, but it increasingly tended to reduce the faith to a subjective inner experience. The real action happened either in private devotions or in *conventicles* or *holy clubs* (what we would today call *small groups*). American revivalism was more radical still, expecting the *real action* of Christian formation to take place outside the ordinary ministry of the church altogether. Christians should still gather weekly, of course, but the Spirit really came down when the evangelist came to town and the extraordinary methods he employed yielded excitement.

In contrast to the logic we have followed in Romans 10, evangelical theologian Stanley Grenz argues that evangelicalism is more a *spirituality* than a *theology*, more interested in individual piety than in creeds, confessions, and liturgies. Experience gives rise to—in fact he says, "determines"—doctrine, rather than the other way around. Evangelicals follow their heart—their converted instincts—"to accept the biblical stories as in some sense true as they are told."[39] The main point, however, is how these stories can be used in daily living—hence, the emphasis on daily devotions.

This emphasis on the inner life of the individual has ecclesiological implications, Grenz recognizes. "Although some evangelicals belong to ecclesiological traditions that understand the church as in some sense a dispenser of grace, generally we see our congregations foremost as a fellowship of believers." We share our journeys (our "testimony") of personal transformation. Therefore, Grenz celebrates the "fundamental shift . . . from a creed-based to a spirituality-based identity" that is more like medieval mysticism than Protestant orthodoxy. "Consequently, spirituality is inward and quietistic," concerned with combating "the lower nature and the world" in "a personal commitment that becomes the ultimate focus of the believer's affections."

Nowhere in this account does Grenz locate the origin of faith in an external gospel; rather, faith arises from an inner experience. "Because spirituality is *generated from within the individual*, inner motivation is crucial"—more important, in fact, than "grand theological statements."

> The spiritual life is above all the imitation of Christ. . . . In general we eschew religious ritual. Not slavish adherence to rites, but doing what Jesus would do is our concept of true discipleship. Consequently, most evangelicals neither accept the sacramentalism of many mainline churches nor join the Quakers in completely eliminating the sacraments. We practice baptism and the Lord's Supper, but understand the significance of these rites in a guarded manner.

In any case, he says, these rites are practiced as goads to personal experience and out of obedience to divine command.

> This view marks a radical shift in the relationship of soteriology and ecclesiology, for it exchanges the priority of the church for the priority of the believer. . . . "Get on with the task; get your life in order by practicing the aids to growth and see if you do not mature spiritually," we exhort. In fact, if a believer comes to the point where he or she senses that stagnation has set in, evangelical counsel is to redouble one's efforts in the task of exercising the disciplines. "Check up on yourself," the evangelical spiritual counselor admonishes.

The emphasis on the individual believer is evident, he says, in the expectation to "find a ministry" within the local fellowship.

All of this is at odds with an emphasis on doctrine and especially, Grenz adds, an emphasis on "a material and a formal principle"—referring to the Reformation slogans, *sola fide* (justification by Christ alone through faith alone) and *sola scriptura* (by Scripture alone). In spite of the fact that the Scriptures declare that "faith comes by hearing and hearing by the word of Christ," Grenz says, "Faith is by nature immediate."

In fact, Grenz goes so far with the emphasis on an inner experience over an external Word that he locates the origin of the Bible's inspiration in the experience of individuals and the community (past, present, and future) rather than in God. Obviously this requires "a revisioned understanding of the *nature* of the Bible's authority." Our own religious experience today needs to be included in the process of inspiration. Accordingly, Grenz believes that this will "chart the way beyond the evangelical tendency to equate in a simple fashion the revelation of God with the Bible—that is, to make a one-to-one correspondence between the words of the Bible and the very Word of God."

In all of this we clearly recognize that the message cannot be separated from the methods, and soteriology (the doctrine of salvation) cannot be separated from ecclesiology (the doctrine of the church). We must distinguish but we can never separate Christ's person and work (the message) from the way we receive him (the medium).

Once your faith is focused on what happens inside you instead of what happened outside you in history, it is easy to say that what you really need are good resources for private experience and moral improvement rather than any external Word. However weak and foolish in the eyes of the world, God's methods and structures, clearly prescribed in Scripture, are consistent with the message. Preaching is not a bully pulpit for either our personal threats or helpful suggestions; it is a saving advent of Christ by his Spirit through his Word. Baptism is not our act of commitment, based on our decision; it is God's act of commitment to us, based on his decision. God's claim always provokes rather than presupposes our commitment. The Lord's Supper is not our remembering and rededicating but focuses on God's promise to give us his Son as our food and drink—certifying and ratifying our inclusion in the covenant of grace.

In the Lord's Day service, God sets a feast where he is the chef, host, and provider. He provides the bath, clothes, food, drink, and even our fellow guests—all without cost to us. And Christ calls his ministers to represent him as servants, waiting on the guests, providing them with all of the table's delicacies. Toward the end of his earthly ministry Jesus asked Peter, "Do you love me?" Peter replied, "You know that I love you." Jesus responded, "Feed my sheep" (John 21:17). This is the task God has given his ministers: not to make the sheep self-feeders but to give them everything necessary for their pilgrimage to the Holy City. God has spread a table in the wilderness. One day he will not only be the meal but a guest together with us who enjoys our fellowship with him in everlasting joy (Matt. 26:29).

Writing against the "new measures" employed by his contemporary, Charles Finney, John Williamson Nevin points out the contrast between "the system of the bench" (precursor to the altar call) and "the system of the catechism. . . . The old Presbyterian faith, into which I was born, was based throughout on the idea of covenant family religion, church membership by God's holy act in baptism, and following this a regular catechetical training of the young, with direct reference to their coming to the Lord's table. In one word, all proceeded on the theory of sacramental, educational religion." These two systems, Nevin concludes, "involve at the bottom two different theories of religion."[40] Nevin's conclusion has been justified by subsequent history. Driven to and fro with every wind of doctrine and often no doctrine at all, those reared in evangelicalism become accustomed to hype and cataclysmic events of intense spiritual experience that nevertheless wear off. When they do wear off, there is often little to keep them from trying a different form of spiritual therapy or dropping out of the religion rat race altogether.

Toward the end of his ministry, as he considered the condition of many who had experienced his revivals, Finney wondered if this endless craving for ever-greater experiences might lead to spiritual exhaustion.[41] In fact, his worries were justified. The area where Finney's revivals were especially dominant is now referred to by historians as the "burned-over district," a seedbed of both disillusionment and the proliferation of esoteric sects.[42] This has been the vicious cycle of evangelical revivalism ever since: a pendulum swinging between enthusiasm and disillusionment rather than steady maturity in Christ through participation in the ordinary life of the covenant community.

Citing numerous contemporary heirs, Michael Pasquarello goes so far as to suggest that Finney's approach itself represents a "practical atheism" according to which the success of Christian mission depends on human technique, style, planning, and charisma "without having to surrender ourselves and our words to the presence and work of the Word and Spirit."[43] It is no wonder that the expectation of the Spirit's activity shifted from the church to the parachurch, from the ordinary means of grace to the extraordinary methods of *inducing* conversions, as Finney understood it.

With salvation placed in the hands of the rugged American individual, the only challenge was to find the appropriate spiritual, moral, and emotional technology for radical, visible, and immediate results. Like the revivals of Finney and his successors, the *new measures* of the church growth movement have been treated by many as science, like the law of gravity. Those who fail to adopt these new models of ministry will be left behind in the spiritual marketplace.

Following from its radical revisions in its view of sin and salvation, revivalism offers a substantially different understanding of the church's identity and mission. For confessional Protestantism (both Reformed and Lutheran), the church is an intergenerational covenant community of sinners gathered by the Spirit through the gospel preached and the sacraments administered and reaching out to the lost with Good News and to the neighbor in love.

This means that the church is not a club for those with similar cultural tastes, political views, ethnic backgrounds, and moral leanings. They do not meet because they share a hobby called *spirituality* or because they have the same vision for transforming culture. Believers gather to be regularly reconstituted as the body of Christ, receiving Christ as their living Head. They do not gather on their own initiative but are gathered by the Spirit through his ordained means of grace.

Unlike voluntary associations (book clubs, political parties, or fans of the opera or garage bands), the church is not made up of people I chose to be my friends. God chose them for me and me for them. They are my family because of God's election, not mine. Gathered to be redefined by the kingdom of Christ rather than by the kingdoms of this age, we are then scattered again into the world as salt—not huddled together in Christian societies for moral transformation and ecclesiastically sanctioned political causes, but dispersed into the world as doctors, homemakers, plumbers, lawyers, truck drivers, citizens, and neighbors.

If the goal of instruction for children and adults is primarily outreach to the unchurched, service to the neighborhood, or even building a sense of community and fellowship, we will have

226

churches full of people who do not know what they believe or why they believe it but who nevertheless feel an intense burden to do more things that they feel unprepared to do well. Yet if we meet together regularly for "the apostles' teaching and fellowship, . . . the breaking of bread and the prayers" (Acts 2:42), the gospel creates community around Christ rather than around itself and provides exactly what is needed for well-informed and motivated witness and service to our neighbors outside the church during the week.

Of course we all have our different *locations*: ethnic, socio-economic, educational, generational, cultural. But when God is the actor, directing the play from his pulpit, Table, and font, the most decisive location is either *in Adam* or *in Christ*. Although the church growth (or seeker-driven) movement defends its perpetual innovations as more *missional*, there has been no growth in the rate of professed conversions during this period. In fact, there has been decline.[44] And no wonder, when even those raised in the church are victims of "a famine on the land—not a famine of bread, nor a thirst for water, but of hearing the words of the LORD" (Amos 8:11).

Until we reevaluate our commitment to the revivalistic paradigm itself, we will view the church as consumers who have signed a contract for spiritual services rather than as sinners who have been incorporated by God's grace into a covenant community.

Why So Many Christians Are Burned Out on the Church

One of the major reasons so many believers today may experience *Christless Christianity* even in churches that identify themselves as Christ-centered is that the dominant emphasis is on means of service rather than the means of grace. Many Christians today are burned out and they are not sure why, but in many cases that I have encountered, the reason is that they have been subjected to constant demands while the gospel remains in the background.

To be sure, the local church involves fellowship among the saints, which includes works of service to the household of faith. But we have confused the priesthood of all believers with the ministry-hood of all believers, as if Christ had never instituted the offices that we find in the epistles. In this approach to ministry, every sheep must be a shepherd. The call to the sheep to become *self-feeders* is the natural consequence of this impoverished line of thinking.

The church has a very narrow commission. It is not called to be an alternative neighborhood, circle of friends, political action committee, social club, or public service agency; it is called to deliver Christ so clearly and fully that believers are prepared to be salt and light in the worldly stations to which God has called them. Why should a person go through all the trouble of belonging to a church and showing up each Sunday if God is the passive receiver and we are the active giver? It's like being expected to look forward to Christmas when you are always giving but never receiving any gifts. Answering Simon's complaint against the woman who anointed Jesus with costly perfume, Jesus said, "He who is forgiven little, loves little." Then he turned to the woman and said, "Your sins are forgiven" (Luke 7:47–48). When we regularly hear and receive Christ's forgiveness, we are filled with love for him and for others.

When Jesus wrapped a towel around his waist and began washing the disciples' feet, Peter was confused and asked, "'Lord, do *you* wash *my* feet?' Jesus answered him, 'What I am doing you do not understand now, but afterward you will understand'" (John 13:6–7; emphasis added). Afterward? After *what*? Jesus is referring to his ultimate act of service at Golgotha, which Peter so often rebuked Jesus for talking about as they were nearing

Jerusalem. Peter was ready for action: a coronation or a revolution, but not Jesus's crucifixion. True to character, Peter protested, "'You shall never wash my feet.' Jesus answered him, 'If I do not wash you, you have no share with me'" (v. 8).

Not only once upon a time, on a hill far away, but each week the Son of God comes to serve us. We may protest. We may think that it is we who need to serve God rather than vice versa. Nevertheless, Jesus tells us as he told Peter that this is actually an insult, a form of pride. We are the ones who need to be bathed, clothed, and fed, not God.

And now Jesus serves us through each other, and especially through the officers he calls through the church. Both leaders and parishioners need to be reminded that this public ministry of pastors and teachers is not an authoritarian obstacle to the gifted work of the whole body but the gift from the ascended Christ that prepares the saints to live together in love and to live out their callings in the world (Eph. 4:8–15). Ministers deliver Christ through their ministry of the Word, not only in well-prepared sermons but throughout the service. In fact, the main purpose of singing in church is not to express our inner experience, piety, and zeal but to serve each other by making "the word of Christ dwell in you richly, teaching and admonishing one another in all wisdom, singing psalms and hymns and spiritual songs, with thankfulness in your hearts to God" (Col. 3:16). We hear the Word, sing the Word, and meditate on it in the fellowship of saints. We teach this Word daily to our children in family instruction and as we live out our confidence in Christ before our children. All of this is so vital because to trust in Christ alone is to swim against the stream of human nature.

Pastors and teachers are not cruise directors who provide venues for everyone to channel all of their gifts and energies to the church, but they are deliverers of the message of Christ. "Him we proclaim," writes Paul, "warning everyone and teaching everyone with all wisdom, that we may present everyone mature in Christ. For this I toil, struggling with all the energy that he powerfully works within me" (Col. 1:28–29).

If people are withering on the vine with perpetual exhortations without Good News, praise without being reminded what they are praising God for, calls to active imitation of Christ before they are first of all called to receive Christ and his good gifts, then it is no surprise that they lack godly motivation for loving and serving their neighbor in the world. And if they are not being regularly immersed in the teaching of the Scriptures, should we be surprised that our witness to Christ among our neighbors is shallow, confused, and confusing? Those who are richly fed at the Lord's banquet will want to (and be prepared to) feed others with the daily bread of their ordinary secular vocations and the Bread of Life in their witness to Christ. However, self-feeders will always burn out eventually—if they don't wander off into strange paths first. Before they feed others, they must be fed; before they serve, they must be served—and not just once but every week.

The church is not the gospel. Whether packaged in *high church* forms (with the church as an institutional place) or *low church* versions (the church as transformed individuals), the idea is rife among us today that the church is engaged in a *redemptive* mission, extending Christ's saving life and mission in the world. But if we are ever to get the focus off us and back onto Christ (much less, to properly interpret Scripture), we will have to stop giving ourselves so much credit. We do not redeem; we were redeemed. The incarnation (God the Son becoming flesh) is not a prototype for us and our incarnational living and ministry in the world; it is a unique event of a unique person, of which we have been made *witnesses* rather than *co-agents*. Neither as a sum total of *born-again* Christians nor as a historical institution with a postal address is the church the savior; it is always

the sinful body that is saved. The church does not testify to its
own holiness or zeal but to Christ, who "justifies the ungodly"
(Rom. 4:5).

Nevertheless, as an institution founded by Christ, who gave it
the gifts of preachers, teachers, elders, and deacons, the church is
indeed our mother throughout our pilgrimage. Far from setting
the church against individual experience of Christ, confessional
Protestantism has recognized that all of our experience with
Christ is communal, historical, and mediated through ordinary
creaturely agency. Echoing the church father Cyprian, Calvin
says, "Whoever has God for his Father has the church for his
mother." Enthusiasm (God-within-ism) opposes the inner witness of the Spirit to the outward ministry. Yet it is a "singular
privilege," Calvin writes, that God has condescended "to con-
secrate to himself the mouths and tongues" of sinners so that
"his own voice may resound in them."

> For although God's power is not bound to outward means, he
> has nonetheless bound us to this ordinary manner of teaching.
> Fanatics, refusing to hold fast to it, entangle themselves in many
> deadly snares. Many are led either by pride, dislike, or rivalry to
> the conviction that they can profit enough from private reading
> and meditation; hence they despise public assemblies and deem
> preaching superfluous. But . . . no one escapes the just penalty of
> this unholy separation without bewitching himself with pestilent
> errors and foulest delusions.[45]

Miroslav Volf points out that the Separatist leader John Smyth
counseled that those who are "born again . . . should no longer
need means of grace" since the persons of the Godhead "are
better than all scriptures, or creatures whatsoever." By contrast,
as Volf notes, the Reformers strongly affirmed God's saving
activity through creaturely means—even to the point of calling
the church the mother of the faithful.[46]

Enthusiasm has taken all sorts of forms in the modern age: from the sophisticated rationalism of the Enlightenment to the anti-intellectual emotionalism of the American frontier. The effect of pietism (especially culminating in the Second Great Awakening), as William McLoughlin observes, was to shift the emphasis away from "collective belief, adherence to creedal standards and proper observance of traditional forms, to the emphasis on individual religious experience."[47] If the Enlightenment shifted "the ultimate authority in religion" from the church to "the mind of the individual," pietism and romanticism located ultimate authority in the *experience* of the individual.[48] All of this suggests that for some time now evangelicalism has been as much the facilitator as the victim of modern secularism.

It is interesting that in the Willow Creek study cited earlier, the analogy of church-as-parent was actually employed to suggest that when believers reach maturity they find the church less important. This is a far cry from the New Testament picture of regularly meeting for preaching, teaching, sacrament, fellowship, and prayers.

Growing up, in this conception, is a never-ending process in this life. We grow up *into* Christ and his body. To grow *out of* the church is to lose our connection with its Head (Eph. 4:12–15). Our faith is never strong enough, our hope is never bright enough, and our love is never warm enough for us to become self-feeders. The mature do not find the church less important, for they know that the source of their faith and maturity is always the ministry of Christ through his ambassadors. As a faithful parent, the church will never make its children fend for themselves, tossed back and forth with every wind of doctrine, but will lead Christ's flock throughout their earthly pilgrimage.

The Call to Discipleship: Is There Anything for Us to Do?

The ministry of the church is God's service to us through pastors, teachers, elders, and deacons, which generates a thankful community of genuine gift giving that overflows to the world. The kingdom of God is something we are *receiving*, not something we are *building* (Heb. 12:28). The Lord of the church did not say, "Build my church"; he said that on the "rock" of the confession that Jesus is the Christ, "I will build my church, and the gates of hell will not prevail against it" (Matt. 16:18).

In his Great Commission, the risen Christ did not say, "I'm leaving now, but you will take my place and extend my redeeming work by following my example." Rather, he said, "All authority in heaven and on earth has been given to *me. Go therefore* and make *disciples* of all nations, *baptizing* them in the name of the Father and of the Son and of the Holy Spirit, *teaching* them to observe *all* that I have commanded you. *And behold, I am with you always, to the end of the age*" (Matt. 28:18–20; emphasis added). The indicative comes first and gives rise to the imperative—and even then, God always concludes with another indicative! The gospel goes behind us, before us, and ahead of us.

The church is first of all created by the gospel and then led back into the world as justified and renewed people to love and serve their neighbors and offer witness to Jesus Christ. Therefore the church is both a *place* where God acts in judgment and grace and a *people* who are judged and justified, living out their callings in the world.[49] It is both a historical *organization*, founded by Christ, where Christ gives himself to sinners in baptism, preaching, and the Lord's Supper, and a spiritual *organism* that is united through faith to its living Head. This means the gospel has priority over all human action, and any particular church is only truly a church if Christ is ruling it by his Word and Spirit.

Nevertheless, the Emergent Church movement has reminded us that there is a serious call to discipleship in the New Testament. Its leaders are right to challenge the consumeristic individualism of a lot of contemporary evangelicalism. Yet can this noble goal be attained by offering various stations in the worship space for individuals to experience their own private religious experience? One person finds an icon attractive, while another chooses a labyrinth, and still another elects to sit and listen to some teaching, while a friend breaks away to take communion. How does this reflect *community* more fully than a whole congregation of young and old, rich and poor, well-educated professionals and high school drop-outs being called away from their choices to be seated at a common Table, receiving common gifts, through common means?

Jesus had disciples, which means *students*. Of course a student in first-century Israel was different from a student in a university today. A teacher (rabbi) drew followers who met regularly for instruction and personal fellowship. Unlike the distant professor today who lectures and leaves the class (as pastors too often do), such teachers spent time with pupils so they could not only be informed but be formed by the wisdom and example of the rabbi. I've always been impressed that when Luther was appalled by the ignorance among the common people even of the Apostles' Creed, the Ten Commandments, and the Lord's Prayer, he did not pass them off to underlings but wrote and personally taught the children the catechism during the week. This expectation of the pastor as the main *catechist* was picked up by Calvin and other Reformers—and it connected the youth to the community that they were a part of and growing up into. By contrast, today people are clamoring for spiritual directors, coaches, and mentors as if they were orphans rather than heirs of the covenant. If as pastors, teachers, and elders we fulfilled our ministry more faithfully, this understandable craving for guidance in the Christian life would be satisfied by the ordinary ministry of the church.

Philosopher of science Michael Polanyi has explained how the physical sciences have progressed in a similar fashion. Though it is less a matter of accumulating data than learning a craft, successful scientists submit themselves to the authority of their seniors. Becoming a good scientist has always been a lot like becoming a good violinist or a good winemaker. You have to spend time *learning the ropes*. In our age that values efficiency and volume over maturity and quality, we would rather have an expert write down the rules of *how to play the violin* or *how to make wine* in four easy steps. What we need, however, are practices that value long-term commitments to a craft.

Christian discipleship is a lifelong process of being built up into "the body of Christ, until we all attain to the unity of the faith and of the knowledge of the Son of God," through the gift of pastors and teachers (Eph. 4:11–13; see also vv. 14–16). This ministry shapes parents and family friends, grandparents and Little League coaches to be servants of the Word to children as they are growing up in the church. We are also called to "grow in the grace and knowledge of our Lord and Savior Jesus Christ," so that we do not "lose [our] own stability" (2 Peter 3:17–18). The *gift* necessary for ministry, says Paul, was given by God but recognized and confirmed by the church through examination and ordination (2 Cor. 5:18; 2 Tim. 2:14–25; 4:1–5; Titus 1:5–2:2; cf. Acts 6:4–6). An authorized gospel comes with an authorized ministry. It is ministers of God's Word—not people who like to carve out their own niches, share their own experiences, and determine their own emphases—whom God qualifies by training, testing, and approving and who bring us God's gifts in his name. Our goal is not to leave our own legacy but to dole out Christ's inheritance.

If the church is God's creation, the result of his electing, redeeming, and renewing grace, then why should we allow the demographics of our culture of marketing undermine its catholicity or unity in Christ?

A Call to the Resistance

Winding up his lecture tour in the United States before returning to Nazi Germany, where he would eventually be sent to a concentration camp and executed, Dietrich Bonhoeffer summarizes American religion as "Protestantism without the Reformation." Although the influence of the Reformation in American's religious history has been profound (especially prior to the mid-nineteenth century) and remains a counter-weight to the dominance of the revivalist heritage, Bonhoeffer's diagnosis seems justified:

> God has granted American Christianity no Reformation. He has given it strong revivalist preachers, churchmen and theologians, but no Reformation of the church of Jesus Christ by the Word of God. . . . American theology and the American church as a whole have never been able to understand the meaning of "criticism" by the Word of God and all that signifies. Right to the last they do

not understand that God's "criticism" touches even religion, the Christianity of the church and the sanctification of Christians, and that God has founded his church beyond religion and beyond ethics. . . . In American theology, Christianity is still essentially religion and ethics. . . . Because of this the person and work of Christ must, for theology, sink into the background and in the long run remain misunderstood, because it is not recognized as the sole ground of radical judgment and radical forgiveness.[1]

Time and again the church has proved a willing accomplice to its own captivity, in the new covenant as well as the old. Observing this tendency in his day, Martin Luther wrote *On the Babylonian Captivity of the Church*, in which he argues that the church desperately needs to be liberated by its Lord from bondage to the very things it regards as benign or even hopeful.

Is the word *captivity* too strong? After all, there is nothing like an Office of Religious Affairs controlling the church's discourse in America. In his book *Amusing Ourselves to Death*, Jewish writer Neil Postman (a communications professor at New York University) points out the difference between two apocalyptic scenarios. George Orwell's *1984* predicts a society ruled by "Big Brother"—a totalitarian regime. Congratulating ourselves on having dodged Orwell's prophecy, at least in America, we have forgotten Aldous Huxley's slightly older *Brave New World*, with a quite different scenario. While Orwell predicts an externally imposed oppression, Huxley imagines a self-imposed captivity:

As he saw it, people will come to love their oppression, to adore the technologies that undo their capacities to think. What Orwell feared were those who would ban books. What Huxley feared was that there would be no reason to ban a book, for there would be no one who wanted to read one. Orwell feared those who would deprive us of information. Huxley feared those who would give us so much that we would be reduced to passivity and egoism. Orwell feared that the truth would be concealed from us. Huxley feared the truth would be drowned in a sea of irrelevance. Orwell feared we would become a captive culture. Huxley feared we would become a trivial culture, preoccupied with some equivalent of the feelies, the orgy porgy, and the centrifugal bumblepuppy.[2]

If we are slaves, it is not to an external oppressor but to our own trivial desires. We are willing captives—until God appears on the scene and utters his solemn command to the powers and principalities we have enthroned: "Let my people go!"

A Discourse of Resistance

A *discourse of resistance* is called for in these circumstances, but we have to be careful on this score. There is, of course, an anti-modernist spirit whose strategy of resistance is as dangerous as it is simplistic. The enemy is easily identified: secular humanism, public schools, Democrats, liberals, and gays; or on the other side of the aisle, fundamentalism, Christian schools, Republicans, conservatives, and patriarchalists. And since culture—our shared public life—is reduced to the spectacle of politics, the only way to resist is to win the culture wars.

The discourse of resistance I am suggesting, however, concerns the recovery of Christian faith and practice within the church itself. It begins by challenging not only weak views of God, sin, and grace but the plausibility structures, paradigms, or world-views that make biblical views increasingly incomprehensible even for most Christian laypeople and pastors. In the Christian discourse of resistance, God is the speaker. It is time to start listening to God's voice in Scripture again, taking our covenant Lord more seriously than we do ourselves and the wider secular audience that needs to be saved from its *self-talk*.

It may just be that the most relevant strategy, especially in our context, is to highlight rather than downplay those points at which God's truth challenges our own half-truths and lies. "In a culture where religion is functional both socially and psychologically," sociologist Peter Berger argues, "Christian preaching itself ought to call people to a confrontation with the God who stands against the needs of society and against the aspirations of the human heart."[3]

Like the gospel itself, this strategy seems counterintuitive—especially after being thoroughly indoctrinated in strategies of compromise masquerading as mission. No more *translating* the gospel! The gospel is an offense at precisely the same points and for the same reasons as always. Efforts to translate the gospel into contemporary language actually aim at making the gospel not only more understandable but more believable. The problem is that the gospel is so counterintuitive to our fallen pride that it cannot be believed apart from a miracle of divine grace. And because it is through the gospel itself that the Spirit accomplishes this feat, we remove the one possibility for genuine conversion that we have in our arsenal. Lost in translation is the gospel itself—and therefore the only hope of genuine transformation as well as forgiveness.

We need to recover that sense so pervasive in other periods: namely, that even Christians do not know what they really need or even want and that attending to their immediate felt needs may muffle the only proclamation that can actually satisfy real needs. Berger judges that "the more general personal consequence of the abandonment of theological criteria for the Christian life is the cult of experience. . . . Emotional pragmatism now takes the place of the honest confrontation with the Christian message."[4] But this means that people remain hopelessly trapped within their own inner psyche and resources, suppressing the truth about themselves that might drive them to Christ. No longer objectively guilty before a holy God, they only feel a sense of guilt or shame that they deny by changing the subject to something lighter and more upbeat. No longer saved from damnation—which is the source of their deepest sense of anxiety—they are now saved from unpleasantness.

We are the walking dead, forgetful that our designer-label fashions of religion and morality are really a death shroud. To paraphrase Jesus, we go through life like corpses with lipstick, not even aware that all of our makeovers and self-improvement are just cosmetic (Matt. 23:25–28).

Our fig leaves may have become more sophisticated (and expensive), but they are no more successful in covering our nakedness in God's presence than the homespun wardrobe of our first parents. Not only our sins but "all our righteous acts are like filthy rags" (Isa. 64:6 NIV). Isaiah 59 records the court trial: Yahweh versus Israel. Although the people have complained that so many calamities have unjustly fallen upon them, the prophet as God's attorney exposes the ones bringing the complaint as perpetrators rather than victims: "Their cobwebs are useless for clothing; they cannot cover themselves with what they make. Their deeds are evil deeds, and the acts of violence are in their hands" (v. 6 NIV). Only after the evidence is brought forward do the people confess their sin and recognize that they have brought God's judgment upon themselves (vv. 9–15). In this situation, the Judge, seeing "that there was no one to intervene," takes it upon himself to don the garments of battle and win the salvation of his people at his own expense. "'The Redeemer will come to Zion, to those in Jacob who repent of their sins,' declares the LORD" (vv. 16, 20). The church has not only allowed us to change the subject; it has changed the subject for us.

It is the false prophets who "dress the wound of my people as though it were not serious. 'Peace, peace,' they say, when there is no peace" (Jer. 8:11 NIV). "They fill you with false hopes," he adds. "They speak visions from their own minds, not from the mouth of the LORD. They keep saying to those who despise me, 'The LORD says: You will have peace'" (Jer. 23:16–17 NIV). It is not compassion for the people or zeal for God's house but their own thirst for popularity that renders the false prophets constitutionally incapable of telling the truth about the crisis.

Enclosed in our own narrow world of personal *spin*, we are never introduced to the real world created by God's Word. Instead of something new and surprising that might actually bring genuine transformation at our roots, we hear only more of the background Muzak that softly affirms the status quo. Instead of being brought to the end of our rope so that we will let go of all other securities and fall into the merciful arms of God, we are encouraged to have another go at saving ourselves (however defined) with God's help. Both sin and redemption are trivialized when we write the script.

In his messages to the churches in Revelation 3, Christ addresses the church of Laodicea. Unlike the churches of Pergamos and Thyatira, this church is not a haven of heresy and immorality; nor is it dead, like the church of Sardis. More like the Ephesian church, the Laodiceans have lost their first love, Christ, and so have become *lukewarm*—neither hot nor cold and therefore good for neither warmth nor refreshment.

> Because you say, "I am rich, have become wealthy, and have need of nothing"—and do not know that you are wretched, miserable, poor, blind, and naked—I counsel you to buy from Me gold refined in the fire, that you may be rich; and white garments, that you may be clothed, that the shame of your nakedness may not be revealed; and anoint your eyes with salve, that you may see. As many as I love, I rebuke and chasten.
>
> Revelation 3:17–19 NKJV

A church that is deeply aware of its misery and nakedness before a holy God will cling tenaciously to an all-sufficient Savior, while one that is self-confident and relatively unaware of its inherent sinfulness will reach for religion and morality whenever it seems convenient.

The Pharisees thought that if they could just get everyone to follow the correct rules, they could usher in the messianic kingdom. Yet when the Messiah himself actually appeared, they were confronted with their own unrighteousness and helplessness. Christ came not to help good people become better but "to seek and to save that which was lost" (Luke 19:10 NKJV). If this is a crushing blow to our pride, it is also the most hopeful and marvelous news we could hear. Salvation is not something to achieve ("seeking to establish their own righteousness") but something to receive: "the righteousness of God" through faith in Christ (Rom. 10:3 NKJV; see vv. 1–4). Although Paul brought apostolic discipline to bear on the immorality, division, and immaturity of the Corinthian believers, he did not question their status as a church, as he did the Galatian church for verging on a denial of the gospel.

Confident in ourselves, we will naturally incline toward moralism, asking Jesus, along with the rich young ruler, "What is the one thing that I must do in order to inherit eternal life?" And until we are, like that ruler, faced with the real intention of the law, we will naturally assume with him, "All this I have done since my youth" (see Luke 18:18–21). We do not naturally assume that we are wretched, poor, blind, and naked. We do not like being brought to the end of our rope any more than that rich young ruler did. Even the disciples asked, "'Who then can be saved?' But Jesus looked at them and said, 'With man this is impossible, but with God all things are possible'" (vv. 25–26).

Secularism cannot be blamed on the secularists, many of whom were raised in the church. We are the problem. If most churchgoers cannot tell us anything specific about the God they consider meaningful or explain basic doctrines of creation in God's image, original sin, the atonement, justification, sanctification, the means of grace, or the hope of glory, then the blame can hardly be placed at the feet of secular humanists. If, for example, privatization entails "the transfer of truth claims from the objective world to the subjectivity of the individual,"[5] then American Protestants have not only adapted to a secular culture but are part of a revivalistic heritage that helped to create it.

All that is necessary for us to become unwitting Pelagians is less preaching and teaching of the law and the gospel—downplaying the means of grace (Word and sacrament) in favor of our means of transforming ourselves and our world. Since self-trust is our default setting, we can never assume that we really *get* the gospel and can now move on to our own works. Even when we talk about our obligations to God and neighbor, it must be grounded first of all in the gospel of salvation by grace apart from works. So when the church loses its interest in doctrine (a word that simply means "teaching"), it is no surprise that we will drift back to our most familiar religious and moral assumptions.

If pietism emphasized the importance of deeds over creeds, liberalism finally dispensed with the latter altogether. Like Barth, J. Gresham Machen had been awakened from the spell of their teacher, Wilhelm Herrmann. He speaks of a "pragmatist skepticism, this optimistic religion of a self-sufficient humanity," which has taken the place in Protestantism of "the redemptive religion hitherto known as Christianity."[6] He adds,

> These questions take us into the very heart of the situation; the growth of ignorance in the Church, the growth of indifference with regard to the simple facts recorded in the Bible, all goes back to a great spiritual movement, really skeptical in its tendency, which has been going forward during the last one hundred years—a movement which appears not only in philosophers and

theologians such as Kant and Schleiermacher and Ritschl, but also in a widespread attitude of plain men and women throughout the world. The depreciation of the intellect, with the exaltation of the feelings or of the will, is, we think, a basic fact in modern life, which is rapidly leading to a condition in which men neither know anything nor care anything about the doctrinal content of the Christian religion, and in which there is in general a lamentable intellectual decline.[7]

Americans, as we have already seen, have a fairly pronounced anti-intellectual streak. We are doers, not believers; pragmatists, not thinkers. Impatient with tedious study and reflection, we would rather be overcoming obstacles, conquering nature, and putting it to use more than understanding and enjoying it.

Yet if moralism—self-help salvation—is our default setting, we need to be regularly preached and taught out of it. Baptism, communion, and preaching all call us out of ourselves and our self-trust and guide us to cling to Christ in faith and to serve our neighbors in love. Machen points out that "the Christian movement at its inception was not just a way of life in the modern sense, but a way of life founded upon a message. It was based, not on a mere program of work, but upon an account of facts. In other words, it was based upon doctrine."[8]

When we examine the ecumenical creeds and the confessions and catechisms of the Reformation traditions, one thing is clear: Christ is central, the Alpha and Omega of faith and practice. Teaching the faith to each generation through such standards, however, has become increasingly suspect of *formalism* and *intellectualism* in a culture that prizes autonomy and self-referential expression. Ann Douglas observes, "Nothing could show better the late nineteenth-century Protestant Church's altered identity as an eager participant in the emerging consumer society than its obsession with popularity and its increasing disregard of intellectual issues."[9] Across our entire cultural landscape, the only law left seems to be "keep it light." If we expect to reach the unchurched (in other words, sell our product to a wider market), we will have to get rid of everything with rough edges, everything that offends and puts people off.

As much as I would like to imagine otherwise, I am my most familiar and enjoyable topic, and my personal well-being is my most pressing felt need. I would like to come to church primarily to talk about my felt needs and express my pious experience. And as a preacher with an entrepreneurial streak, it would be a lot easier for me to create my own ministry paradigm than sit in a study preparing a meal for the sheep from Holy Writ. It would be a lot easier if I could just share my experience and some of the life principles that have worked in my life and family with a few verses thrown in. Shifting the focus to God and the story of his unyielding faithfulness to save me despite myself, inserting me into the wider story of his covenant people, will always make me bristle. Because of my natural tendency to turn inward, it requires a lot of patience and work to understand much less accept this script. If I am ever going to say *amen* to God's story, and be ushered into it, nothing short of a miracle will be necessary. Only the Spirit, rescripting me according to the gospel, can accomplish this feat.

Coming to God as consumers saved by following the instructions on the product label rather than as sinners saved by grace is not only the essence of human sin, it does not even deliver on its promise of liberation. Instead it drives us deeper into ourselves, into the solitary confinement of the convictions, longings, felt needs, experiences, and assumptions that we already have. It keeps us from ever being disrupted by someone greater than ourselves or by something more wonderful than our own half-hearted achievements.

I think of that marvelous scene in *Babette's Feast* when the bleak huddle of Pietist villagers is treated to a meal that is beyond their wildest dreams. At first fearful of indulging, they become delighted and grateful companions in an exchange of joy. If the world does not know how to mourn or dance properly, our only truly loving course of action is to perform in front of it, to preach and practice what it means to be sinners who are justified. We and our churches need to recover the fundamental presupposition that God cares for us too much to leave us to ourselves or to affirm us in our ignorance, lies, spin, and casual acceptance of the world's interpretation of reality. In his fourth volume of *Church Dogmatics*, Karl Barth brilliantly observes that sloth is as much the heart of sin as pride. We do not have to be heretics to be unfaithful; we can be too lazy to swim against the tide. As C. S. Lewis puts it memorably, "We are like an ignorant child who wants to go on making mud pies in a slum because he cannot imagine what is meant by the offer of a holiday at the sea."[10]

When our churches assume the gospel, reduce it to slogans, or confuse it with moralism and hype, it is not surprising that the type of spirituality we fall back on is moralistic, therapeutic deism. In a therapeutic worldview, the self is always sovereign. Accommodating this false religion is not love—either of God or neighbor—but sloth, depriving human beings of genuine liberation and depriving God of the glory that is his due. The self must be dethroned. That's the only way out.

A Politics of Resistance

This passing age has its power regimes, generated by its own words and sacraments. Through its constant bombardment of advertising, marketing, politics, and entertainment—swirling together in the whirl of Vanity Fair—its discourse of accommodation aims at making us passive consumers of its parodies of abundant life. With its sacraments of virtual reality and rituals

247

of instant gratification, this age of sin and death seduces us into thinking that this is the *real world*.

So where did we ever get the idea that the best way to ensure the relevance of Christian faith and practice is to accommodate in this present age the discourse and practices of the age to come? How could we ever have imagined that the best way to win the world to Christ is to surrender the only legitimate tools that God has given for the breakthrough of Christ's kingdom in the very heart of this world's history of vanity?

This present evil age has not only its discourse of accommodation but also its politics of accommodation. Combined, they are powerful—but not powerful enough. Not only the message but the gospel's method of delivery itself is *Good News*. God did not merely speak about the incarnation. Still less did God speak of the incarnation as a general principle for anything and everything that God does in the world. No, God actually became flesh, fulfilled all righteousness, conquered sin and death, and in his resurrection inaugurated the new creation as the firstfruits of the entire harvest. A new power regime is afoot in this passing age: the power of life over death, justification over condemnation, righteousness over the dominion of sin. *God's politics* is his work: the cross and the resurrection—and the confident expectation of Christ's return in glory to make all things new.

And now, as we are reminded in Ephesians 4:8–16, the ascended King moves his gifts of this subversive revolution down to us; we do not have to climb up to him. Here the apostle Paul teaches that the same one who descended to the uttermost depths for us and ascended "far above all the heavens, that he might fill all things" (v. 10), does not keep the treasures of his conquest to himself but liberally distributes them to his liberated captives below. The original Greek emphasizes, "The gifts that *he himself* gave. . . ." They originate with Christ, not with individual members or the body as a whole. The gifts he gives are apostles, prophets, evangelists, pastors, and teachers (v. 11). They are not given as a hierarchy of control, like "the rulers of the Gentiles" who "lord it over" their subjects instead of serving (Matt. 20:25; see vv. 25–28). Rather, Paul says they are given

> for the perfecting of the saints, for the work of the ministry, for the edifying of the body of Christ: Till we all come in the unity of the faith, and of the knowledge of the Son of God, unto a perfect man, unto the measure of the stature of the fulness of Christ: That we henceforth be no more children, tossed to and fro, and carried about with every wind of doctrine, . . . but speaking the truth in love, may grow up into him in all things, which is the head, even Christ.
>
> Ephesians 4:12–15 KJV

More recent translations typically render the clause in verse 12, "to equip the saints for the work of ministry" (e.g., ESV, NRSV, RSV), which has been used as the chief proof-text for *every member ministry*. For various reasons, I am persuaded that the older translations (especially of verse 12) are more accurate and also capture better the logic of the argument.[11]

This does not mean, of course, that the official ministry of the Word (now exercised by pastors and teachers) is the only gift or that ministers rank higher in the kingdom of Christ than everyone else. Rather, this *gift* of the ministry of the Word is given so that the whole body may be *gifted*: brought together in the unity of the faith and of the knowledge of the Son of God. Only then can each member receive the additional gifts that make them function together as one mature body with Christ as its living Head (Eph. 4:15–16). The gifts flow down from Christ; the Great Shepherd serves his flock through undershepherds who minister his gospel through preaching and sacrament.

Of course in other places Paul expands the list of gifts that are exercised by the wider body (see Rom. 12:3–8; 1 Cor. 12). A church that is lacking in generosity, hospitality, and other gifts of mutual edification is unhealthy; a church that lacks the Word is not a church. Therefore we come to church first of all to receive these gifts, realizing more and more our communion with Christ and therefore with each other as his body.

Think of this in terms of a lavish dinner where gifts are exchanged. First, we are guests, enjoying the meal that has been generously provided by the host (Christ) through his servers (ministers). Then grateful guests become active participants in the exchange of gifts. Having received much, they give much, and the mutual giving and receiving of gifts continues throughout the week as believers care for each other in all sorts of informal ways and then share these gifts with their unbelieving neighbors in their secular callings. We can reverse this flow of gifts not only by turning the gospel message itself into exhortations to climb ladders of experience and moral activism but by turning the means of grace into means of works, pre-empting God's gracious service to us by focusing almost exclusively on *our* service.

I have already underscored the ways our message has been transformed from good news to good advice. The effects of confusing law and gospel in *content* has wide-ranging effects in church *practice* as well. If the message is *deeds, not creeds*, focusing on "What Would Jesus Do?" while assuming that everybody already knows what Jesus has done (and is doing and will do), it only stands to reason that the flow of gifts from Christ to us will be reversed in the way we live out our personal and corporate life as God's people.

Christ has not only appointed the message but the methods that he deems consistent with that gospel. Paul says our salvation "depends not on human will or exertion, but on God, who has mercy" (Rom. 9:16). If our salvation is due entirely to God's electing, redeeming, regenerating, sanctifying, and preserving grace, then the methods that he has chosen to deliver Christ and all of his benefits will be means of grace (God serving us) rather than means of works (our serving God). Once again, this is not to exclude works or our service; it is to say that only when we are saved and served by God can we be instruments through whom God brings his saving news and loving service to others.

Combining the Pelagian emphasis on self-salvation with the Gnostic emphasis on inner experience and enlightenment over the external ministry of preaching, sacrament, and discipline, much of contemporary practice across the ecclesiastical spectrum seems to assume that mission is one thing and the marks of the church (preaching and sacrament) are another. If the message of a lot of preaching has already shifted from God and his work to us and our activity, it is no wonder that many today finally wonder why preaching is even necessary in the public service. Being *missional* often seems not only to mean the appropriate pursuit of methods of informal witness and service in addition to the official gathering of the covenant people but also to dispense with all formal elements of the public service itself. Again, this is nothing new or especially *postmodern*. Those of us raised in conservative evangelicalism are familiar with the contrast often made between *getting saved* and *joining a church*, as if evangelism could be separated from baptism and discipleship and as if union with Christ could be separated from union with his visible body.

But no such dichotomy is found in the book of Acts, where we read, "The Lord added to the church daily those who were being saved" (Acts 2:47 NKJV). Those converts were immediately baptized and incorporated into the ordinary life of the church's public gathering, where "they devoted themselves to the apostles' teaching and fellowship, to the breaking of the bread and the prayers" (Acts 2:42). In fact, repeated throughout the book of Acts is the expression: "The Word of God spread." Therefore, the mission and marks of the church were never separated. Based on this history of the apostolic witness, the church is successful in its mission to the extent that it proclaims Christ, baptizes, teaches, gathers around the Lord's Table, and is then scattered out into the world as his witnesses.

Because believers remain saint and sinner simultaneously, they never outgrow their need to be fed by the gospel through these divinely instituted means of grace. Not only at their conversion but throughout their pilgrimage the gospel alone is "the power of God for salvation" (Rom. 1:16). If Christ is clearly proclaimed each Lord's Day from Genesis to Revelation, believers will be strengthened in faith and good works and unbelievers will be exposed to his regenerating Word.

If baptism and the Lord's Supper are ordinary events in the public service instead of being shunted aside to weekday services to avoid alienating the unchurched with unfamiliar rites, not only will believers be regularly renewed in Christ but unbelieving visitors will witness the bath and banquet to which they too are invited. By encountering this divine visitation among his people, they may be brought to conviction of sin and faith in Christ and be led by members to the elders, where they make their profession of faith, are baptized and instructed, and then join the fellowship of saints in communion. Outsiders become insiders through the Word and Spirit. Not by eliminating the strangeness that makes them outsiders, but by prayerfully anticipating God's powerful work through the strange message and methods he has appointed, we see the mission succeed through the marks of preaching and sacrament.

Furthermore, in the name of mission we seem to be unchurching the churched (substantiated by studies revealing that over half of those raised in evangelical churches become unchurched by their sophomore year in college). So the discipline of the church through its officers is essential to genuine mission. Pastors preach, teach, and administer the sacraments; elders care for the flock's spiritual needs, including correction of faith and practice; deacons distribute the collective material gifts of the body to those with temporal needs. Churches that bear these marks and endeavor to grow in their faithfulness to them *are* missional.

At no point in our pilgrimage do any Christians mature beyond this ministry so that they can become *self-feeders*. Christ does not deliver us from one tyrant only to leave us weak and isolated prey to weather, wolves, and our own wanderings. "Obey your leaders and submit to them," Scripture exhorts, "for they are keeping watch over your souls, as those who will have to give an account. Let them do this with joy and not with groaning, for that would be of no advantage to you" (Heb. 13:17). Even our submission to the elders, then, is grounded in God's loving service to and care for us. "Let us hold fast the confession of our hope without wavering, for he who promised is faithful. And let us consider how to stir up one another to love and good works, not neglecting to meet together, as is the habit of some, but encouraging one another, and all the more as you see the Day drawing near" (Heb. 10:23–25).

The Word Spread: A Missional Church

Not only is the ministry of Christ by his Spirit through Word and sacrament sufficient for building up the body of Christ, it is sufficient for our mission to the world. The same means appointed by our ascended King for making lifelong believers recipients of the kingdom works in ever-widening circles to draw in those who are far off.

After warning Timothy of the self-centered orientation of the *last days*, Paul's charge is neither to conform the gospel to the felt needs of his hearers nor to substitute deeds for creeds.

Rather, it is to "preach the word; be ready in season and out of season"—that is, when it is popular and when it's not.

> Reprove, rebuke, and exhort, with complete patience and teaching. For the time is coming when people will not endure sound teaching, but having itching ears they will accumulate for themselves teachers to suit their own passions, and will turn away from listening to the truth and wander off into myths. As for you, always be sober-minded, endure suffering, do the work of an evangelist, fulfill your ministry.
>
> 2 Timothy 4:2–5

The answer to narcissism is not more talk about us, but bringing God's Word to the world.

If the focus of our testimony is our changed life, we as well as our hearers are bound to be disappointed. Certainly the apostles could have told us more about themselves and their changed lives: Peter the fisherman, to Peter the rock, to Peter the denier of Christ, to Peter the apostle; Saul the persecutor of the church, to Paul the apostle, and so forth. Yet aside from these personal details, we know relatively little. We aren't even sure what Paul had in mind when he spoke about his "thorn in the flesh" (2 Cor. 12:7 NASB). What we are sure of is the fact that the apostles knew they too needed the gospel—Christ's personal absolution—throughout the dusty road filled with doubts, fears, suffering, and moral failure.

The apostles were too overwhelmed by Jesus Christ and the events that had taken place in history to be preoccupied with focusing on their own spiritual autobiographies. They knew that it was their testimony to *Christ's* life, death, and resurrection that had the power to convert people from death to life. Without in any way denying their inward transformation or experience, even this was the result of the gospel. It was not by following a formula of steps that they were born again but "through the living and abiding word of God. . . . And this word is the good news that was preached to you" (1 Peter 1:23, 25). Their testimony was to Christ, not to themselves.

Throughout the book of Acts, even at a time when all Christians can agree that there were living apostles and an extraordinary ministry of signs and wonders, the success of the church's mission was consistently attributed to the fact that "many of those who had heard the word believed" (Acts 4:4) and "the word of God continued to spread" (Acts 6:7 NRSV). The church "was built up" in the word and "increased in numbers," and "the word of God continued to advance and gain adherents. . . . As many as had been destined for eternal life became believers. Thus the word of the Lord spread throughout the region" (Acts 9:31; 12:24; 13:48–49 NRSV). The mission and the marks—conversion and the official ministry—went together:

> When they had preached the gospel to that city and had made many disciples, they returned to Lystra and to Iconium and to Antioch, strengthening the souls of the disciples, encouraging them to continue in the faith, and saying that through many tribulations we must enter the kingdom of God. And when they had appointed elders for them in every church, with prayer and fasting they committed them to the Lord in whom they had believed. . . . So the churches were strengthened in the faith and increased in numbers daily. . . . [Paul argued] in the marketplace every day with those who happened to be there. . . .
>
> Acts 14:21–23; 16:5; 17:17

> Many of the Corinthians who heard Paul became believers and were baptized. . . . This continued for two years, so that all the residents of Asia . . . heard the word of the Lord. . . . So the word of the Lord grew mightily and prevailed.
>
> Acts 18:8; 19:10, 20

God creates worlds by speaking. God's Word is never dead, waiting to be supplemented by (or made subordinate to) our own moral activity. Rather, it is "living and active" (Heb. 4:12), always accomplishing its intended mission (Isa. 55:11). In fact, Christianity is a missionary faith precisely because it is a doctrine, an announcement heralded by ambassadors.

God knows what he is doing. Neither the message nor the methods of delivery are our creation. If Christ is not the King of the church, then before long he also will not be its Prophet or Priest. We need to look to him to define not only the church's message but also its nature, mission, and methods with which it is delivered. While revivalism from Finney to the contemporary church growth movement has located *new measures* in pragmatic techniques, a new generation—understandably thirsting for a more transcendent orientation—looks for new means of grace in more mystical practices.[12] Once you get hooked on your own means of ascent, you'll always be looking for a new drug.

Churches that focus only on the nurture of their members, without a passion for reaching outsiders, unfaithfully narrow the mission entrusted to them. Yet churches that focus primarily on the unchurched often forget Christ's command to Peter: "Feed my sheep" (John 21:17). The proper balance is found in Peter's Pentecost sermon: "The promise is for you and for your children and for all who are far off, everyone whom the Lord our God calls to himself" (Acts 2:39). If in all of our missional zeal we are losing the children and failing truly to reach those who are far away, perhaps it is time to rethink our ministry.

What is called for in these days, as in any other time, is a church that is a genuine covenantal community defined by the gospel rather than a service provider defined by laws of the market, political ideologies, ethnic distinctives, or other alternatives to the catholic community that the Father is creating by his Spirit in his Son. For this, we need nothing less than a new creation, where the only demographic that matters is *in Christ*. When our churches are once again located *there*, both the converted and those whom we have yet to reach will become recipients of grace who can, in turn, love and serve their neighbors in the world. When that happens, we too should expect to hear fresh reports, even in America, that "the word of God spread, and the number of disciples multiplied greatly" (Acts 6:7 NKJV).

Why the Reformation Changed Things

Martin Luther pointed out that there were many Reformers in his day, however they were all trying to clean the outside of the cup. Some, like the Brethren of the Common Life (in which Erasmus and Luther were schooled), wanted to return to the primitive simplicity of the early church, emphasizing mutual love and service to each other, fellowship, and the example of Jesus—with a more active role for the laity. They challenged the hypocrisy of Rome (as in Erasmus's sarcastic works, *In Praise of Folly* and *The Colloquies*).

Yet the Reformation was unique—and uniquely effective—because, as Luther said, it went to the heart of the problem: the doctrine. It called people out of themselves, away from their *good works* as well as their sins, to cling to Christ alone through faith alone. The entire worship service was transformed to give clear priority to the gospel of Christ. No longer was it to be seen as the church's sacrifice to God but as God's redemptive service to the people, who then left the service to love and serve their neighbors through their ordinary callings. There were still sacrifices of praise and thanksgiving, but no more sacrifices for sin, and even the former were simply the *amen* of faith to God's Good News.

The Reformation initiated by Luther went to the heart of what he called the Babylonian captivity of the church. Just as Paul observed that Israel did not find the righteousness it was looking for because it was seeking it by works rather than through faith in Christ, the Reformers knew that genuine transformation—that is, sanctification in Christ—can only be the result of abandoning one's own righteousness and being found in Christ.

After elaborating Calvin's treatment of the preached Word as the living voice of God through a weak messenger, Elizabeth Achtemeier adds,

> No one believes that God speaks through his Word until they hear it. And no argument can convince the unbeliever apart from the work of the Spirit. "Faith comes from what is heard," writes Paul, "and what is heard comes by the preaching of Christ" (Rom. 10:17, RSV). And it is the preaching of Christ—the testimony of faith that there is beyond our human words a transcendent Word—it is that alone which can awaken and renew the church.

She also says, however, "Because much of the church in this country no longer believes or expects to hear God speaking through its Scriptures, it therefore is not very Christian anymore."[13]

We live in an age that is simultaneously cynical and credulous—unable to believe in anything in particular while open to everything in general. Conflict is bound to develop within the church itself when Christians and churches deny civil religion and embrace the scandal of a particular gospel that arises from the narration of God's disruptive and disorienting intrusion in our world and our lives. But it needs to happen.

It is interesting that in his ministry Jesus always drew crowds by his miraculous signs, but he drove most away when he began to preach. We see this especially in John 6, in which Jesus announces that what the people are not even looking for is what they need most: the everlasting "bread from heaven" (v. 31), which is Jesus himself. When the people begin to peel away from the crowd, disappointed that Jesus is not going to satisfy their felt need for another meal, Jesus adds, "No one can come to me unless the Father who sent me draws him" (v. 44). Even the disciples respond, "This is a hard teaching. Who can accept it?" (v. 60 NIV). Nevertheless, that day Jesus forces a choice between being consumers or disciples, and Peter responds, "Lord, to whom shall we go? You have the words of eternal life. We believe and know that you are the Holy One of God" (vv. 68–69 NIV).

The church in America will have to learn what it means to mourn before it can dance. Sticking to the story, fixing our eyes on Christ—even if it means distracting us from what we have diagnosed as our real issues—is the kindest thing a pastor can do for a congregation, the most precious gift we can receive and pass along to our neighbors, and the most relevant mission on earth. In the words of Dorothy Sayers,

> It is the dogma that is the drama—not beautiful phrases, not comforting sentiments, nor vague aspirations to loving-kindness and moral uplift, nor the promise of something nice after death— but the terrifying assertion that the same God who made the world lived in the world and passed through the grave and gate of death. Show that to the heathen, and they may not believe it; but at least they may realize that here is something that one might be glad to believe.[14]

Notes

Foreword: Liberating a Captive Church

1. Flannery O'Connor, *Wise Blood* (New York: Harcourt, Brace, 1952; repr., New York: Farrar, Straus & Giroux, 2007), 101.

Chapter 1: Christless Christianity

1. George Barna, *The Second Coming of the Church* (Nashville: Word, 1998), 67.

2. Michael S. Horton, *Made in America: The Shaping of Modern American Evangelicalism* (Grand Rapids: Baker, 1991); Michael S. Horton, ed., *Power Religion: The Selling Out of the Evangelical Church?* (Chicago: Moody, 1992); Michael S. Horton, *Beyond Culture Wars* (Chicago: Moody, 1994).

3. Interview with John R. W. Stott, *Christianity Today*, October 2006, 96.

4. William H. Willimon, *Peculiar Speech: Preaching to the Baptized* (Grand Rapids: Eerdmans, 1992), 9.

Chapter 2 Naming Our Captivity

1. Barna, *Second Coming of the Church*, 7.

2. Ibid., 8, 21.

3. Ibid., 21–22.

4. President George W. Bush in an October 4, 2007, interview with Al Arabiya, reported by Molly Iverson, "Between the Times," *Modern Reformation*, November–December 2007.

5. Barna, *Second Coming of the Church*, 23.

261

6. Ibid., 25–28.

7. Ibid., 60–61.

8. Robert Schuller, *Self-Esteem: The New Reformation* (Waco: Word, 1982), 12–15, 64, 75.

9. C. S. Lewis, *The Weight of Glory* (San Francisco: HarperCollins, 2001), 26.

10. David Brooks, *Bobos in Paradise: The New Upper Class and How They Got There* (New York: Simon and Schuster, 2000).

11. Kenneth Woodward, *Newsweek*, September 1984, 26.

12. Kenneth Woodward, *Newsweek*, November 28, 1994, 62.

13. Karl Menninger, *Whatever Became of Sin?* (New York: Hawthorn Books, 1973).

14. Katherine A. Kersten, "To Hell with Sin: When 'Being a Good Person' Excuses Everything," *Wall Street Journal*, September 17, 1999.

15. Robert Jay Lifton, "The Protean Self," in *The Truth about the Truth*, ed. Walter Truett Anderson (New York: Putnam, 1995), 130–35.

16. Bishop C. FitzSimons Allison, "Distractions," *Modern Reformation*, September–October 2007.

17. Philip Rieff, *The Triumph of the Therapeutic: Uses of Faith after Freud* (New York: Harper & Row, 1966), x–xii.

18. Neil McCormick, *Killing Bono* (New York: Simon & Schuster, 2004), 12.

19. Cathy Lynn Grossman, "Is Sin Dead?" *USA Today*, March 19, 2008.

20. Christian Smith with Melinda Lundquist Denton, *Soul Searching: The Religious and Spiritual Lives of American Teenagers* (New York: Oxford University Press, 2006), 162–71, 258, 262.

21. Ibid., 42.

22. Smith explored his findings with us on the *White Horse Inn* radio broadcast, available at www.whitehorseinn.org.

23. Smith with Denton, *Soul Searching*, 27.

24. Ibid., 162–63.

25. See especially James D. Hunter, *Evangelicalism: The Coming Generation* (Chicago: University of Chicago Press, 1987), chapter 2.

26. Interview by Michael Cromartie, "What American Teenagers Believe: A Conversation with Christian Smith," in *Books & Culture*, January–February 2005, 10.

27. David Briggs, "More Sinners Are Lining Up at the Virtual Confessional," Religion News Service, *San Diego Union-Tribune*, Sunday, April 14, 2007, Religion and Ethics section.

28. Ibid.

29. Roger Olson, *Arminian Theology* (Downers Grove, IL: InterVarsity, 2005), 28 (including footnote 20). Furthermore, I have been amazed that Arminian friends like Methodist theologian Thomas Oden have defended core evangelical (i.e., Reformation) teachings like justification even while some conservative Protestants

seem to be losing their interest in the doctrine. Clearly, the theological divide in our day is less denominational than it is theological.

30. Charles G. Finney, *Finney's Systematic Theology* (repr., Minneapolis: Bethany, 1994), 31, 179–80, 236.

31. Ibid., 206, 209.

32. Ibid., 46, 57.

33. Ibid., 320–22.

34. Ibid.

35. William Willimon, *The Intrusive Word: Preaching to the Unbaptized* (Grand Rapids: Eerdmans, 1994), 53.

36. Ibid., 20.

37. Ibid., 21, citing George Barna, *Marketing the Church: What They Never Taught You about Church Growth* (Colorado Springs: NavPress, 1988), 50.

38. Ibid., 38, 43, 52.

39. B. A. Gerrish, "Sovereign Grace: Is Reformed Theology Obsolete?" *Interpretation* 57, no. 1 (January 2003): 45.

40. Marsha Witten, *All Is Forgiven: The Secular Message in American Protestantism* (Princeton: Princeton University Press, 1993), 3–4.

41. Ibid., 4.

42. For Weber's argument, see his essay, "Science as a Vocation," in *From Max Weber: Essays in Sociology*, ed. H. Gerth and C. W. Mills (New York: Oxford University Press, 1946), 129–60. By the way, the literature on this question is vast, but two books are especially critical for getting a bead on contemporary sociological interpretations of Weber's theory: Peter Berger, *The Sacred Canopy* (Garden City, NY: Doubleday, 1967) and Thomas Luckmann, *The Invisible Religion* (London: Collier-Macmillan, 1967).

43. William James, *Pragmatism* (reprint, New York: Meridian, 1955), 192–95.

44. Quoted in Richard Hofstadter, *Anti-Intellectualism in American Life* (New York: Vintage, 1963), 115.

45. Hofstadter, *Anti-Intellectualism in American Life*, 55.

46. Garry Wills, *Head and Heart: American Christianities* (New York: Penguin, 2007), 294.

47. Ibid., 302.

48. Ralph Waldo Emerson, quoted in ibid., 273.

49. Quotations in this and the following five paragraphs (except for Scripture references) are from Witten, *All Is Forgiven*, 5–6, 15, 20–23, 131.

50. Quotations in this and the following twenty paragraphs (except for Scripture references) are from ibid., 24, 30, 33–35, 40–41, 44–47, 50, 53, 63, 76, 80–81, 84–85, 92, 95, 101, 104–7, 109–15, 117, 119, 120, 125, 127.

51. Barna, *Marketing the Church*, 145.

52. Donald Bloesch, *God, Authority, and Salvation*, vol. 1 of *Essentials of Evangelical Theology* (San Francisco: Harper & Row, 1978), 10.

53. G. K. Chesterton, *Orthodoxy: The Romance of Faith* (New York: Doubleday, 1990), 15, 158.

54. Ibid., 157.

55. Ibid., 157–58.

Chapter 3 Smooth Talking and Christless Christianity

1. George Lindbeck, "The Church's Mission," in *Postmodern Theology: Christian Faith in a Pluralist World*, ed. Frederic B. Burnham (San Francisco: HarperSanFrancisco, 1989), 45.

2. Wanyeki Mahiaini, "A View from Africa," in *One World or Many? The Impact of Globalisation on Mission*, ed. Richard Tiplady (Pasadena: William Carey Library, 2003), 161.

3. D. R. McConnell, *A Different Gospel: Biblical and Historical Insights into the Word of Faith Movement* (updated ed.; Peabody, MA: Hendrickson, 1995). A Pentecostal who did graduate work at Oral Roberts University, McConnell offers ample citation and evaluation of this claim.

4. Kenneth Copeland, "The Force of Love," *Praise the Lord* broadcast (TBN), recorded February 5, 1986; audio tape # 02-0028, 1987.

5. This position is extensively documented in Michael Horton, ed., *The Agony of Deceit* (Chicago: Moody, 1990).

6. Joel Osteen, *Your Best Life Now: Seven Steps to Living at Your Full Potential* (New York: Warner, 2004), 41–42, 57, 66, 119.

7. Ibid., 262.

8. Karl Marx, "Bourgeois and Proletarians," in *The Communist Manifesto*, 1848.

9. David Van Biema and Jeff Chu, "Does God Want You to Be Rich?" *Time*, September 10, 2006.

10. Quotations in this and the following thirty-six paragraphs (except for Scripture quotations) are from Joel Osteen, *Become a Better You: 7 Keys to Improving Your Life Every Day* (New York: Free Press, 2007), 5, 9, 37, 39–41, 45–46, 50, 56, 67, 69, 86–87, 89, 91, 101, 103–5, 129–30, 218, 236, 301–2, 308, 316.

11. Dietrich Bonhoeffer, *Life Together* (Minneapolis: Fortress, 1996), 62.

12. Quoted in "A Church That Packs Them In, 16,000 At a Time," *New York Times*, July 18, 2005.

13. Audio clip on *The Bible Answer Man* radio broadcast, April 26, 2004.

14. C. S. Lewis, "Answers to Questions on Christianity," *God in the Dock* (Grand Rapids: Eerdmans, 1970), 58.

15. Lewis, "Christian Apologetics," *God in the Dock*, 91.

16. Lewis, "Cross-Examination," *God in the Dock*, 261.

17. Karl Barth, *Church Dogmatics*, IV, 3.2, 803.

Chapter 4 How We Turn Good News into Good Advice

1. J. Gresham Machen, *Christian Faith in the Modern World* (New York: Macmillan, 1936), 57.

2. Brian McLaren, *A Generous Orthodoxy* (Grand Rapids: Zondervan, 2004), 206.

3. Ibid., 260.

4. Ibid., 264.

5. Ibid., 61.

6. Steve Chalke, *The Lost Message of Jesus* (Grand Rapids: Zondervan, 2003), 182–83; Brian McLaren, *The Story We Find Ourselves In: Further Adventures of a New Kind of Christian* (San Francisco: Jossey-Bass, 2003), 102.

7. Brian McLaren, *Everything Must Change: Jesus, Global Crises, and a Revolution of Hope* (Nashville: Thomas Nelson, 2007), 79.

8. Ibid., 79–80.

9. Dan Kimball, *The Emerging Church: Vintage Christianity for New Generations* (Grand Rapids: Zondervan, 2003), 26.

10. Mark Oestreicher, quoted in ibid., 35.

11. Kimball, *The Emerging Church*, 79, 81.

12. Ibid., 185, 194.

13. Ibid., 214.

14. David Gibson, "Assumed Evangelicalism: Some Reflections En Route to Denying the Gospel," Reformed University Fellowship at Lehigh University, http://www.ruf-lu.org/articles/Assumed%20Evangelicalism.htm.

15. Robert Robinson, "Come, Thou Fount of Every Blessing," *Hymns for the Living Church* (Carol Stream, IL: Hope Publishing, 1974).

16. J. Gresham Machen, *Christianity and Liberalism* (Grand Rapids: Eerdmans, 1923), 47.

17. Cornelis Hulsman with Prince Hassan, "The Peacebuilding Prince," *Christianity Today*, February 2008, 64.

18. Steve Padilla, "Rabbi, Atheist Debate with Passion, Humor," *Los Angeles Times*, December 29, 2007, B2.

19. Richard Dawkins, *The God Delusion* (New York: Houghton Mifflin, 2006), 99.

20. The Heidelberg Catechism, Lord's Day 23, Q. 60, in the *Psalter Hymnal: Doctrinal Standards and Liturgy of the Christian Reformed Church* (Grand Rapids: CRC Board of Publications, 1976), 30.

21. Martin Luther, *Word and Sacrament*, vol. 35 of *Luther's Works*, American ed. (Philadelphia: Muhlenberg Press, 1960), 358, cited by Graeme Goldsworthy, *The Goldsworthy Trilogy* (Carlisle, UK: Paternoster Press, 2000), 129.

22. Goldsworthy, *The Goldsworthy Trilogy*, 128–29.

23. Ibid., 131, 136–37.

24. Ibid., 137.

25. George Barna, *Grow Your Church from the Outside In* (Ventura: Regal, 2002), 161.

Chapter 5 Your Own Personal Jesus

1. Jeff Gordinier, "On a Ka-Ching and a Prayer," *Entertainment Weekly*, October 7, 1994.
2. Curtis White, "Hot Air Gods," *Harper's*, December 2007, 13.
3. Ibid.
4. Ibid., 13–14.
5. Ibid., 14.
6. Alexis de Tocqueville, *Democracy in America*, trans. Henry Reeve, ed. Francis Bowen vol. 1, (New York: Century, 1898), 66.
7. C. Austin Miles, "In the Garden," *Hymns for the Living Church* (Carol Stream, IL: Hope Publishing, 1974), 398.
8. Gerhard Forde, *On Being a Theologian of the Cross: Reflections on Luther's Heidelberg Disputation, 1518* (Grand Rapids: Eerdmans, 1997), 5.
9. H. Richard Niebuhr, *The Kingdom of God in America* (Chicago: Willett, Clark, 1937; repr., Middletown, CT: Wesleyan University Press, 1988), 193.
10. Cited in Wade Clark Roof, *A Generation of Seekers: The Spiritual Journeys of the Baby Boom Generation* (San Francisco: HarperCollins, 1993), 75.
11. As in *The Apocalypse of Adam*, or the Trimorphic Protennoia concept, found among the Nag Hammadi discoveries.
12. Marilyn Ferguson, *The Aquarian Conspiracy: Personal and Social Transformation in the 1980s* (New York: J. P. Tarcher/Putnam, 1980), 18.
13. On the rising interest in Gnostic and pagan spiritualities, see especially Peter Jones, *The Gnostic Empire Strikes Back* (Phillipsburg, NJ: Presbyterian and Reformed, 1994). In addition to his books on this subject, Jones has launched *Christian Witness to a Pagan Planet*, www.cwipp.org.
14. Robert N. Bellah et al., *Habits of the Heart: Individualism and Commitment in American Life*, rev. ed. (Berkeley: University of California Press, 1996), 221, 235.
15. Depeche Mode, "Personal Jesus," songwriter Martin L. Gore, *Violator* album, Grabbing Hands Music/EMI Music, 1989.
16. Harold Bloom, *The American Religion: The Emergence of the Post-Christian Nation* (New York: Simon and Schuster, 1992), 26–27.
17. Ibid., 15, 17.
18. Ibid., 22.
19. Ibid., 25.
20. Quoted in ibid., 260.
21. Ibid., 264.
22. Ibid., 65.
23. Wilhelm Herrmann, *Communion with God* (New York: Putnam's Sons, 1913), 16.

24. Edgar Young Mullins, *The Christian Religion in its Doctrinal Expression* (Philadelphia: Roger Williams Press, 1917), 73; cited by Bloom, *The American Religion*, 204.

25. Ibid., 199.

26. Edgar Young Mullins, *The Axioms of Religion: A New Interpretation of the Baptist Faith* (Philadelphia: American Baptist Publication Society, 1908), 53–54; cited by Bloom, *The American Religion*, 213.

27. Ibid., 214.

28. "Triumphalism is the only mode in which Mullins and the Baptists read Romans," moving quickly through the incarnation and the cross to Romans 8: "In all these things we are more than conquerors through him that loved us" (v. 37 NIV), (Bloom, *The American Religion*, 213).

29. Ibid., 133.

30. Ibid., 213.

31. Ibid., 228–29.

32. Ibid., 259.

33. Roof, *A Generation of Seekers*, 195.

34. James Davison Hunter, *American Evangelicalism: Conservative Religion and the Quandary of Modernity* (New Brunswick: Rutgers University Press, 1983), 75.

35. Roof, *A Generation of Seekers*, 195.

36. Chuck Smith, *New Testament Study Guide* (Costa Mesa, CA: Word for Today, 1982), 113.

37. Philip Lee, *Against the Protestant Gnostics* (New York: Oxford University Press, 1987), 144.

38. Ibid., 255.

39. Roof, *A Generation of Seekers*, 23, 30, 67.

40. J. I. Packer cites Warfield's criticism and concurs in "Keswick and the Reformed Doctrine of Sanctification," *Evangelical Quarterly* 27, no. 3 (July 1955): 153–67.

41. Nathaniel Hawthorne, cited in Vernon L. Parrington, *The Romantic Revolution in America*, vol. 2 of *Main Currents in American Thought* (New York: Harcourt Brace, 1959), 441–42.

42. C. FitzSimons Allison, "Reflections on Modern Reformation," *Modern Reformation* 16, no. 1 (January–February 2007): 13.

Chapter 6 Delivering Christ

1. See, for example, Michelle Boorstein, "Megachurch Pastor Warren Calls for a Second Reformation," *Washington Post*, February 5, 2008, 1.

2. Quotations in this and the following three paragraphs are from Greg L. Hawkins and Cally Parkinson, *Reveal: Where Are You?* (Northbrook, IL: Willow, 2007), 4, 39, 42–44, 47, 49, 53, 65.

3. Doug Pagitt, *Preaching Re-Imagined* (Grand Rapids: Zondervan, 2005), 31.

4. McLaren, *A Generous Orthodoxy*, 185.

5. Pagitt, *Preaching Re-Imagined*, 139.

6. McLaren, *A Generous Orthodoxy*, 23.

7. Kimball, *The Emerging Church*, 91.

8. Ibid., 93.

9. Charles Finney, *Systematic Theology* (Minneapolis: Bethany, 1976), 31; cf. Keith J. Hardman, *Charles Grandison Finney: Revivalist and Reformer* (Grand Rapids: Baker, 1987).

10. Charles G. Finney, *Letters on Revivals*, 2nd ed. (New York: Wright, 1845), 142.

11. Ibid., 204.

12. Whitney R. Cross, *The Burned-Over District: The Social and Intellectual History of Enthusiastic Religion in Western New York, 1800–1850* (Ithaca: Cornell University Press, 1982), 182–84; cf. 179.

13. Quoted in Hardman, *Charles Grandison Finney*, 380.

14. Charles Finney, quoted in ibid.

15. George Barna, *Revolution: Finding Vibrant Faith beyond the Walls of the Sanctuary* (Carol Stream, IL: Tyndale, 2005), back cover copy.

16. Ibid., 180.

17. Barna, *Second Coming of the Church*, 96.

18. Ibid., 68, 138–39, 140.

19. Ibid., 177.

20. Ibid., 65.

21. Barna, *Revolution*, 17, 22, 203, 208, 210.

22. Ibid., 175.

23. Ibid., 62–63.

24. Reported in *USA Today*, Ellison Research, August 2007.

25. Ibid., 70.

26. Steven J. Keillor, *God's Judgments: Interpreting History and the Christian Faith* (Downers Grove, IL: InterVarsity, 2007).

27. The Constitution of the Presbyterian Church (USA), *Book of Order*, W-7.4002d.

28. http://les-pcusa.org/Business/Business.aspx?iid=297.

29. "Covenanting for Justice in the Economy and the Earth Project," PC(USA) resolutions, Twenty-Fourth General Council, http://warc.jalb.de/warcajsp/side.jsp?news_id=1154&navi=45; emphasis added.

30. "On the Liberation of Iraq," http://www.sbc.net/resolutions/amResolution.asp?ID=1126, June 2003.

31. "Resolution on Exportation of Alcohol and Tobacco," http://www.sbc.net/resolutions/amResolution.asp?ID=95, June 1988.

32. "On Global Warming," http://www.sbc.net/resolutions/amResolution.asp?ID=1171, June 2007.

33. John de Gruchy, *Liberating Reformed Theology: A South African Contribution to an Ecumenical Debate* (Grand Rapids: Eerdmans, 1991), 21–46, 216–17.

34. The interview with Sherwood Wirt in *Decision* magazine is included in Lewis, *God in the Dock*, 265.

35. C. S. Lewis, *The Lion, the Witch, and the Wardrobe* (New York: HarperCollins, 2005), 132–33.

36. Martin Luther *Church Postil* of 1522, quoted in Stephen H. Webb, *The Divine Voice: Christian Proclamation and the Theology of Sound* (Grand Rapids: Brazos Press, 2004), 143.

37. Westminster Shorter Catechism in *The Book of Confessions*, General Assembly of the PC(USA), 1991, Q. 89.

38. Bloom, *The American Religion*.

39. Quotations in this and the following six paragraphs are from Stanley Grenz, *Revisioning Evangelical Theology: A Fresh Agenda for the 21st Century* (Downers Grove, IL: InterVarsity, 1993), 17, 30–34, 38, 41–42, 44–46, 48, 51–52, 55, 62, 77, 80, 88, 122; emphasis added.

40. John Williamson Nevin, *The Anxious Bench* (London: Taylor & Francis, 1987), 2–5.

41. See Hardman, *Charles Grandison Finney*, 380–94.

42. See, for example, Cross, *The Burned-Over District*.

43. Michael Pasquarello III, *Christian Preaching: A Trinitarian Theology of Proclamation* (Grand Rapids: Baker Academic, 2007), 24.

44. "The proportion of the unchurched has been slowly rising since the late eighties," according to George Barna, *The Index of Leading Spiritual Indicators* (Dallas: Word, 1996), 34.

45. John Calvin, *Institutes* 4.1.5.

46. Miroslav Volf, *After Our Likeness* (Grand Rapids: Eerdmans, 1993), 161–62.

47. William McLoughlin, *Revivals, Awakenings, and Reform* (Chicago: University of Chicago Press, 1980), 25. I am grateful to Toby Kurth for providing this and the following reference.

48. Ned C. Landsman, *From Colonials to Provincials: American Thought and Culture, 1680–1760* (New York: Twayne, 1997; Ithaca, NY: Cornell University Press, 2000), 66.

49. See Gene Edward Veith, *The Spirituality of the Cross: The Way of the First Evangelicals* (St. Louis: Concordia, 1999).

Chapter 7 A Call to the Resistance

1. Dietrich Bonhoeffer, "Protestantism without the Reformation," in *No Rusty Swords: Letters, Lectures and Notes, 1928–1936*, ed. Edwin H. Robertson, trans. Edwin H. Robertson and John Bowden (London: Collins, 1965), 92–118.

2. Neil Postman, *Amusing Ourselves to Death: Public Discourse in the Age of Show Business* (New York: Penguin, 1985), vii.

3. Peter Berger, *The Noise of Solemn Assemblies: Christian Commitment and the Religious Establishment in America* (Garden City, NY: Doubleday, 1961), 125–26.

4. Ibid.

5. Ibid., 131.

6. J. Gresham Machen, *What Is Faith?* (New York: Macmillan, 1925), 282.

7. Ibid., 23.

8. Machen, *Christianity and Liberalism*, 21.

9. Ann Douglas, *The Feminization of American Culture* (New York: Knopf, 1977), 7.

10. Lewis, *Weight of Glory*, 26.

11. For a discussion of the wording of Ephesians 4:12, see Andrew Lincoln, *Word Biblical Commentary*, vol. 42, *Ephesians* (Waco: Word, 1990).

12. McLaren, *A Generous Orthodoxy*, 225–26.

13. Elizabeth Achtemeier, "The Canon as the Voice of the Living God," in Carl E. Braaten and Robert W. Jenson, eds., *Reclaiming the Bible for the Church* (Edinburgh: T & T Clark, 1995), 120, 122–23.

14. Dorothy Sayers, *Creed or Chaos?* (New York: Harcourt, Brace, 1949), 25.

Michael Horton (PhD, University of Coventry and Wycliffe Hall, Oxford) is the J. Gresham Machen professor of apologetics and theology at Westminster Seminary California and associate pastor at Christ United Reformed Church in Santee, California. He is also the editor-in-chief of *Modern Reformation* magazine, the co-host of *The White Horse Inn* radio program (whitehorseinn .org), and the author of several books, including *A Better Way* and *God of Promise*.